Investigating Business

Investigating Business

Christina Poulter

First published 1996 by
MACMILLAN PRESS LTD
Houndmills, Basingstoke, Hampshire RG21 6XS
and London
Companies and representatives
throughout the world

ISBN 0–333–66488–4

A catalogue record for this book is available
from the British Library.

10	9	8	7	6	5	4	3	2	1
05	04	03	02	01	00	99	98	97	96

Typeset by Footnote Graphics, Warminster, Wilts

Printed in Great Britain by
Butler and Tanner Ltd, Frome, Somerset

To my mother
and those who have been patient
during the construction of this book,
David, Richard, Cathryn and Matthew

About the author

Christina Poulter is an experienced teacher of
business and related subjects. For six years she was
Head of Business and Economics at St Edmund's
School in Portsmouth. Prior to this she was a
business studies lecturer at the Isle of Wight College
of Arts and Technology. She is currently manager of
the Prison Education Service at the Isle of Wight
College.

Contents

List of Boxes

Preface

A constantly changing world is motivated by the need for individuals to survive economically. In this context, trade or business is part of the central social structure. Any analysis of the business needs to move beyond the concept of the quest to purely maximise profit to a deeper understanding of businesses objectives and their operation in a wider social context. Businesses are part of society, and so are responsible for and accountable for their actions.

Businesses operate in a dynamic environment and are pushed into action by external forces beyond their control. Successful business students need to be able to absorb and apply the established theory to an ever-changing scene. They need to be aware of issues and be able to respond to events, using their skills and knowledge to analyse and evaluate business opportunities.

This book encourages students to be proactive. Each chapter covers the essential text whilst the Focus articles challenge, question and evaluate topical issues. Their role is to stimulate discussion and debate and initiate further research. An active response is required for the practical application and critical analysis tasks whilst the case studies challenge the students' ability to apply their skills and make informed decisions. Integrated case studies are set at intervals throughout the book which involve the student in the business process.

The use of IT as a tool for business is encouraged and facilitated throughout and can be effectively used to set coursework assignments in which the student's business skill is applied. It also encourages a cross-curricular approach.

CHRISTINA POULTER

Acknowledgements

The authors and publishers would like to thank the following for permission to reproduce copyright material:

The Associated Examining Board (AEB)
University of Cambridge Local
   Examinations Syndicate
Transport 2000
Central Office of Information
Abbey National Plc
The Observer
PA News.

The author would also like to thank Geoff Wade at the Portsea Island Co-operative and Keith Haywood, Personnel Manager at the Isle of Wight College for their help.

Box 16.8 is reproduced by permission of the Controller of Her Majesty's Stationery Office and the Office for National Statistics.

Every effort has been made to trace all the copyright-holders, but if any have been inadvertently overlooked the publishers will be pleased to make the necessary arrangements at the first opportunity.

Section 1
Business Organisation

1.1 Business Organisation Past and Present

FOCUS

The vanished empire

The costs of the reforms initiated by Mr Gorbachev were a high price to pay for the Russian people, and perhaps for the political stability of the world.

The original aims of the Gorbachev reforms were twofold:

- 'Perestroika' – the restructuring of the inefficient state sector;
- 'Glasnost' – a spirit of 'openness' allowing the Soviet workforce more control of their destiny.

Once the wheel was set in motion, events overtook plans and control was lost. The old USSR has disintegrated and the 'Russia' which remains is now set on a precarious path towards a market economy.

The USSR was built on the collectivist ideology that the means of production should be controlled by the Government for the collective good of all the people and not by individuals motivated by profit. The dictator Stalin preached the philosophy of 'shop labour', workers laboured for the collective good of the state, not for themselves as individuals. In reality, whilst the poor queued for food the politicians and bureaucrats lived a very different lifestyle.

The archaic 'Gosplan' computer was used by the Russians to forecast supply and demand, taking the place of market mechanisms. Its failure led to chaotic production plans which resulted in queues and general shortages of supplies. The price of sustaining an empire was immense and included the cost of the space race, the nuclear deterrent and the suppression of counter-cultures. When the pressure became too great there was a desperate economic and hence political change of direction. An economic revolution has been planned, but to achieve its economic vision Russia needs capital investment from the West to help build a productive private sector. Yet of the $24 billion promised to Russia by the G7 nations only approximately half has been received whilst the IMF is still considering a $6 billion loan. World recession and fear of political and social instability in the Eastern bloc have stalled the flow of much-needed investment from the West.

The danger is that Russia may have to go through one last cycle of repression in order to abate the economic and social disorder that has developed. Whilst drug barons exploit the new trade routes the exportation of guns and plutonium are posing a real threat to the rest of the world.

Source: National newspaper reports and author's research.

Preview

In this chapter we shall investigate the following key areas:
- the basic economic problem
- production
- the chain of distribution
- the structure of trade
- resource allocation
- economic models
- types of organisation

The entrepreneur

In earliest times man laboured alone or in small family groupings. The development of the tribal system proved that if individuals pooled their skills and resources man could become more efficient.

The concept of the division of labour, where individuals specialise in what they are efficient at achieving, is central to the development of trade.

From self-sufficiency to barter, to the use of money as a means of exchange, this is the path to a developed economic and business structure.

For any good to be produced, or service to be provided, there needs to be a combination of what economists call the factors of production, our economic resources.

These factors are defined in economics as land, labour and capital.

But before production can take place, there is a need for someone to take the initiative and decide what will be produced, where, when and how.

This vital link in the production process is often called the fourth factor of production, the entrepreneur, or risk-taker.

- In a market economy it is the entrepreneur who decides what products or services are in demand and then creates a supply. The motivation is profit and the cost of profit is risk.
- In a planned economy it is the Government which makes the production decisions.

Hence the allocation of resources will depend on the type of economic system in operation. Although the two extreme models are the market and planned economies, in reality most economies are a mixture of both. The type of economic system in operation will usually be based on the political motivation of the Government. Economic aims and objectives are inevitably bound up with politics.

The basic economic problem

If all our productive resources were free and plentiful there would be no need for economists.

The basic economic problem is that there are too few resources to satisfy our unlimited needs and wants. Choices about how to use our limited resources need to be made by individuals, businesses and governments.

Individuals can earn income by supplying labour, interest by investing capital and rent by providing land. A successful entrepreneur can achieve profit as a reward for taking risks. Money is only the measure of the value of each of these productive inputs and money value is affected by many other variables which we will look at later when we investigate 'the economy' in Chapter 6.15. Once income is earned, decisions need to be made about spending.

Economists state that our choice is based on the opportunity cost of each possible decision – the real cost. The real cost of each decision that we make is what we forgo. If a government spends more money on defence schemes the opportunity cost may be a reduction in the living standards of its people.

Production

Production is not just the making of a tangible good, it is also the provision of a service: anything for which someone is prepared to pay.

The factors of production are the resources which contribute to the production process:

- Land   All natural resources which can be used in the process of production

- Labour   All human effort, both mental and physical
- Capital   All man-made items which go into producing further output – money plus that which is purchased with the monetary surplus
- Entrepreneur   The initiator who links up the factors of production and starts the productive process

Box 1.1 gives two practical examples.

The factors of production

For a crop of rape seed   **Land** = The field
Labour = Farm workers
Capital = The tractor and other equipment
Entrepreneur = The farmer

In car production   **Land** = The factory site
Labour = Car workers
Capital = The machinery
Entrepreneur = The car company

Classification of production

Production is usually classified into three sectors – primary, secondary and tertiary:

- Primary sector   Resources which are *extracted* from nature – e.g. agriculture, fishing, mining
- Secondary sector   Resources which are *converted* into tangible goods – e.g. manufacturing and construction

- Tertiary sector   The provision of a *service* e.g. direct services to individuals – leisure, police, defence. Services to businesses – insurance, banking, transport

This is a very simplistic division into categories of production. The production of one good or service could encompass all of the sectors.

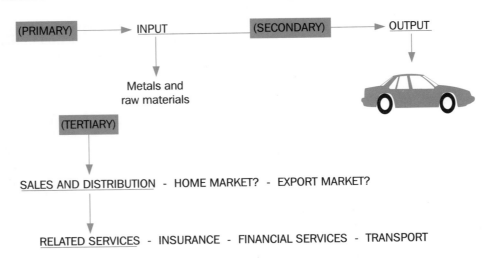

The chain of distribution

The chain of distribution is the process by which a good is directed from its source of production to the market.

The standard chain of production and distribution can now be examined:

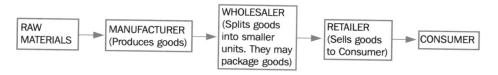

An example of this standard chain can be seen operating in some smaller retail outlets. Organisations like Spar and Wavy Line are wholesalers who provide a supply to retailers packaged under their own name. The name is nationally or regionally known but the goods are cheaper than major 'brand' names. This means that if smaller sole trader units operate under for example the Spar name they are able to offer a range of standard but cheaper produce.

Here are two typical variations on the chain of distribution:

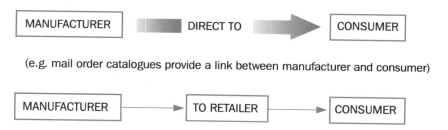

(e.g. mail order catalogues provide a link between manufacturer and consumer)

(e.g. many goods are supplied direct to retailers who sell to consumers)

The structure of trade

One way of looking at the types of businesses operating in the UK economy is by looking at the proportion of the population employed in each area. However, it must be remembered that labour is only one factor of production, and whilst in earlier times it was often the most important factor, now it has been replaced in many sectors by capital. Look at Box 1.2.

BOX 1.2	Employment by sector, 1993	
	Production and construction	26%
	Services	63%
	Agriculture, fisheries and forestry	10%
	Other	1%

Source: Author's research.

Industrialisation: an historical perspective

The process of industrialisation started in the UK in the early eighteenth century. UK agriculture had already undergone a revolution in the early sixteenth century when European farming was still carried out by peasants with subsistence levels of output. After 1750 the enclosure of common land and open fields led to an increased output of food to support a growing population. By 1800 the UK had a highly efficient and commercialised agricultural system. The raw materials of industry including coal, iron, tin and copper were to be found in the UK, whilst the developed ports, toll roads and canal system provided the essential infrastructure for trade. A well developed system of commerce provided banking and loans for prospective business ventures, while

Europe was still hampered by local taxes and other barriers to trade. Industrialisation in the UK was accelerated in the late eighteenth century by a series of inventions and innovations which increased output of consumer and capital goods: the steam engine was a major contributor to the development of the 'factory' system. In 1750 it is estimated that 80% of the workforce were employed in agriculture. By 1811, it is thought, the number of agricultural workers had fallen to 33%, releasing workers for industry, in particular mining and textiles. The increased agrarian prosperity had led to a demand for consumer goods whilst overseas market opportunities were expanded by the effects of British colonisation. Look at Box 1.3.

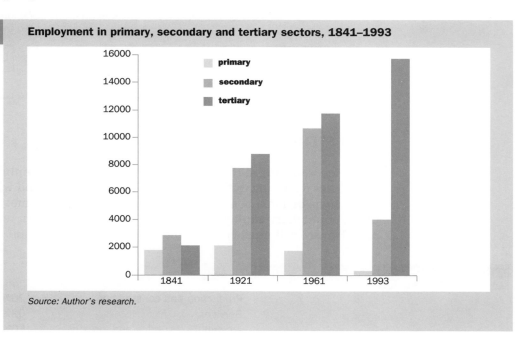

BOX 1.3

Employment in primary, secondary and tertiary sectors, 1841–1993

Source: Author's research.

How resources are allocated

Resources are allocated according to the type of economic system in operation.

The economic system will often be dependent upon the political philosophy of the Government.

In analysing economic structure it must be understood that the planned and market structures which we are going to compare are only models. In reality any economic system will be a mixture of planning and free enterprise (market) with an emphasis either way.

The planned model

In a planned economy, the decisions about the allocation of resources are made by the Government.

It is the politicians or bureaucrats who decide on what is produced, how, where and when. The political ethos behind the planned (or otherwise termed 'command') economy is that of collectivism: a belief that the means of production should be used for the collective good of all the people, not just those who have the means to pay. The reputation of this political and economic structure has been much tarnished by its failures in the Eastern bloc, where the practical application of its policies resulted in the suppression of other political beliefs and counter-cultures. Powerful state politicians and bureaucrats formed an upper-class elite who did not always practice the egalitarian 'equality of mankind' policies which they preached. Resources were ineffectively allocated, which led to shortages and queuing for even basic foodstuffs. We can summarise the advantages and disadvantages of the planned economy in Box 1.4.

BOX 1.4

The planned economy
- The state can set its objectives aimed at the collective good of the community and has the power to control business and economic activity
- Longer-term strategies can be developed, resources can be directed and productive output can be supported
- The wasteful duplication of resources, which can be an outcome of competition between businesses, is avoided

Disadvantages of a planned economy
- Business decisions are made by those who are not entrepreneurs and who may lack the necessary skills and motivations
- The absence of market mechanisms means that arbitrary decisions about levels of demand, and therefore supply, are made using market simulations and models which may not always prove to be efficient
- The absence of the profit motive to encourage enterprise may mean that there is no incentive to increase production
- Price controls which are initiated by the Government can lead to distortions in the market and a shortage of supply of goods which may be in demand
- These price controls may lead to a thriving '**black economy**' where goods are supplied illegally, at a price.

The market model

The market model or free enterprise system is based on the interaction of supply and demand

If there is a demand for a good or service, a supply should be created by the entrepreneur linking up the factors of production.

The individual quest for wealth and the acquisition of capital is encouraged in this system, which is otherwise known as capitalism. In a free enterprise economy the profit motive is seen as both an incentive to produce and an indicator of success. Look at the demand and supply diagram:

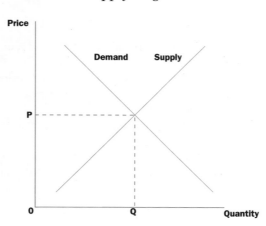

In general, more will be demanded as price falls. As price rises it is likely that the entrepreneur will increase supply. Box 1.5 now summarises the advantages and disadvantages of the market economy.

If we hold these two market models up to the mirror of current economic systems, we can see that the former USSR was close to the planned economy whilst the USA has strong capitalist beliefs. However, the reality is that economies tend to be a mixture of both planned and market sectors. The free market assumes that all aspects of the market are perfectly competitive but in reality this is untrue. Resources (or the factors which create production) cannot be automatically directed into the production output which reaps the highest reward. Mobility, or the ability for a factor of production to change to another occupation or geographical area, is severely limited. If a shipyard closes on the Tyne it is not easy for workers to become financial advisers in the South East. A machine (capital) may be producing a certain good but it may not be possible for it to produce another type of good if demand increases.

Increased competition can eventually lead to its own elimination. As smaller companies fail to compete with larger-scale organisations, the big companies can eliminate the competition and eventually control the whole market.

The mixed economy

Most economies throughout the world, have a mixture of free enterprise and planning, private and public sectors – the former created by individuals seeking profit and the latter controlled by the Government for the provision of certain services.

BOX 1.5

The market economy

Advantages of a market economy
- Consumer demand and its fluctuations are automatically accommodated through market mechanisms
- The profit motive can be an effective incentive to encourage output and a straightforward measurement of business success
- Competition between suppliers can lead to an increase in efficiency and lower prices

Disadvantages of a market economy
- Consumer choice is dependent upon the ability to pay; hence, demand can only be created by those with purchasing power
- Goods or services which may be necessary for the collective good of all citizens, for example education and health care, may be severely neglected
- If success is judged purely on a profit basis, the quality of services to society may suffer
- Society needs the provision of public or **non-excludable goods or services** such as defence and the police.

Non-excludable goods or services are those which are supplied on a national basis and which benefit all citizens, not just those who have chosen to pay.

For example the police force and the armed services cannot be there to protect some of the people whilst others are excluded.

Box 1.6 shows how organisations may be structured into sectors in a mixed economy giving examples of different types of business and organisational units.

We shall now examine the private sector in some detail. The public sector is considered in Chapter 1.3.

BOX 1.6

Types of organisations in the mixed economy

Type of organisation	Private sector	Public sector	Other
Definition	Run by individuals for profit	Owned by the Government	Fits into neither the public nor the private sector
Examples	• Sole traders • Partnerships • Limited companies (private and public)	• Government departments • Local authorities • Public corporations	• Building societies • Trade associations • Trade unions

The private sector

The private sector of the economy incorporates business units which are normally set up in the pursuit of profit.

The types of businesses range from a sole trader, which is usually described as the smallest unit of ownership, to a public limited company, which includes large companies whose shares are quoted on the Stock Exchange.

Sole traders

A business can be set up as a sole trader without any legal formalities. Sole traders need to inform the relevant bodies, for example their local tax office or perhaps the local authority if a trading licence is needed (for example a market trader). They also need to comply with any regulations, for example in the case of a restaurant, food hygiene regulations and health and safety rulings. The process of establishing a sole trader is relatively simple because the owner *is* the business.

- the business has no legal identity
- The owner has unlimited liability if the business should collapse

- unlimited liability means that the owner is totally liable for any debts the business has incurred
- they can lose their personal assets and possessions.

Look at Box 1.7, which summarises the advantages and disadvantages of this business form.

The partnership

A partnership consists of two or more individuals who go into business together.

- In a normal partnership formation the partners have unlimited liability in the same form as the sole trader
- Partnerships also have no legal identity.

The main reasons for the formation of partnerships is that they allow specialisms to merge, capital input to be increased and workload and responsibility to be shared. Partnerships tend to be more prevalent in the

---

BOX 1.7

The sole trader
Advantages
- The setting up process is simple with no legal formalities
- Decisions are made by the sole trader alone, so business organisation is less problematic than in organisations where many individuals are involved
- All the profit goes to the sole trader
- The accounts do not have to be sent to Companies House or be audited

Disadvantages
- Because they make all the profit they must also bear any loss – in effect they have 'unlimited liability'
- The capital input is limited by the owner's ability to raise funds
- The trader's specialisations or skills may be limited
- Personal accident or injury could prove to be a major problem.

professions, e.g. solicitors, dentists, doctors, accountants and in skilled trades, e.g. builders. The main reason for this is that if, for example, a solicitor was working on his own and he wanted to offer a much wider service to his clients he would need to take on another specialist, another solicitor. Now if a sole trader, for example a corner shop, was in the same situation, the trader could employ additional part-time checkout staff or other employees. A solicitors' practice would need another person of equal status, and in this situation it is unlikely that someone of equal professional status would want to be an employee. It is also likely that they would be able to inject their own capital resources into the business. Similarly, if a plumber joins with a bricklayer and a 'chippy' their scope for construction is increased, they can become housebuilders. Partnerships provide a good example of specialisation.

Decision-making

A sole trader can make all decisions personally without a situation of conflict developing. However, once other people are involved the mechanisms become more complex:

- Who puts in the capital, and how much?
- How is the profit shared?
- Who does what duties?
- What about holidays?
- Who makes the decisions?
- Who works what hours?

Many partnerships when they are first established may not feel that these decisions will be a problem, but the reality can prove to be very different. Although there are no formal legal requirements when a partnership is established it is always advisable to visit a solicitor and get a legal contract agreement drawn up. This document is called a Deed of Articles.

If a contract is not drawn up the Partnership Act 1890 will come into force in the case of any difficulties. This Act states that there should be equal profit-sharing and liability for debts. If each partner has contributed in varying degrees this may not be seen as equitable and it may be much more sensible to get a contract drawn up and signed by everyone involved.

Box 1.8 summarises the advantages of this business form.

BOX 1.8

The partnership

Advantages
- Partnerships can be formed easily
- They can benefit from increased specialisation
- They can result in a pooling of effort and resources and a spreading of risk
- As they have unlimited liability, there is no monitoring or auditing of accounts
- Partners may be able to increase their access to loan funds

Disadvantages
- Even when a contract is drawn up, conflict can still arise
- Unlimited liability for partners means that personal assets and possessions can be lost
- Capital contribution and access to loan funds is restricted compared with a limited company (see below)

Limited partnerships

Generally partnerships have unlimited liability, but in some cases there are sleeping partners

If investors feel that a business is a good proposition but do not want to be involved in its operation, they may want to put capital into a business without taking part in its everyday operation ('sleep'). It would, therefore, be unfair for a sleeping partner to have unlimited liability, and it can be written into the contract that the sleeping partner will have limited liability. While it is possible to have partners with limited liability, in any partnership there must always be one partner with unlimited liability.

Limited companies

In the nineteenth century when the industrial revolution was well established, the Government needed to encourage enterprise and one way of achieving this was to eliminate some of the risks involved in business as a result of unlimited liability. They therefore passed the Limited Liability Act. This Act gave protection to entrepreneurs to ensure that their personal assets could no longer be seized if the business failed.

Limited liability companies are now the most widely formed type of business unit.

- the company has its own legal identity existing in law as a separate entity to its owner
- the owners are called shareholders and are liable *only for the amount of their shareholding*
- they can only lose what they invest

Because of the protection involved, the way a limited company is set up is more complex than one with unlimited liability. As the company is a legal entity it has to be registered with Companies House. Certain documents need to be completed which provide information to the Registrar of Companies. Accounts have to be sent off periodically to be monitored and audited.

The process of incorporation

The following documents need to be sent off to the Registrar of Companies before a business can become incorporated:

---

1 MEMORANDUM OF ASSOCIATION – External matters

- Name
- address
- aims and objectives

---

2 ARTICLES OF ASSOCIATION – Internal management

- Definition of directors' powers and how they are appointed
- the dates of meetings and their frequency
- the way shares are transferred and how company accounts are kept

---

3 STATEMENT OF NOMINAL (STARTING) CAPITAL

---

4 A LIST OF DIRECTORS AND THEIR CONSENT

---

5 A DECLARATION THAT THE COMPANIES ACT HAS BEEN COMPLIED WITH

---

6 CERTIFICATE OF INCORPORATION

The private limited company

This is the smaller type of limited company.

A private limited company tends to be one set up by family or friends.

The reason for this is that shares (or ownership) cannot be freely transferred to the general public.

- The shareholders have limited liability and, by agreement with the shareholders, additional shares can be issued to expand the capital available
- 'Ltd' is usually stated after the company name.

The public limited company

This is the larger type of limited company.

- Shares can be traded publicly on the Stock Exchange so more capital funding is available.

- They have the term 'plc' after the company name.

The process of formation is the same with both types of limited companies, but when incorporation takes place a public limited company needs to issue a prospectus

A prospectus is like an advertisement which gives information about the company to prospective share purchasers (owners).

Shares are then publicly quoted and floated on the Stock Exchange. There are two other organisations which sell shares, the Unlisted Securities Market (USM) and the Over the Counter market (OTC)

Shares

Shareholders are the owners of a business.

Shares have two values, first as a potential asset which can be sold on the share market, and secondly as a source of income earned through dividend The Stock Exchange deals in shares for newly quoted companies and also acts as a market for second-hand shares. Shares traded on the open market may either increase or decrease in value and transaction fees also need to be considered, so that which may have seemed to be an asset could prove to be a liability. The income, or dividend value, of the shares will depend on the profitability of the company. When a company makes a profit it is not all distributed to shareholders as dividend. Each company will declare the amount of profit which it intends to distribute to its shareholders; the rest will be reinvested back into the company or held as reserves

There are two main types of shares with different levels of risk involved.

Preference shares

Preference shareholders are entitled to a fixed rate of return on their investment.

They therefore have the first claim on any profit made. However, because their return is fixed, if a company does well they still only receive the same fixed rate.

Ordinary shares

Shares, profits and dividends

Ordinary shares are the most common form of shares issued.

Because the return is not fixed, they may receive much less than the preference shareholders or much more, depending on the profitability of the company. Most ordinary shareholders can vote at shareholders' meetings. They also vote for the board members and can have a say in the profit distribution (see Box 1.9.). These shares are known as the equity or ownership of a company.

In a family business, which is a private limited company, founder shares are sometimes issued. These have more voting rights than the ordinary shareholders and can be used to enable the initiators of the business to keep control.

BOX 1.9

Profit distribution

If a company had a capital structure of 34 000 £1 7% preference shares, how would the dividend be distributed if the following profits were announced?

Year	Profit for distribution (£)	Preference	Ordinary
①	25 000		
②	26 595		
③	24 689		

The preference share dividend will always be constant if any profit is made. The preference share dividend will be:

Step 1

7/100 of 34 000, which is £2380

Year	Profit for distribution (£)	Preference	Ordinary
①	25 000	2380	?
②	26 595	2380	?
③	24 689	2380	?

Step 2

Whatever is left after the preference dividend has been deducted will be given out to the ordinary shareholders. If there is no profit to be distributed the preference shareholders will not receive any dividend.

	(£)		(£)
①	25 000 – £2380 to Preference shareholders leaves		22 620
②	26 595 – £2380 to Preference shareholders leaves		24 215
③	24 689 – £2380 to Preference shareholders leaves		22 309

Debentures are not share capital, they are a **loan**. Therefore the loan interest on debentures needs to be paid back before any profit is distributed.

Shareholdings are known as risk capital.

Investors put in money hoping for a profit but could lose their capital. In a private limited company shareholders are more closely linked. In a publicly quoted company, however, it is very easy for the initial shareholders to lose control of the company and therefore take-overs can occur. This will be looked at later in Chapter 1.2 on 'Growth or Focus?'.

BOX 1.10

Example: How to work out the following profit distribution

A company has the following capital structure:

£10 000 9% Unsecured loan stock (debentures)
5000 £1 8% Preference shares
30 000 Ordinary shares of £1 each

	Year 1 (£)	Year 2 (£)	Year 3 (£)	Year 4 (£)
Trading profit	8000	10 000	10 500	11 200
Loan interest	?	?	?	?
Residual profit	?	?	?	?
Preference dividend	?	?	?	?
Left for equity	?	?	?	?
Ordinary dividend	?	?	?	?

Step 1

Debentures are a loan which have to be paid back first. Therefore 9% of 10 000 is £900 for each year.

Step 2

The residual profit is the amount which is left after the loan is taken out of the trading profit. Therefore:

	(£)	(£)	(£)
Year 1 –	8000 –	900 =	7100
Year 2 –	10 000 –	900 =	9100
Year 3 –	10 500 –	900 =	9600
Year 4 –	11 200 –	900 =	10 300

Step 3

The residual profit is the amount which is left for preference shareholders to have the first share. Preference shareholders have a fixed amount which is:

8% of £5000 = £400

Therefore £400 is taken out of the residual profit for each year:

	(£)	(£)	(£)	
Year 1 –	7100 –	400 =	6700	left for equity (Ordinary shareholders)
Year 2 –	9100 –	400 =	8700	left for equity (Ordinary shareholders)
Year 3 –	9600 –	400 =	9200	left for equity (Ordinary shareholders)
Year 4 –	10 300 –	400 =	9900	left for equity (Ordinary shareholders)

The ordinary dividend for each year will be as above.

Yield

The amount the shareholder actual receives, or the yield, is not always the same as the dividend. This is because the dividend is based on the face or 'par' value of the share. For example, a share issued 5 years ago at a 'face' value of £1 is now be likely to be traded on the market at a very different price.

The yield is the actual rate of return.

For example if someone buys shares with a face value of £1 but pays £2 per share and the dividend is 20p in the pound, the actual yield is half of 20%. The formula is:

$$\text{Yield} = \frac{\text{Face value} \times \text{Dividend}}{\text{Price}}$$

$$\frac{1 \times 20}{2} = 10\%$$

Shareholders and the organisational structure

Shareholders, as we have seen, are the owners of a business. They vote on major policy issues but delegate the power of general decision-making to the directors. Executive directors take an active part in the day-to-day running of the company whereas non-executive directors do not but may act in an advisory role.

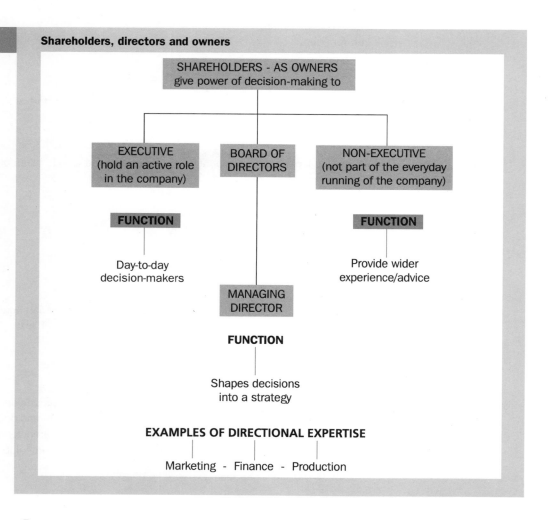

BOX 1.11   Shareholders, directors and owners

SHAREHOLDERS - AS OWNERS
give power of decision-making to

| EXECUTIVE (hold an active role in the company) | BOARD OF DIRECTORS | NON-EXECUTIVE (not part of the everyday running of the company) |

FUNCTION   **FUNCTION**

Day-to-day decision-makers   Provide wider experience/advice

MANAGING DIRECTOR

FUNCTION

Shapes decisions into a strategy

EXAMPLES OF DIRECTIONAL EXPERTISE

Marketing - Finance - Production

REVIEW

After reading this chapter you should understand the need for economic decision-making in the allocation of resources for production. You should also know how business is structured into organisational units in what is called the 'private sector'.

REVIEW TASK

PRACTICAL APPLICATION

Complete the following company share calculation.

A company has the following capital structure:

Loan capital £200 000   7% debentures
Share capital £200 000   6% preference £1 shares
800 000 ordinary shares of 50p

Year	Profit	Debentures	Preference	Ordinary
①	£78 000			
②	£110 000			
③	£42 000			
④	£16 000			

2. Complete the following table on share dividends.
The capital structure of a company is made up of:

12 000 £1 ordinary shares
5500 of 8% preference shares
13 200 9% debentures

Year	① (£)	② (£)	③ (£)	④ (£)
Trading profit	2980	4650	5749	9548
Loan interest				
Residual profit				
Preference				
Dividend				
Ordinary				
Dividend				

REVIEW TASK

CRITICAL ANALYSIS

Analyse the differences between a partnership and a limited company (private and public) from each of the following aspects:

(a) Formation formalities
(b) Ownership
(c) Legal status
(d) Liability
(e) Control
(f) Management.

QUESTIONS

Essay questions

1 The mixed economy can provide the best features of the Planned and Market models. Discuss this statement.

2 Explain the benefits and problems of operating as a sole trader.

3 Describe the process involved when a company becomes incorporated.

CASE STUDY

Sugar and the price of being public

Alan Sugar, creator of multi-million pound company Amstrad (Alan Michael Sugar Trading), and Tottenham Hotspur Company Chairman, profited greatly from the 1980s consumer boom. It is said he once held ordinary equity stock in Amstrad worth £600 million. The financial situation in recent times has been more problematic with £90 million losses in 1992–93, though forecast losses for 1994 are expected to be less than £5 million. Sugar believes that this decline is the outcome of a diminishing market for Amstrad. His business fortune was founded on cheap products assembled in the Far East, reaching its peak with the personal computer. He has been criticised by the business world for producing poor-quality products and not re-investing his money on new product development. In 1992 Sugar attempted to buy back his company at 30p a share, seeking the security of private limited status. He tried to convince Amstrad's 60 000 shareholders to opt out of the Stock Exchange. He was unsuccessful.

Sugar's £113 million bid for the company was opposed by both private and institutional investors. Dividend in Amstrad was never high. In 1986, when pre-tax profit rose, 300% dividend amounted to just 49p. In its most profitable year, 1988, with pre-tax profits of $160.4 million, dividends were £1.87. Amshold is the Jersey-based Private Limited Company which acquired Sugar's 35% stake in Amstrad. It is said that he and his wife Ann are the only two directors of the company. Sugar had initially floated off a quarter of the company in 1980 netting £2 million. He is estimated to have pulled £34 million out of the company in March 1991, but is still thought to own 35% stock at a value in October 1994 of 28p per share, being worth £57 million.

The company has now been bought by Psion.

Source: National newspaper reports and author's research.

CASE STUDY TASKS

1. Explain the difference between profit, dividend and yield.
2. Why should assembling and selling computers direct to the public be a high-current growth area?
3. Define the term 'ordinary equity' and contrast it with other types of stock.
4. Differentiate between private and institutional investors.
5. Design and produce a personal message to Amstrad shareholders on behalf of Alan Sugar explaining the positive advantages of opting out of the Stock Exchange. Use a computer or wordprocessor if possible.

Growth or Focus?

FOCUS

The 1980s rush for growth

Date	Company	Acquisition	Price
1986	Saatchi & Saatchi	Ted Bates	$450 m
1987	MFI	MFI (buyout)	$718 m
1988	News Corporation	Triangle Publications	$3 bn
1988	Maxwell Communications	Macmillan Inc.	$2.6 bn
1988	Lowndes Queensway	Harris Queensway	£477 m
1988	Mecca	Pleasurama	£750 m
1988	Coloroll	John Crowther Carpets	£217 m
1988	British & Commonwealth	Atlantic Computers	£400 m
1989	Brent Walker	William Hill & Mecca	£685 m

Source: Author's research.

The entrepreneurial high-fliers of the 1980s once had the best performing shares on the Stock Market. Former Young Business Man of the Year, John Ashcroft of Coloroll, and John Gunn of British & Commonwealth fell when the investment community began to become concerned about how they would service and repay their borrowing. The huge debts were the price of their acquisitions. When Maurice Saatchi went on a buying spree in the late 1980s swallowing up other advertising agencies, massive debts accrued to the company

In 1988 when some of the business gurus were at their peak of activity, interest rates were low and it was a seller's market. Buyers overstepped what they could afford and when the economic climate changed, with high interest rates and an increasing concern over the USA recession, their **high gearing** was totally exposed.

In 1988 John Ashcroft launched a £217 million bid for John Crowther Carpets, doubling the size of his empire. Within a year his business had failed, the victim of a slump which had led to a dramatic fall in consumer spending aggravated by high interest rates. That same year British & Commonwealth went a step too far and purchased Atlantic Computers, whilst Mecca's £750 million bid for Pleasurama was doomed to fail when they had to meet 15% interest charges and ultimately became easy prey to a take-over of £500 million by Rank. The Saatchi Brothers diversified into Market Consultancy, but when speculation hit the City of London that they were possibly set to take over the Midland Bank, it was too much for investors to envisage. Their share price fell from over £50 to under £2 between 1985 and 1993.

In the early 1990s the business climate became more cautious. The questionable accounting practices and the rush for growth have been replaced by an emphasis on focus; concentrating on the areas in which a business has proved to be efficient. The dangers of capital expansion via share floatations had been exposed as the road to a possible take-over by predators and a loss of control. Both Alan Sugar (Amstrad) and Richard Branson (Virgin) fought to take their companies back to private limited status (see Chapter 1.1). Only Richard Branson was successful.

Source: National newspaper reports and author's research.

Preview

In this chapter we investigate the following key areas:
- the advantages and disadvantages of growth
- types of growth
- integration
- mergers and take-overs
- capital expansion
- the Stock Exchange
- the developments in investment markets
- the European factor

The price of growth

The 1980s were the decade of the acquisitive entrepreneur – growth was the key target and many businesses diversified and grew too large on an increasing burden of debt.

Many of the business moguls like Robert Maxwell and Kerry Packer found that as the economic climate changed they became financially over-exposed. As interest rates rose, demand fell, along with company profits. Some, like the newspaper baron Rupert Murdoch, experienced difficulties but survived, others, the most notorious being Robert Maxwell, did not. Maxwell dug himself deeper into debt with his purchases of Macmillan (the American company) for $2.6 billion and the Official Airline Guide for $750 million. He sought ways out by complex financial juggling that eventually collapsed around him.

Positive growth theories are based on the principles of diversification, market control and economies of scale. In simple terms, if a company grows large enough it has the power to move into new areas, eliminate the competition and operate at a cheaper unit cost.

However, *growth has a price*, not just in the financial liabilities it incurs, but in the organisational complexities it creates.

Therefore some companies prefer a more 'focused' approach, concentrating their efforts in areas where they feel they have a specialism or concentrating on their 'core' business. This led in the early 1990s to an increase in corporate divestment, companies scaling down their organisations to smaller autonomous units. In 1994 there was an resurgence of interest in mergers and take-overs. The privatised regional electricity companies look ripe for take-overs whilst more building societies are likely to join together to gain the advantages of scale needed to compete in the financial services market.

We can look at some of these elements more closely.

● **Growth or focus?**

Historically we see that as empires expand and grow they eventually reach a point at which they fragment, become uncontrollable and crumble. Attempts to bind diverse cultures and beliefs from a distance are doomed to fail. An organisation can have similar problems. Business can over-expand, and what we call the benefits of economies of scale can actually become diseconomies of scale. The benefits achieved by the smaller units include increased flexibility and the ability to adapt to market changes. As with empires, the problems are largely ones to do with management control: coordination, communication and motivation. All of these can be difficult to achieve on a larger scale.

● **Communication**

To be effective, communication must work up and down the line management structure. If the structure is too complex and diverse, communication can become blurred and messages distorted.

● **Coordination**

If an organisation is too diverse the coordination process can become over-cumbersome and difficult to monitor.

● **Control**

Market and economic indicators, to which firms need to respond, are often unpredictable and untimely. Response in a large organisation can become ineffective and delayed action can mean missed opportunities.

● **Focus**

Companies in recent years have seen the value of developing their core interests, focusing on their efficient and well developed units. Businesses have become less interested in integration but more in forming working partnerships with compatible organisations. However, there are some sectors in which integration has become a key issue. The financial services sector is an area where competition has intensified and there is a need for organisations to integrate to consolidate their power.

Another factor is that companies are attempting to cut back borrowing and repair damaged balance sheets. In a recessionary period a firm will adopt a more conservative approach to development. The risk-taking that goes hand in hand with a boom period will be replaced by caution.

The cycle of growth and focus is directly related to the business cycle from boom to gloom. The smaller company can be much more flexible, adjusting to changes in the market and responding to developments needed. Nevertheless it can also be more vulnerable.

How to grow

A business can increase its size through internal expansion, capital growth or external expansion.

Internal expansion is achieved by increasing production output or sales. This is also known as organic growth The expansion is incorporated within the same structure but there would normally be an increase in the factors of production. As we know, the factors of production are the resources that go towards producing a unit of output and they are defined as land, labour, capital and enterprise

A company producing a good or service may take on more employees (labour), an additional site (land), extra investment in machinery (capital) and the person that would initiate this move for growth would be the entrepreneur A company could also increase its internal growth by increasing the efficiency of its factors of production, e.g. a more highly skilled workforce, an increased use of technology or a more efficient management of its structure of production. A business can also expand by increasing its capital structure

Why grow?

Advantages of increasing scale

Companies should aim for a scale of output at which they obtain the maximum benefits.

Firms will usually benefit if they operate on a larger scale because, put simply, as output increases costs decrease – i.e. if a company produces 2000 goods on a machine and decides to produce an extra 1000 articles, as the machine is already in production, the extra cost would be minimal. This costing exercise will be looked at further when we analyse fixed and variable costs in Section 2 on 'Finance and Business'. In simple terms, this is an example of what is known as economies of scale, but a firm can

benefit from economies of scale only if the market will absorb the increased output

Economies of scale

Economies of scale are categorised into two groups, internal and external

● Internal economies of scale are the benefits a firm experiences from the effective organisation of its own productive resources.
● External economies of scale are the benefits the firm experiences as a result of the growth of the whole industry of which the firm is an integral part.

Look at Boxes 2.1 and 2.2.

BOX 2.1	**Types of internal economies of scale**

- **Financial** – Larger companies would usually have increased financial status and therefore a greater credit rating because they would be deemed less of an investment risk by creditors. They can raise extra capital on the Stock Exchange and their greater selling potential and larger assets lead to greater all-round financial security, flexibility and bargaining power.
- **Human resource management** – A large firm allows for increased specialisation because it has a greater capacity to break its functions down into specialised areas. For example, if you look at a simple situation in a small office, a clerk or secretary may perform many functions as an all-round office administrator. In a large company these functions would be broken into specialised areas – i.e. word-processing, reception, post, cash control, etc. This could allow for increased division of labour and specialisation. It can also prove easier to attract better qualified staff because the larger company can offer increased potential for advancement and wider opportunities within the same company.
- **Technical** – The capital resources of larger companies means that they can invest in increased technological development.
- **Decreased risk** – Spreading risk is easier for a large company because they can diversify and are less dependent on specific market areas which may prove vulnerable at certain times.
- **Commercial** – Because larger firms have more resources available it means they can use the resources to gain benefits for the organisation. For example, they can derive benefits from bulk purchasing of raw materials; their communication networks are much wider so outlets can be operated on a more diverse scale whilst still gaining benefits from, for example, national advertising.

BOX 2.2	**Types of external economies of scale**

- **Concentration** – Benefits can be gained by industries locating in areas where colleges and other agencies have developed specialised training courses which develop skills needed by the workforce in local industries.
- **Ancillary services** – In areas where there is a high degree of industrial concentration ancillary services develop to support the industries. This may be in the form of the supply of raw materials, distribution channels or other aids to trade.

How to expand: external growth

Diversification and integration

Diversification

The benefits of diversification are simple to grasp. The old adage, 'Don't put all your eggs in one basket' seems to have a natural logic in this context. If a company concentrates in a specific market and that market then goes into decline it is difficult to switch direction, whereas if a company sees room for potential development in another market area and diversifies into that area, then resources can be more easily shifted from one area to another within the same structure. This is a way of spreading risk.

Integration

When companies join together integration is said to take place.

When some companies join together there can be a more positive outcome and 'synergy' is said to occur, the whole being greater than the sum of the parts.

Synergy can take place when two companies have complementary markets or production processes. When the car manufacturer SAAB integrated with Scania, the production processes and research base were complementary, so synergy occurred. In the case of Saga, the holiday company for the over-50s, it made 'synergetic sense' for them to take over a company dealing in retirement homes because their markets were complementary. In other words, Saga could capitalise from the contacts they had made, particularly their communication links with their holidaymakers, which include a magazine distributed to their customers.

Integration can either be on a vertical or horizontal basis:

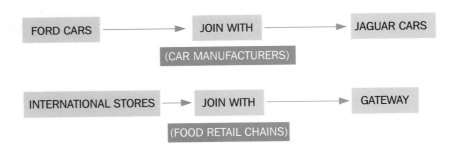

Vertical   A coming together of firms who are at different points in the productive process. This integration can occur either forward or backwards in the process:

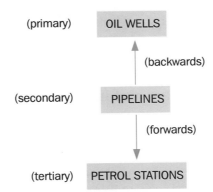

Mergers and take-overs

'Two firms coming together' can either take the form of a merger or a take-over. A merger is a form of integration which is a two-sided agreement whereby companies join together for mutual benefits.

The company that has a controlling interest is called a holding company. Another form of merger is a conglomerate merger whereby a firm may enter into a totally different field of operation. This is also called 'conglomerate growth'.

A take-over is very different in that a company is taken over against its wishes by another company often termed a predator.

This is a far more hostile situation, as the term implies. If a company is publicly quoted there is no reason why another company cannot buy up shares in it if they are interested in holding ownership. This can be a disadvantage of becoming a publicly floated company.

The take-over scene is one which developed momentum in the 1980s.

BOX 2.3

The Rowntree take-over

Rowntree were an old British chocolate-making firm which was set up in the nineteenth century. Joseph Rowntree built up his company on his Quaker beliefs, similar to cooperative ideals, which included supporting and housing his workforce. The take-over of Rowntree began when Suchard (another Swiss-based chocolate company) built up a 14.9% share stake. Suchard stated its intention to hold a 25% stake in Rowntree unless a third party moved on to the scene. Nestlé's then started their eventually successful take-over bid.

Throughout the 1980s Nestlé had been buying up companies which owned international brand names. For example in 1984 it bought out Carnation, the USA food processing firm, and shortly afterwards Buitoni, the pasta group. Apart from the benefits of scale, diversification and an acquisition of successful brand names like Kit Kat, another factor must be considered – entry to the Single European Market (SEM). The Swiss, like the Japanese, were not in the Single European Market and therefore were looking at ways of gaining entry. By producing their goods within Europe they could achieve this. Also the importance of such successful **brand names** cannot be understated. For any company to develop newly branded goods the risk factor is very high: to buy successful brand names is much more lucrative. In buying out Rowntree Nestlé gained internationally famous names such as After Eights and Lion Bars, both big sellers in Europe. These were the biggest prize.

Capital expansion: the Stock Exchange

The Stock Exchange is a market where stocks and shares are bought and sold. The value of shares is determined by the interaction of the demand for the shares and the supply available. The Stock Exchange appears on our televisions like a household name, but in reality few understand the complexities of its operations. Like many institutions it is happy to maintain its own mystique.

When the Stock Exchange has problems economic gloom descends, but what is it really all about?

The Stock Exchange has two major roles, one as a market for raising funds for business and government (primary) and another as a speculative stage for investors (secondary). The former is subject of this section.

Raising funds for business (new issues)

A principal role of the Stock Exchange is to allow companies to raise capital by selling securities in the primary market. Equity finance gives business the opportunity to fund expansion programmes, develop new products and reduce borrowings. Any company applying for a full listing needs to provide in its listing particulars a full picture of the company, its management, financial records, trading history and business prospects. Companies are able to raise capital at the time of going to the market but also subsequently by issuing securities for cash. Look at Box 2.4.

A company can sell shares up to its authorised levels as stated in the Memorandum of Association. Any amount above that level needs the agreement of the

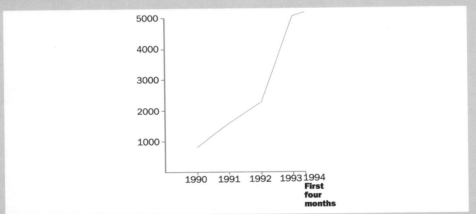

BOX 2.4

New Issues

Source: Author's research.

- A public issue is normally processed through an 'issuing house', usually a merchant bank, who acts as agent for the share sale
- A **prospectus** is placed in the media, which outlines the major aims and objectives of the company and shares are then sold to investors through the issuing house
- The advantage of this process is that if the shares are not sold the issuing house 'underwrites' them, in other words, they take over the responsibility for their sale. If they are not all sold it is the issuing house which bears the risk.

shareholders. A positive aspect of share issues over the past decade has been the increased use of employee share schemes. They are used by companies to encourage workers to become financially involved with the company's successes and failures.

A rights issue

A rights issue is an invitation to **existing shareholders to buy additional shares**; they are usually offered at a relatively low price and can form a good investment, dependent upon the performance of the company.

From the company's viewpoint, this can be a safer way of obtaining capital because no new shareholders are recruited.

The players in the Stock Market

The Stock Exchange Council

The role of the Stock Exchange Council is to:

- Control the admission of new members
- Formulate the rules
- When necessary discipline members
- Settle disputes
- Provide information.

The investor

The investor can follow one of two procedures.

SEAQ is the Stock Exchange Automatic Quotation Screen, showing up-to-the-minute buying and selling prices for shares.

- The deal will be carried out through a **market maker**
- The Stock Exchange **central control system** will process the deal
- The **Registrar of the company** will record the ownership.

We need to consider this process in some detail.

The process of investing

An investor goes to a broker (an agent who deals with the public) who in turn refers to SEAQ. The SEAQ computer screen gives out a buying and selling price for each share. The majority of shares are ordinary shares; preference shares are rare. The investor may go to a bank manager who will then go to a broker, who will consult SEAQ, as the diagram above demonstrates.

The broker processes the deal through the Stock Exchange central system and at the end of the day a check is made to ensure that each sale is matched by a purchase. The broker then needs to get the funds, but in the meantime the shares are temporarily owned by the Stock Exchange pool nominee account (SEPON).

The investor has to pay for the shares on settlement day, which is approximately 2 weeks later. At the end of the account the Stock Exchange informs the Company Registrar of the transfer of ownership. The Registrar keeps a log of who owns the shares in the company. The settlement period can take much longer: during the privatisation boom of the 1980s the volume of work passing through the Stock Exchange meant the process was taking months not weeks. Box 2.5 explains this process.

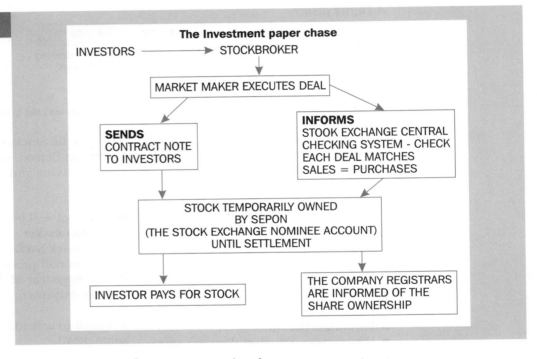

BOX 2.5

The Investment paper chase

INVESTORS → STOCKBROKER

MARKET MAKER EXECUTES DEAL

SENDS CONTRACT NOTE TO INVESTORS

INFORMS STOOK EXCHANGE CENTRAL CHECKING SYSTEM - CHECK EACH DEAL MATCHES SALES = PURCHASES

STOCK TEMPORARILY OWNED BY SEPON (THE STOCK EXCHANGE NOMINEE ACCOUNT) UNTIL SETTLEMENT

INVESTOR PAYS FOR STOCK

THE COMPANY REGISTRARS ARE INFORMED OF THE SHARE OWNERSHIP

Recent developments in investment

'Big Bang'

The Big Bang of October 1986 was a catchword to express the changes which occurred in the Stock Exchange dealing system. The Stock Exchange came into line with international practices. The system of fixed commissions for brokers was eliminated and competition was introduced with an opening up of dealing to both corporate and international membership.

This development saw the arrival of Japanese dealer Nomura; the closed 'club' atmosphere disappeared and the Stock Exchange became a high technology industry. Dealers were no longer on the floor of the Stock Exchange operating the 'hue and cry' system where brokers approached jobbers, who in effect had stalls set up to sell their services. The hustle and bustle, which was associated with the floor of the Stock Exchange, was gone. The dealing moved to the backrooms of stockbroking companies and was carried out by market makers via computer terminals.

The Financial Services Act, which came into force during this period, was also designed to open up competition in the financial world, allowing building societies to compete with banks and causing a mushrooming of so-called 'financial advisers' all eager to compete for investment funds.

The predators

Before the flow of trade into the Stock Exchange with the extensive privatisations of the 1980s and the changes involved with the 'Big Bang' initiative, most registrars were managing to get new share certificates out within the statutory 14 days. However, after the new influx in trading activity, the process began to take months. A disturbing aspect of this for any company is the fact that a predator can build up a stake in a company before it even realises this is happening because ownership is not stipulated on the share registers. However, the City code requires a purchaser to make a full bid for the company if they hold 30% of the shares. Technically a broker does not have to sell stock until a client can prove ownership by providing a share certificate, but in reality when fund managers are continually making large deals with brokers and even smaller investors still constitute important trade, brokers are unlikely to refuse a deal.

TAURUS: a load of old bull?

Because of the intense amount of paper created by share transactions at one point in the boom period it was rumoured that the Stock Exchange would have to close down for a few days to clear the backlog. TALISMAN is the name of the main stock exchange settlement system; in an average week TALISMAN could handle transactions in 1.5 billion shares, but it was felt that another system was necessary.

The alternative investment markets (USM and AIM)

The Unlisted Securities Market (USM) was set up as a stepping stone for smaller and younger companies who were not yet ready for a full listing on the Stock Exchange. This is a simpler and cheaper way of achieving capital growth as the regulations are less stringent and the fee is smaller. The USM was eventually being replaced by the Alternative Investment Market (AIM), which was launched in January 1995.

BOX 2.6

TAURUS

A new computer system called 'TAURUS' was meant to herald the beginning of the era of the paperless transaction. The idea was that investors would become a member of TAURUS, with each having their own code. Transactions would then be moved in and out of the member's account. This system would have required a change in the law which stipulates that a company must issue share certificates every time ownership changes.

However, TAURUS proved a non-starter. Ironically, a system intended to simplify share settlement procedure and bring down the costs involved was plagued by controversy, with suggestions that the original cost figure of a few million to set up the system was likely to become a figure nearer £60 million. TAURUS was finally abandoned and a new approach to designing a system was initiated. The new system being developed by the Bank of England is called CREST, and will not be a totally paperless system.

Pro-Share

Popular capitalism is a term which is used to describe the involvement of the 'man in the street' in the stock market and investment world.

It evolved from the Government's privatisation issues. One of their objectives was to involve more small investors in equity dealing. Their opponents argued that the policy could also be used as an effective vote-winner with equity holdings forging political allegiances. Although there was an initial period when the small investor did become actively involved in stock market trading, this was relatively short lived. It is the 'institutional' investor, the insurance companies and pensions funds, who holds the major equity in the UK market. Indeed the pension funds have approximately £200 million invested on the Stock Exchange, whilst insurance companies own about a quarter of shares traded. Pro-Share was set up to promote wider share ownership. It was established with funding from the Government, the Stock Exchange and industry. Now it is totally separate, with a diverse range of activities including research into UK share ownership, running investment clubs and providing a forum for individual share owners to voice their opinion.

The Government as competitor

The Government also needs to raise funds to cover its spending. The funds the Government borrows for public sector spending is called the Public Sector Borrowing Requirement (PSBR) Up until the mid-1980s the public sector was constantly in debt. The privatisations of the 1980s and the revenue raised enabled some Public Sector Debt Repayment (PSDR). The revenue also enabled the Government to repay some of the accumulated debt, or the National Debt, which dated back to the seventeenth century.

When the Government raises funds, most are obtained through the City of London. Therefore the Government competes for funds with the private sector. Government stock is called 'gilt edged' – the Government is seen as a safe source of investment and this relative security is reflected in the returns on the investment. The Government has many types of investment sources, including Treasury Bills, Index Linked Bonds and National Savings Certificates.

The role of the Government as competitor was demonstrated when they issued their First Option Bond. The interest rates on the bond were so competitive that the Government came under pressure from the building societies to withdraw the bond – investors drew funds out of their building society accounts to go to post offices and buy bonds. The building societies threatened to increase their own interest rates, which would have had a knock-on effect on home ownership loans. The increase in mortgage rates would have been extremely unpopular in a housing market which incorporates a fast increasing number of individuals with negative equity (they owe more than their property is worth). The Government were compelled to withdraw the bond.

Investment problems for companies

Share values are not purely a reflection of the efficiency and prospective profit output of a company – indeed some would say that in many cases they are quite unrelated. There are other factors which have little to do with individual company performance but have a lot to do with the rise and fall of equity values. Other factors include the world economic climate, confidence in the national government, responses to national economic indicators or Government policy and speculation on the exchange. Stock Exchange fluctuations can demonstrate how ineffective it can be as an indicator of company performance. Look at Box 2.7.

Shareholders are often concerned with making quick profits; long-term objectives are much harder to justify. Yet for a company, risks in the short term can reap better rewards in the longer term. When Richard Branson floated the Virgin Group in 1986 he believed the falling value of his group's shares was based on a misconception of his own image and risk-taking tendency, by the stock market. He felt that the City's short-termism was inappropriate to his own business and ultimately staged a buy-out of the group's shares. Virgin the private company was reborn.

BOX 2.7

The BP share issue

The BP share issue is a prime example of how the mechanics of the Stock Exchange can actually have a regressive effect on a company which is performing efficiently. British Petroleum (BP) had been partially privatised with a portion of shares being held back by the Government. When the second tranche (or block) of shares were put out to public issue, the timing was ill-fated. The flotation occurred just after the Stock Exchange crash on 'Black Monday' (16 September 1992). The price of the second tranche of shares had been pre-set before the crash and ironically when the new shares were floated the price was higher than the original BP shares from the first issues, which were trading on the Exchange: the market value of these shares was lower than the issue value of the newly floated shares. The fact that some members of the public rushed to buy these shares demonstrates a lack of understanding, by the small investor, of how the Stock Exchange works.

The shares had been **underwritten**. This is when a financial broker, usually a merchant bank, guarantees to buy up any unsold shares for a fixed price in return for an underwriting fee. The Stock Market was seen by the general public as an ever-rising star in the investment world. BP hardly deserved this embarrassment but the fate of its shares was beyond its control.

Source: National newspaper reports and author's research.

The European factor

The CBI (Confederation of British Industry) is a group of UK industrialists who meet to discuss the state of British industry and advise the government on aspects affecting business. They have now expressed their concerns about UK companies being taken over by predatory European companies. A major problem is that in the UK many larger companies are publicly quoted whilst in countries like Italy much of the private sector is made up of family businesses who will often form working partnerships but keep their equity off the stock market. In many countries within the European Union (EU), the Stock Market is much less significant. For example, the Brussels stock market is open for only a few hours a day unlike the London Stock Exchange, and they have only 1/10th the volume of the London stock market listings. Company rules also work differently in some European countries where powers can be given to directors rather than shareholders.

The Rowntree take-over (see Box 2.3) caused an outcry from the CBI and Michael Heseltine (then Minister for Trade and Industry) who called for the take-over to be referred to the Monopolies and Mergers Commission, to assess if Nestlé now held a monopoly position. After the take-over, Nestlé would control 25% of the European chocolate market, this being one of the levels at which a monopoly is said to occur.

A criticism of EU membership is that its regulations are often manipulated or ignored. Cadbury's wanted to merge with Rowntree but they were not allowed to do so by the Monopolies and Mergers Commission because they would have controlled 40% of the UK chocolate market, yet in European terms the proportion would only have been 20%.

This situation is viewed as a potentially serious problem and many UK banks have had to enlist European merger specialists. The fact is, most UK companies are far more at home in the USA where companies operate in a very similar way with a shared language and similar culture. In the European market many UK companies seem ill at ease.

REVIEW

After reading this chapter you should understand the different ways a business can grow, and the implications of growth for the business and consumers.

REVIEW TASK

PRACTICAL APPLICATION
Anatomy of a take-over

On 12 April 1988, Rowntree share price rose to 477p as a result of a take-over bid by the Swiss firm Nestlé. Suchard stepped in and bought shares on 13 April, and the price rose to 630p. On 27 April, Nestlé offered 890p per share to Rowntree shareholders. At that point they did not obtain a majority stake and Suchard bid 980p, obtaining 28% of the shareholding. Nestlé offered 1075p per share on 24 June and obtained Suchard's shares, thus becoming the majority shareholder in Rowntree.

1 Draw a graph to plot the rise of Rowntree's share value.
2 Work out the profit that would have been gained by someone holding 600 shares purchased on 13 April and sold on 27 April, using a 1.5% commission charge.

Essay questions

1 'When the capital development of a country becomes a by-product of the activities of a Casino, the job is likely to be ill done' (Keynes).
Analyse this statement.

2 Evaluate the implications of 'growth' and 'focus' for the modern company.

3 'The benefits to the consumer decline when mergers occur.' Discuss this statement. (AEB)

CASE STUDY

Nestlé bid for Rowntree
Study the list below – and then answer the questions that follow.

Possible reasons why the bid should be rejected
- Rowntree is among the world's 4 largest confectionery companies
- Over the last 10 years Rowntree has invested some £900 million, at 1987 prices, in promoting its brands across the world
- The company has already captured over 24% of the UK chocolate market and is well placed to exploit the opportunities offered by a Single European Market after 1992
- Forecasts for 1988 show UK confectionery profits up 26% to £64.5 million, with profits in Continental Europe reaching £15.3 million, a rise of 39%
- Earnings per share look poised to rise from 40.8p to 47p with dividends increased by 19% to 18.5p
- Rowntree will continue to invest in its brand with a record advertising and promotional spend next year of £138.9 million.

CASE STUDY TASKS
1. Given the information, explain the implications of this take-over for:
   - Rowntree shareholders
   - The Rowntree management team
   - Rowntree staff
   - Nestlé shareholders
   - Nestlé management team
   - Nestlé staff
   - Chocolate consumers.
2. What are the implications of the Single European Market in the Nestlé takeover of Rowntree?
3. You work for a private limited company which is, at present, contemplating a public flotation of its shares. As a business studies student, write a report to the Managing Director, stating the implications of a public flotation. Prepare your report and accompanying documentation on a computer or word processor, if possible.

FOCUS

The changing face of the public sector

The National Health Service

In 1990 legislation was passed to reform the National Health Service and by 1991 the reforms had begun to be implemented. The Government believed that in order to increase efficiency the hospitals providing health care would need to be separated from the large general practitioners that were its commissioners – the establishment of an **internal market**. A **weighted capitation system** (funding based on the needs of the area) is being used to allow extra Government funding for health services in deprived areas. Hospitals are also being encouraged to take on 'Trust' status.

Trust hospitals are not controlled by local regions but by a Hospital Trust Committee made up of medical and non-medical members. Although management is devolved to the committees, the Chairman is appointed by the government department and the finances come directly from central government.

Schools

Under the present 'Local Management of Schools' system, headteachers are now responsible for their own budget which has been devolved from local government. Headteachers and governors are also taking on increasing responsibility for decision-making. Schools have also been given the opportunity to 'opt out' of local authority control. The Parents' Charter gives parents the opportunity to place their child in the school of their choice rather than the one that is in their 'catchment' (local) area, and the controversial League Tables of results are meant to be used as the benchmark of academic success.

Further education

Since April 1993, Further Education colleges have had **corporate status** and operate as registered charities. This means that they no longer come under the control of the county council but obtain their funding indirectly from central government through the Further Education Funding Council. In theory, the management and governors of each college have the powers of decision-making but, in effect, the Government can place restrictive financial controls which may leave them unable to manage as they would wish.

Prisons

On 1 April 1993 the Prison Service became an 'Executive Agency'. The Director-General of Prisons is responsible for operational matters and the Home Secretary is responsible for policy decisions. The idea is that in future the service will have much greater autonomy. Each prison governor will control their own budget and the recruitment of staff will take place at a local level. The devolved structure has created the opportunity to privatise some prisons. The Criminal Justice Act 1991 encouraged **market testing** to take place, which resulted in some areas of the service, e.g. court escort service and education of inmates, being put out to contract.

Source: National newspaper reports and author's research.

A perspective

It could be argued that the breaking down of these large public sector organisations into smaller accountable units allows more direct management by those central to the organisation. It also opens the structure to allow the process of privatisation and market testing. The new financial flexibility may mean that funds can be allocated by the managers of the service, but if the Government are imposing tight financial constraints decision-making may be severely restricted. The increasing emphasis on public sector 'managers' as opposed to 'professionals' within the organisation has caused much internal concern. School headteachers, college principals and prison governors are expected to act as business managers whilst those on governing bodies are taking on the responsibility and role of company directors. The final question which needs to be asked is: can patients, students and prisoners really be seen as 'customers' and, through the segmentation of the public sector, can a social policy be fully developed?

There is a large question-mark over Agency status. Can an Agency structure function in areas of high political sensitivity? Two such areas are the Prison Service and the Child Support Agency. The sacking of the Director-General of the Prison Service, Derek Lewis, by the Home Secretary, Michael Howard, has brought this problem to the fore.

In an Agency the Government Minister devolves responsibility for operational matters to the civil servant in charge through the framework document. The Minister is responsible for policy decisions and the civil servant for operational matters. Derek Lewis was sacked by Michael Howard for operational failures over the escape from Parkhurst following the publication of the Learmont Report. Derek Lewis intended to take the Home Secretary to court because he maintained that Michael Howard had interfered directly in operational matters and therefore should take responsibility for any failures that occurred. In the event, an out-of-court settlement was agreed. The Civil Service Code states that civil servants do as ministers instruct.

Civil servants fear that under this system they are being made scapegoats for ministers and are being used as a way for government to escape political liability. Blurred lines of responsibility may always be useful in areas where political capital can be won or lost.

Preview
In this chapter we shall investigate the following key areas:
- government departments and social ownership
- local authorities
- the business rate

The modern public sector

The public sector consists of organisations run by central and local government. Some would argue that these organisations provide a service to the people paid for by taxation, without the need for the profit motive. Others would say that the profit motive of the private sector is the only true indicator of efficiency. The public sector incorporates

- government departments, which control specific areas of the economy
- public corporations, which are partly controlled indirectly by the Government
- Local Authorities.

The present public sector has been much diminished, with the Government transferring ownership of the majority of the nationalised industries to the private sector (privatisation) and the lifting of Government protection from certain trading activities (deregulation). Local authorities have lost control of many aspects of health and education whilst much of their trading activities and local services are being contracted out to the private sector. Central government now controls many areas which were previously devolved to local authorities, a control often established by setting up tight financial restrictions.

Government departments

How governments are elected

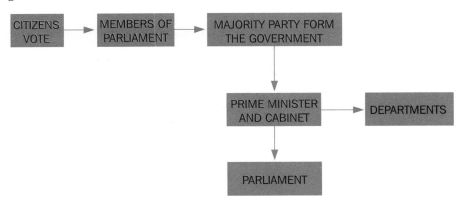

- The public vote to elect their local members of parliament
- The majority party form a Government
- The party leader becomes the Prime Minister who then selects the Cabinet of Ministers
- The Cabinet members each have responsibility for a certain area of the UK economy.

Examples of government departments include:

- Treasury (finance)
- Environment
- Health
- Education and Employment

Public corporations

Public corporations are set up by Act of Parliament. To dissolve them another Act must be passed. The management structure is:

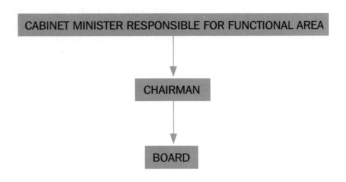

The Chairman is appointed by the Minister, so the appointment will tend to be a political one on a fixed-term contract.

Public corporations are not just nationalised industries. 'Public corporation' is a wider term which also incorporates, for example, the BBC, which was set up by Charter not an Act of Parliament. The newly incorporated Further Education Colleges were also set up by Charter.

BOX 3.1

The UK public sector

The public sector of the UK economy has been cut back dramatically since 1979. Most **nationalisation**, which moved private sector companies into the public sector, took place after the Second World War and was carried out by a Labour Government. However, some industries were nationalised by the Conservative Government of the early 1970s. They include British Aerospace, Rolls Royce and British Shipbuilders. If we look at some of the industries that were brought into the public sector it gives us some idea of the scale of its contraction:

1945–9	● British Airways
	● Gas
	● Electricity
	● Steel
	● Coal
	● Railways
1970s	● Leyland Cars
	● Rolls Royce
	● British Aerospace
	● British Shipbuilders

Social ownership

In support of social ownership it could be argued that:

- Some industries are natural monopolies. They benefit from economies of scale (remember Chapter 1.2). It may be in the public interest that these industries remain public sector monopolies rather than become private sector monopolies. The public utilities, for example, gas, electricity and water, could be used as prime examples.
- It is possible for the Government to **control the economy** through the public sector – for instance, creating or cutting back employment. Once the public sector is marginalised, this economic tool is lost.
- **Essential services** can be maintained through the public sector and the infrastructure of the country can be developed, for example, by a publicly owned public transport system.
- Some industries are 'capital-intensive', needing **investment in** research and development (R & D) which means that funding for long-term projects is vital. In the private sector shareholders are likely to be more interested in short-term profits. One reason for the original nationalisation of the coal and railway industries was the lack of investment when they were private sector businesses.
- **National security and defence** industries can be preserved in the state sector.
- Some industries may suffer from **short-term market problems** which could threaten their existence but

their loss could be detrimental to the economy. Governments may therefore bring these industries into the protection of the public sector for a short period. This was the case with Leyland (Rover) cars and Rolls Royce in the 1970s.

Privatisation

The rationale for privatisation is that:

- Industries in the public sector can charge higher prices because they are **protected from market forces**.
- Protection from the market can lead to **management complacency and overmanning**.
- In the public sector, **politicians**, not **entrepreneurs**, will ultimately make business decisions.

The process of privatisation

The process of privatisation involves the selling of public sector corporate ownership to the private sector.

Deregulation is the breaking down of government regulations which had given certain public sector concerns protection from the free market.

For example, bus services had been controlled by the National Bus Company and weekly information on television and radio programming was restricted to the *Radio Times* and *TV Times*. The lifting of the controlling regulations has led to bus companies' competing for passengers, but often only on the busiest routes, and a mushrooming of periodicals printing weekly details of programmes to be broadcast. Look at Box 3.2.

| BOX 3.2 | **Bus deregulation** |

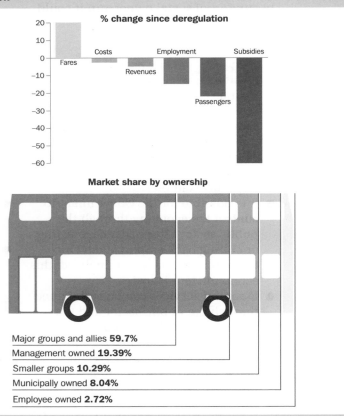

% change since deregulation

Market share by ownership

Major groups and allies **59.7%**

Management owned **19.39%**

Smaller groups **10.29%**

Municipally owned **8.04%**

Employee owned **2.72%**

Up until 1985 local bus services were run by the National Bus Company which was a government body. The Transport Act 1985, which came into force in 1986, made it possible for anyone to run a bus service as long as they:

● Obtained an operator's licence from the Department of Transport

● Ensured their vehicles met the safety standards set by the Department

● Registered their routes with the Regional Traffic Commissioners.

The original bus service operators are now private sector companies and if local authorities want a particular service to be provided on a specific route they will invite tenders from bus operators. The objective of deregulation was to create more competition in the provision of local bus services. To some extent this has happened: through the use of competitive tendering local authorities can obtain cheaper services. However, it has also meant that services on loss-making routes have been cut whilst services on more popular routes have in many areas reached saturation point, with a number of bus companies competing for the same passengers.

The regulators

In order to protect the consumer from the dangers of the old public sector monopolies becoming private sector monopolies, regulatory bodies were established for the public utilities:

- OFTEL – British Telecom
- OFGAS – British Gas
- OFFER – Electricity.

Some of the regulators have been quite effective at exposing actions that are detrimental to the consumer. However, the work of the regulators often relies on using information supplied by the corporate giants they are attempting to monitor. The privatised public utilities have had regulations placed upon them, including price controls, in an attempt to curb their monopoly position. For example, British Telecom are obliged to keep their pay phone services despite their unprofitability. They are also forced to allow cable operators to interconnect to their systems, but are prohibited from offering a cable TV service themselves for a 10-year period. These restriction may seem futile when the profits of the privatised public utilities are announced and the salaries of their top executives are rising. The share options handed out to these executives is another factor the public has questioned. The success of their operations are not necessarily a reflection of their competitive performance, but often an outcome of their monopoly situation.

Local authorities

Local government allows local people to vote to determine how their own communities are governed. Residents elect councillors who then form into committees to make decisions about the running of local services. Decisions made will have an impact on the environment in which businesses operate:

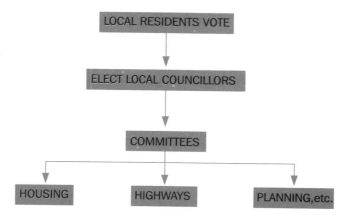

Some of the services which local authorities operate are mandatory (they have to provide them by law) and some are discretionary (they have the option to provide them). Mandatory services include refuse collection, education and the fire service, whilst examples of discretionary provision are nursery schools and cycle training.

Local government organisational structure is split into a two-tier system, with a county and district level:

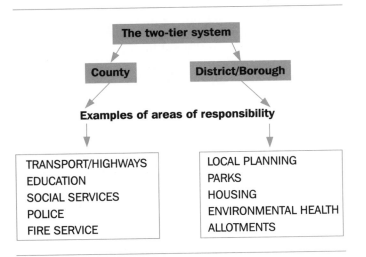

Local authorities receive funding from central government and income from trading but they also raise funds by local taxation. They can now also obtain European regional funding.

The business rate

Businesses used to pay rates in the same way as domestic premises, based on the rateable, or rentable, value of the property. Each property had an assessed rentable value based on the size, the facilities and the location. Local authorities would then set a poundage rate based on the amount of funding they needed. This system enabled the council to gather the funding they needed by calculating the total rateable value of all the properties in the area and dividing that figure by the amount they needed to collect, so establishing a poundage levy.

Discrepancies occurred because some councils had higher spending budgets than others. The boundaries of local areas meant that in one street residents on one side of the road could be paying a much higher rate than residents on the other side.

In April 1991 a new system for setting a business rate was started, called the Uniform Business Rate. It works in a similar way. Each business property has an assessed rateable value but the rate per pound is set nationally not locally. In order to implement this system the rentable value of all properties was re-assessed by the Inland Revenue between 1988 and 1990. The problem was that property reassessment had not been done since the 1970s so the rateable value jumped up significantly although in many cases the national rate (uniform rate) or multiplier was much lower than the previous local rate. To ease the burden on businesses a system of transitional relief was established. Transitional relief is based on the last rateable value under the old rating system of 1989/90. If a business paid less under the old system, it would be entitled to Transitional Relief.

The rateable values of businesses are reassessed every 5 years and a revised uniform rate or multiplier will be set annually. The uniform business rate up to April 1995 was 42.3p.

BOX 3.3

Transitional relief

If a business had a rateable value of £1000 in 1989/90 and the local rate was set at £2.77:

   £1000 × £2.77 = £2770 per annum to pay

If the newly assessed rateable value was £10000 in 1990/91 and the Uniform Rate was set at 34.8p:

   £10000 × 34.8p = £3480 per annum to pay

The Government established that the maximum increase could be 15% plus inflation (which at the time was 7%):

   15% of £2770 = £415.50   + inflation = £29.08

Therefore £2770 + £415.50 + £29.08 = **£3214.58** would be the maximum amount.

If a business paid more under the old system the amount of reduction was also set at the same level. This helped to offset the cost of the transitional relief.

Current developments in privatisation

The Government has encouraged public/private sector partnerships, with many local authority services being 'contracted out' to the private sector. This process involves local authorities offering the contract for a particular services to the private sector by requesting quotations for the provision of the service. Refuse collection and school meal services are areas where contracting out has been used. Leisure centres are often owned by the council but the management is carried out by private sector companies who it is considered would have better management expertise.

The defence industry is not exempt from this pattern of development. The Army Catering Corps has been replaced, with private companies providing this service and the provision of security to some defence sites has also been contracted out. However, the question of defence site security was raised when the IRA bombed a defence base which was using a private contractor. An enquiry found that the effective provision of the service had been undermined by the cutting of costs.

There are two principles which underline these moves – Competitive Tendering and Indirect Labour.

Competitive tendering

Competitive tendering means the whole provision of a service can be handed over to another provider who bids for the job on a competitive basis. The justification for this system is based on the fact that firms will compete to offer the service and hence costs can be cut. However, some firms that compete for these tenders put in bids at unrealistic prices in order to win and the standard of the service provided may fall or the contractor may be unable to survive.

Indirect labour

An advantage of contracting out a service is that the workforce become the responsibility of the private contractor. In the past public sector workers have had relative job security, which has been criticised for encouraging overmanning and complacency. It also allowed an increase in the power of public sector unions. The workers of contract companies often have little job security and are often employed on a 'self-employment' basis, which means they do not get paid holidays or sick pay. The use of indirect labour is increasingly being used by big private sector companies. Companies which include British Telecom and British Gas put much of their work out to competitive tendering rather than using a direct labour force.

A case was taken to the European Court by three Eastbourne refuse collectors whose service was put out to tender by the local authority. They called for the protection of workers whose jobs are transferred from one form of ownership to another. They claimed protection under the European Directive of TUPE (Transfer of Undertakings and Protection of Employment). The UK government had always stated that TUPE applied only to commercial ventures. The European Court overruled the UK interpretation, and this ruling could have serious implications for privatisation and competitive tendering contracts.

REVIEW

After reading this chapter you should understand the role of the public sector within the economy, its changing function in society and the effects of these changes on the whole of business activity.

REVIEW TASK

PRACTICAL APPLICATION 1

Privatisation of electricity

Shares began trading on the Stock Exchange on 11 December 1990. The price of the shares was fixed at 240p, with 100p payable on application and two further instalments of 70p payable at a later date. At the close of the first day's trading the 240p partly-paid shares were changing hands at premiums of between 42p and 66p:

● What sort of discount were the shares sold at by the Government?
● What does this imply about the sell-off?

PRACTICAL APPLICATION 2

A High Street business property has been reassessed for the new business rate at £125 000 with a multiplier of 34.8p for each pound of rateable value. However, the old rateable value was £60 305 with a multiplier per pound of value of £2.77. The Government set a maximum increase of 12.5% plus an inflation rate of 6%. Work out:

● The amount due per annum under the old system
● The new amount due under the new system
● The amount of payment after transitional relief.

REVIEW TASK

CRITICAL ANALYSIS

Consider the affects of privatisation on:
- The taxpayer
- The Government
- The company structure.

QUESTIONS

Essay questions

1 'Privatisation is like selling off the family silver to pay for the shopping' (Harold Macmillan, Conservative Prime Minister, 1957–63). Discuss this statement.

2 'Competitive tendering has brought down the cost of public sector services.' Discuss this statement.

3 The most effective action open to the regulatory bodies in the public sector is to expose irregularities to public scrutiny. To what extent is this true?

Data response question
Read the article and answer the questions which follow.
Training and Enterprise Councils (TECs) were set up in local areas by the government to co-ordinate business training and development.

Updata

Norfolk and Waveney TEC

Market Research Findings - December 1991

TABLE 1

Norfolk & Waveney - Consumer Spending
(% change)
Constant 1985 Prices (£m)

	Total	Durables	Non-Durables
1989	3993	440	3553
% change	4.0	0.6	4.4
1990	4055	408	3647
% change	1.5	− 7.4	2.6
1991	4044	412	3632
% change	− 0.3	0.9	− 0.4

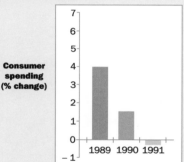

TABLE 2

Norfolk & Waveney GDP
(% change)
Constant Prices (£m)

	1989	1990	1991
Total GDP	4803	4821	4783
% change	2.9	0.4	− 0.8

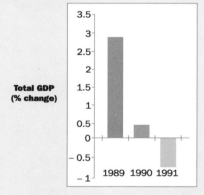

Source: Business Strategies Ltd (London, December 1991)

Trends and projections in local consumer spending in **TABLE 1** clearly show the effects of the recent recession. Similar trends and projections can be seen when looking at Gross Domestic Product (GDP) for the TEC area in **TABLE 2**.

It is important to note that there is also a delay expected between the economy showing sustained signs of recovery and businesses feeling confident enough to take on more staff. It is for this reason that rising unemployment could be expected at least in the short term.

Norfolk and Waveney TEC envisages local economic recovery to begin in the first half of 1992 and although short term labour and skill shortages are not expected, past experience suggests that labour market problems associated with strong economic growth will eventually emerge. The TEC fully appreciates the importance of planning early for the skills needed in a growing economy.

(Adapted from *Updata, Edition 2,* Norfolk and Waveney TEC, December 1991)

Using only data from Tables 1 and 2, discuss 'the effects of the recent recession' in the area, already visible in December 1991.

Explain how these 'effects' might have an impact upon employment in

an independent local supermarket

a medium-sized engineering firm making components for washing machines and spin dryers

the local tourist industry.

Discuss the 'labour market problems associated with strong economic growth' as mentioned in the article. (AEB), June 1993

CASE STUDY

Nuclear fall-out!

The privatisation of the electricity industry did cause some red faces at Westminster. The assurance by the then Energy Minister Cecil Parkinson that the nuclear power industry would be part of the privatisation programme looked set to be a hollow promise.

Nicholas Ridley, the then Trade and Industry Secretary, who is believed to have been the architect of the Government's privatisation programme, argued that the privatisation of public utilities created competition and would ultimately provide a better service to the consumer. He later found his privatisation programme under threat from the pillar of the private sector establishment – the City. In the run-up to the privatisation of the electricity industry, the City came to the conclusion that the nuclear power industry was unsellable. The potentially immense, and as yet unknown, decommissioning costs, plus the safety implications in the aftermath of Chernobyl, led to the City blocking the privatisation.

National Power, the successor to the Central Electricity Generating Board, was to have taken nuclear with it into the private sector. Ironically if it had not been for the privatisation attempt the real costs of nuclear power might not have been exposed. Mrs Thatcher and Sir Arthur Marshall, the then Chairman of the electricity industry, were both champions of nuclear power. The ultimate threat to the nuclear industry of being eliminated from the privatisation process was thought to be too much for Sir Arthur Marshall to accept, and he eventually departed from his post.

Two years on from the rejection of nuclear power, its status survived. This was largely due to a very effective publicity campaign and events in the Gulf war which saw oil prices double. The increasing environmental worries generated by fossil fuel helped to put forward a more positive case for nuclear energy. Plans are underway to privatise Nuclear Electric. However, the quarter million pound fine which was issued to Nuclear Electric in September 1995, for failing to comply to safety regulations, will not help their case in the eyes of the public.

Source: National newspaper reports and author's research.

CASE STUDY TASK
From a concerned customer

To whom it may concern
OFFER
London

Dear Sir,

I would like to complain about what I consider to be gross overpricing of electricity with a 30% price increase to my business. The electricity industry is exploiting its private monopoly status and your organisation has had little impact.

I believe your main objectives are to ensure that customers are protected and competitiveness is promoted, but how is this possible when Powergen and National Power are the only two suppliers and the National Grid is a total monopoly?

I recently read that you have had 21,000 complaints since 'vesting day' – is this a measure of your success?

Now that British Gas is the subject of a monopoly enquiry, should you not be pursuing a similar type of enquiry of the electricity industry?

The 1995 profits of the National Grid are a disgrace, especially as their top executives are pocketing a large amount of this for themselves based on their free share options. Their further tax avoidance by putting a proportion of their shareholdings in the names of their spouse is a scam the ordinary taxpayer would not have the chance of achieving. Given that these industries were built on taxpayers' money I feel your role as regulator of the industry should become more prominent.

The closing of the old Electricity Board showrooms, now called Powerhouse, is a loss to the consumer but perhaps as it is the only section of the industry which competes directly with other electricity appliance retailers, it is an indication of the industry's inability to compete on a level playing field!

Yours faithfully,

1. Explain the City's rejection of nuclear power.
2. Why did the rejection by the City put the industry in jeopardy?
3. What does the 'concerned customer' mean by 'private monopoly'?
4. Explain the role of OFFER.
5. Create a reply to the above customer from OFFER, using a word processor or computer for the letter.

1.4 Other Types of Organisation

Mutual status

Building societies were initially set up to provide housing for groups of individuals who pooled their funds to create the necessary capital to create homes.

The Building Society Act 1986 was designed to liberate building societies from their non-profit-making mutual status and encourage them to compete in the world of financial services. The initial problem was that to compete with the private sector, mutual status would not provide enough capital. Therefore building societies have been given the power, through the Act, to change their status to plc as long as 20% of all members vote and 75% of those who vote support the change. The Abbey National has changed to plc status, and the Woolwich is also planning to make the same move. Building societies are generally doing badly with a net outflow of funds.

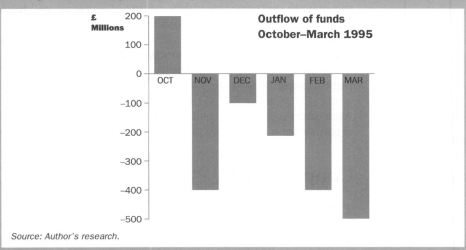

Outflow of funds October–March 1995

Source: Author's research.

The Government has now decided to look again at building society status. The review could go as far as re-writing the Building Society Act and transforming societies into 'savings banks'. The tradition of mutual societies owned by their members could be coming to a close; ministers are now accepting that the present financial system is not encouraging industrial development and see the building societies with a possible new role as industrial financiers.

The traditional building society market of home loans has been hijacked by the banks whilst the general mortgage market is still contracting. The outflow of funds illustrated above was swollen when the government announced that they were going to place a tax on gas and electricity charges. An estimated £720 million was believed to have been drawn out by consumers to pay their gas and electricity bills early in order to avoid the extra cost that would have resulted from the imposition of the tax. The proposed tax proved so unpopular with voters that the government decided against implementation. The net loss of savings in one month was £500 million triggering concerns about a rise in interest rates and the future constitution of the movement.

Source: National newspaper reports and author's research.

Preview

In this chapter we shall investigate the following key areas:

- co-operatives
- franchising
- mutual status

Types of organisation

Some organisations do not form part of the private sector or the public sector of the economy. They are not covered either by the Companies Act or by Act of Parliament. They are not motivated by profit nor are they contributing to the public purse.

An example of two of these types of organisations are cooperative societies and building societies. They are both registered under the Industrial and Provident Society Act and are mutual bodies. They have open membership and withdrawable, not sellable, share capital. The decision-making process is democratic, with 1 vote per person. Examples of other organisations which do not fit into the two main sectors are trade unions and trade associations.

Cooperatives

The 'Co-op' principle

A cooperative society is an organisation set up to meet the needs of its members. It belongs to them and they generally decide how their society should be run.

It is easy to see this principle operating in a housing, manufacturing or farmers' cooperative, less so in an organisation as large and diverse as a large regional retail society. Look at Box 4.1.

BOX 4.1	A Co-op is a different type of organisation	
	A Co-op	*A company*
	SET UP TO MEET MUTUAL NEEDS	SET UP TO PROFIT FROM A NEED
	BELONGS TO ITS MEMBERS – SHOPPERS	BELONGS TO ITS SHAREHOLDERS – INVESTORS
	CONSTITUTED UNDER INDUSTRIAL AND PROVIDENT SOCIETIES ACTS	CONSTITUTED UNDER COMPANY LAW
	1 MEMBER, 1 VOTE	1 SHARE, 1 VOTE
	SOCIAL PURPOSE	PROFIT MOTIVE
	PROFITS TO USERS OF SERVICE	PROFITS TO CAPITAL HOLDERS
	FIXED PRICE AND WITHDRAWABLE SHARES	VALUES FLUCTUATE NON-WITHDRAWABLE SHARES

Source: Author's research from Co-op Society literature.

Nevertheless, the principles still hold true, since all societies belong to their shareholding members. In fact, becoming a shareholder of a consumer cooperative society is much easier than buying shares in a company. Anyone over 16 can become a shareholder for as little as £1. Unlike in a company,

- Cooperative shares do not fluctuate in value
- can be withdrawn at any time
- attract interest much like a deposit account with a bank or building society.

A big difference in a Co-op, however, is that all shareholders have an equal say, regardless of the size of their holding, and are actively encouraged to play a full part in running their society, so fulfilling the obligations and opportunities that come from being a part-owner of a multi-million pound business.

History

The consumer cooperative movement has its roots in the early part of the nineteenth century. The industrial revolution created many problems. One was the difficulty many ordinary families experienced in obtaining food of acceptable quality at fair prices. The development of shops did not keep pace with the growth of the new industrial communities, and often unscrupulous shopkeepers maintained a monopoly of trade in their localities. The formation of nonconformist churches and the development of political movements such as Chartism gave ordinary people the ability and opportunity to organise aspects of their lives. The retail cooperative movement began in 1844 in Rochdale (see Box 4.2). The need and ability to organise, coupled with the ideas of social reformers Robert Owen and Dr William King, encouraged people to start their own shops, which they ran cooperatively. And so the social needs and self-help values of the Victorian age sowed the seeds for a movement that was to revolutionise retailing during the century ahead.

One of the main difficulties faced by those early cooperative societies was to procure goods to sell in their shops. Individually they had neither the skill nor the buying power to get the best deal for their members. So cooperation was taken a step further and, in 1863, a group of societies formed the Cooperative Wholesale Society (CWS). The CWS eventually extended its activities beyond wholesaling and into the areas of manufacturing, farming, importing and the provision of services which local societies could not undertake individually. The Cooperative Insurance Society – now one of Britain's biggest insurers – and the Cooperative Bank are just two of the offsprings of the CWS.

BOX 4.2

Rochdale principles
- Open membership
- Democratic control
- Payment of fixed interest on capital
- Profit distributed to members in proportion to their trade
- Provision of education
- Cooperation among cooperatives

As the formation of cooperatives gathered momentum, so the need grew for an organisation to coordinate activities and collectively represent the interests of societies. In 1889 the Cooperative Union was formed which remains, to this day, the hub of the Consumer Cooperative Movement.

Modern problems

Throughout this century the cooperative movement has undergone many changes in order to meet the competition from multiple retailers, with societies combining to form larger and more effective organisations.

When considering the problems of the cooperative movement in formulating a corporate plan, it must be recognised that, contrary to its public image, 'The Co-op' is not a single body but a movement of about 80 separate societies. Each society is independent, with its own legal identity, board of directors, management structure and so on. Societies vary enormously in size, environment, history and character. The present structure suffers the following disadvantages:

- It is difficult to create a national or even regional development strategy. This is particularly so in the case of superstores where, in some areas, cooperative superstores are commonplace while, in others, they are non-existent. The wide variety of names under which Co-op superstores operate is another indication of the need for a national strategy.

- There is no overall marketing strategy. Across the UK there are examples of societies operating high quality food stores, with a strong emphasis on fresh foods, whilst neighbouring societies retain an outdated infrastructure or small uneconomic grocery units.

- It is difficult to overhaul the movement's shop structure. In 1989 there were 4671 separate shops of which only 76 were superstores, 189 were supermarkets, over 10 000 sq. ft, and 1429 were food stores of between 2000 and 10 000 sq. ft sales area. Clearly, this is not the best structure for retailing in the 1990s. The average sales area of less than 5000 sq. ft remains in marked contrast to the multiples' average of 15 000 sq. ft.

- There are about 80 Boards of Directors, each pursuing separate and often distinctive policies. The movement is perceived by most people as one organisation, but refuses to behave as such.

- Each of the 80 or so societies requires its own management and administrative operations. This is wasteful and inefficient. The movement's competitors operate highly centralised businesses where the specialist skills of individuals are used to maximum effect.

At various times in the movement's history, the idea of one national cooperative society has been mooted, and although no formal plans have ever been approved, it remains a possibility for the future.

Workers' or producer cooperatives

These involve shared work, responsibility, decision-making and profits. They all adhere to the cooperative democratic principle of 1 person 1 vote. There is some management delegation and there are some pay differentials, but this is kept to a minimum.

The John Lewis Partnership is one of the better-known workers' cooperatives. Another example is the Scott–Bader Chemical Company. Both of these businesses based on Christian Socialist principles were given by the owners to the workforce. More recent workers' cooperatives have tended to be set up by the Industrial Common Ownership Movement (ICOM). Look at Box 4.3.

BOX 4.3

Tower colliery

In December 1994 the last deep coal mine in South Wales operating since the 1930s became a workers' cooperative. The workers at the Tower Colliery won financial backing after raising their own capital with the support of the local community who set up a series of fund-raising activities. The new Goitra Tower Anthracite Company is convinced that the 'employee buyout' will be a success. They state that the operating profit of the pit over the last three years was £28 million. A problem which could arise with a workers' cooperative is the question of who does the 'managing'? The advisers to the Tower workers have set up a clearly defined management structure. Employees will have two roles. They will be voters at the annual general meeting, but employees on a day-to-day basis. There will be three management directors, who will be appointed for their expertise in management and finance, plus two workers' directors.

Source: National newspaper reports and author's research.

Franchising

Franchising has, in its widest sense, existed in the UK for many years, but has also been in a period of rapid growth over the past decade.

The franchising system involves a franchiser who issues a licence to a franchisee allowing them to sell or manufacture a product or provide a service under the name of the franchiser.

Franchise agreements vary widely but usually involve a lump sum being paid to the franchiser on signature of the franchise contract, whilst the franchiser generally provides a complete business package which incorporates supply of stock, training of staff and continual back-up advice. The agreement normally also involves regular payments to the franchiser in the form of royalties, often calculated as a percentage of turnover.

Types of franchise

Types of franchise range from your local Unigate milkman or Dynorod service to the independent television channels. Examples of the oldest types are breweries and car distributors whilst the most common ones seen on our High Streets are the fast food chains of, amongst others, McDonald's and Wimpy.

Advantages

The advantages of a franchise can be seen through the success of famous names like The Body Shop, but to gain the advantage of a well known and often nationally advertised name, a high price has to be paid whilst smaller franchise outfits naturally come cheaper. A major advantage of buying a franchise is that you are trading in a proven good or service.

Disadvantages

The disadvantages can be illustrated through the experience of the health food chain Holland and Barrett, who found that for them as a franchiser it became difficult to initiate change in a fast-moving market using franchise outlets with a devolved management structure. They ultimately withdrew from the franchising world.

The growing franchise market has inevitably attracted many 'cowboy outfits' eager to jump on the franchise bandwagon. Many are only too keen to capitalise on increasing numbers of unemployed individuals, some with redundancy capital to invest in what they believe to be a potential business opportunity.

British Franchise Agency

The British Franchise Agency (BFA) was established to ensure that ethical standards are followed by franchise organisations. It has attempted to increase awareness about the franchise scene by setting up exhibitions so that legitimate franchise organisations can market their goods with the support of the regulatory body. However, only a small proportion of franchisers belong to the BFA and it has no statutory powers as a 'watchdog'. Exploitation of the franchise trade often takes the form of fictitious or unrealistic accounting projections, and other marketing hype.

REVIEW

After reading this section you should understand that there are other organisations apart from those in the private and public sectors. You should also understand how business franchise agreements operate.

REVIEW TASK

PRACTICAL APPLICATION

In 1968 the Cooperative Congress accepted a plan that would reduce the number of societies then in existence from 467 to 50. Progress in achieving this plan was overtaken by events and in 1974 a further plan suggested that therere should be 26 societies. In 1982 Congress accepted that urgent action should be taken to create 25 regional societies by the end of 1984. Now study the following Co-op statistics.

Year	No. of societies	Year	No. of societies
1969	467	**1979**	216
1973	267	**1980**	206
1974	260	**1984**	100
1975	253	**1987**	91
1976	237	**1988**	85
1977	231	**1989**	81
1978	225		

Source: Author's research from Co-op Society literature.

- By what percentage did the Cooperative Society fail to achieve its targets in 1974 and 1984?
- What was the objective of this concentration, and why was it necessary?

REVIEW TASK

CRITICAL ANALYSIS
- Explain the advantages and the disadvantages of the franchise system to the:
- franchisee
- franchiser.
- Identify the main factors that have led to the demise of cooperatives in the twentieth century and draft, on a word processor or computer if possible, a report to their chairman recommending structural improvements that would improve their effectiveness and overall competitiveness.

QUESTIONS

Essay questions

1 'Building societies are part of the financial world competing for customers, and they therefore need to become plcs.' Discuss this statement.

2 Explain how franchise agreements are a good example of the principles of indirect labour and contracting out.

3 Cooperatives are a democratic form of business unit. Compare and contrast them with other types of business unit.

Abbey National plc

Dear Member

From my previous letters to you, you will know that the Board of the Abbey National Building Society is proposing that the Abbey National converts to a Public Limited Company. This proposal is the most important ever made by the Abbey National to its members.

As a plc, Abbey National will have more freedom to provide you with:

● more and bigger branches
● more efficient service and shorter queues
● more space in branches for customer privacy
● more cash machines
● a wider range of products and services.

I would like to reassure you that becoming a plc will not affect the security of your savings – they will not be converted into shares in Abbey National plc.

It is now time for you to decide how to vote. If this proposal goes ahead, you will be entitled to:

● free shares
● a special application form to buy extra shares.

It is important that you vote. Conversion can only take place if a large number of savers – almost 1 million — use their vote. If this number of savers do not vote, conversion cannot go ahead. Your vote counts.

Source: Abbey National plc (1990).

CASE STUDY TASK
1. Explain the process of converting to a plc in general and specifically in relation to a building society.
2. What are the implications of becoming a plc?
3. How far do you feel the second paragraph is valid as an expression of the advantages of being a plc?
4. How would you vote, and why?

1.5 The Social Dimension

FOCUS

Bhopal laments whilst the West forgets

The guilt of the west for its role in the Bhopal tragedy has evaporated like the gas that killed and maimed thousands of Indians, 2500 in the first day alone. Although it happened in 1984, Indians are still dying at the rate of at least one a day. The water that leaked into the chemical tank caused an explosive reaction and all safety devices failed to respond through lack of maintenance.

The chairman of Union Carbide, the American chemical multinational, was arrested for manslaughter on arriving in Bhopal but avoided a prison sentence. Ultimately the fear of the company was for its own survival as the value of its stock fell. It needed to keep the lawsuit out of the American courts if it was to avoid the possibility of a $5–10 billion dollar pay-out, which was more than its equity and would have resulted in bankruptcy. The case was eventually heard in India and the payout was a mere $470 million. Exxon had to pay out five times that amount for the oil pollution off the Alaskan coast, and there not one life was lost.

The question needs to be asked, who decides on the 'value' of a human life, and is the survival of the business more important than its obligations to society? The reality of the matter is that if the Indians, with their relatively well developed legal system, could not deal with this case then there is little hope for other third world nations. Union Carbide's response to Bhopal was one of charity not liability. Compassion without obligation became the corporate public relations strategy. The safety audit at Bhopal had highlighted faults but no investment was put in to rectify them. It is believed that Union Carbide were in fact losing money at the plant and were planning a sell off. Whilst lawyers now challenge the legitimacy of the compensation payments, there is no doubt that their corporate public relations strategy was skilfully handled to avoid maximum damage.

Source: National newspaper reports and author's research.

Preview

In this chapter we shall investigate the following key areas:

- the market model
- supply and demand
- barriers to competition
- the failure of the market
- cost–benefit analysis
- the social audit

The costs and benefits of business

A market can be defined as a place where buyers and sellers meet. It need not be an actual location, but just a situation. It is the coming together of a need or want (demand) and its fulfilment (supply), and is the process within which businesses operate.

Externalities

Businesses provide both a demand for economic resources, or the factors of production (inputs), and a supply of goods or services (outputs). The UK has moved nearer to a free market with less public sector control (see Chapter 1.3). In a market economy the desire for profit is the main motivation for creating output and the consumer is viewed as 'sovereign'. But consumer demand is based on the ability to pay and wants can be more often fulfilled than needs. For a business the main objective is to satisfy market demand and in the process create an excess of income over costs – a profit.

For a business, working out the costs and benefits of its actions could be said to be its primary objective. These costs are what is known as their private costs, the costs for which they have to account. Who is to measure the knock-on effect of what a company does in the process of going about its business? These costs are the ones it does not have to measure because it does not have to account for them. They are called externalities. The measuring of these peripheral, and usually non-monetary, factors is a much more complex business and is in many cases an attempt to measure the unmeasurable. The Bhopal tragedy in India, where thousands of Indians were killed and permanently maimed due to the malfunctioning of the Union

Carbide plant (see Focus 1.5) underlines the absurdity, and indeed immorality, of trying to put a cost on Third World lives. The run-down of the UK national rail network similarly cannot be realistically costed unless the impact of increased road traffic and the implications of extra road traffic accidents and pollution are also accounted for on someone's financial statement.

These are the social or external effects of business activity, the ones that are not costed in a company's financial records. They nevertheless reflect the 'real' costs of their actions on the economy and society. The cost of pollution is an erosion of our natural resources which ultimately affects our productive capacity, whilst an increase in deaths or injuries in our labour force has a knock-on effect, not only on loss of labour, but also the increased burden on the National Health Service.

'Usism': the reaction to consumerism

The 1980s was termed the consumerist decade, where debt was accepted as a natural outcome of what everyone enjoyed most – spending. The cult of the individual flourished and people were encouraged to be self-determined. The 1990s has encouraged what is known as 'usism' – a more philosophically social attitude to life, a reaction to consumerism, and ultimately a call for business ethics in response to social issues. Through consumer pressure, businesses are having to increase their awareness of the external effects of their operations.

At the Earth Summit in Rio 1992 John Major pledged to steer Britain towards sustainable growth – development which can be sustained by the environment. His aim was to look at the impact the UK makes, as a country, on the world's natural resources – the UK's 'ecological footprint'. Whilst governments and businesses show an environmentally aware face, the marketing men have seen an opportunity to sell their products as 'environmentally friendly' and capitalise on 'ecopanic'. The questions need to be asked: has the green consumer been commoditised, and have governments done enough to justify their new greener image?

The market

How the free market model works

In a free market it is assumed that perfect competition prevails. This means that:

- many producers all compete with the same market conditions
- consumers have full information about the products available and the prices on offer.

The reality is that consumers are not always aware of the products available and the prices on offer. If a consumer lives in Hampshire and the cheapest price available on a good is in Manchester, then it is unrealistic to assume they can obtain the most competitive price. The nearest market to a perfect one could be cited as the Stock Market. All shares are on offer at a price of which everyone is aware.

Price, in a free market, is determined by the interaction of buyers and sellers.

- In simple terms, if there is an increase in demand for a particular good its price should be pushed upwards.
- Conversely, if a good is not in demand then the price a supplier will charge has to fall.

This can be seen in evidence in our High Street retailers who reduce prices in order to clear their 'sale' stock. If we look at the situation from a supplier's perspective, in agriculture, at certain times of the year, when some crops are plentiful, their price falls.

Demand for goods and services

Demand represents the amount of a product the market is prepared to buy. Businesses need to be aware of demand patterns so they can adjust output and respond to the market. The graph in Box 5.1 illustrates that a move down the curve is a response to a falling price level and increasing demand.

However, a change in market conditions, rather than purely price levels, will result in a shift of the curve.

What shifts a demand curve?
Income

There may be a general downturn in the level of income for firms or consumers. This could be the result of a recession, whereby demand for goods is reduced because people do not have money to spend. The fall in demand for goods can therefore mean an increase in unemployment which in turn will reduce demand even further.

BOX 5.1

Price, supply and demand

Price	Supply	Demand
3	30	10
2	20	20
1	10	30

At a price of £2, supply and demand meet. Look at Figure 5.1.

At £2 supply and demand meet

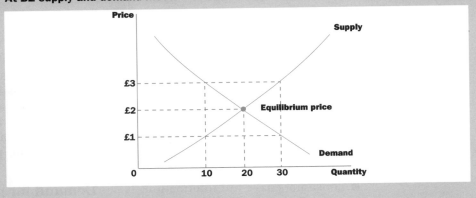

BOX 5.2

As price falls, demand increases

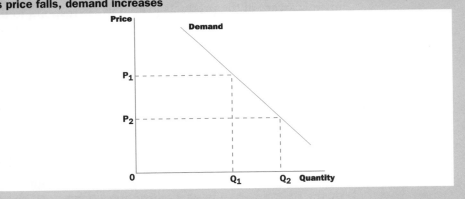

Government action could also result in a drop in the level of income. For instance if the Government increased direct taxation (income tax), this would reduce the amount of disposable income or income that can be spent:

Gross income less statutory deductions (income tax and national insurance) = disposable income

On the other hand, if the government cut income tax the amount of disposable income would be increased, allowing demand to rise. In a more favourable economic climate, companies will tend to expand and take on more labour which in turn should increase consumer income. This can also lead to an increase in demand. Look at Box 5.3.

Population

Forecasts on population fluctuations are important indicators of demand.

Demographers compile forecasts of predicted changes and classify the population into groups which include sex, age, area, and occupation. This knowledge can help businesses develop a supply for an expanding population grouping. Look at Box 5.4.

Choice

Consumer demand may change from one good to another purely because of fashion and preferences. This can be as

BOX 5.3

Demand moves from D_1 to D_2 as extra income is available

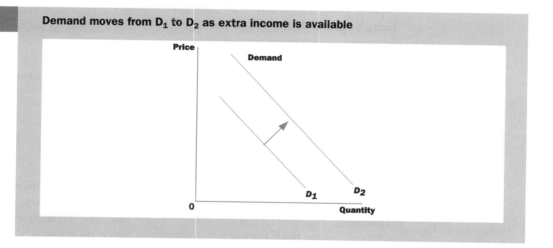

BOX 5.4

Population fluctuation

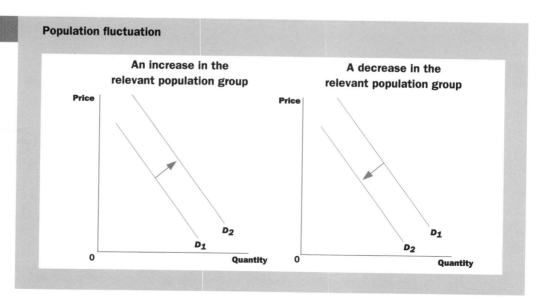

a result of effective marketing or because the utility (satisfaction) a consumer gains from a good may change at any point in time.

Substitutes

There may be a development in substitute goods or resources. For example, if interest rates were to fall it might be cheaper for a firm to substitute capital for labour as a factor of production. The branding of products also leads to differentiation of the same type of good where one may become more popular than another perhaps because of a successful marketing campaign.

Complementary goods

There are some types of goods and services where the demand for them is linked to the demand for other goods and services. For example, the demand for a compact disc player would be linked to the demand for compact discs.

Therefore, changes in the condition of demand rather than purely price means that the actual curve will shift to the right or left. Look at Box 5.5.

Elasticity of demand

Forecasting the responsiveness of demand to a change in price is important to business because it needs to know how much flexibility it has in setting the price of a good, and the effect this will have on its demand.

Elasticity is the term used to measure this responsiveness. To calculate whether demand is elastic or inelastic:

$$\frac{\% \text{ Change in demand}}{\% \text{ Change in price}} = \text{Price elasticity of demand}$$

If the result is less than 1, demand is inelastic – or unresponsive to price changes

A result of 1 and above means that demand is elastic in response to price changes.

Therefore a business can increase the price of goods which are inelastic because the demand response to the price increase will be minimal. But if the product is elastic, the response will be far greater.

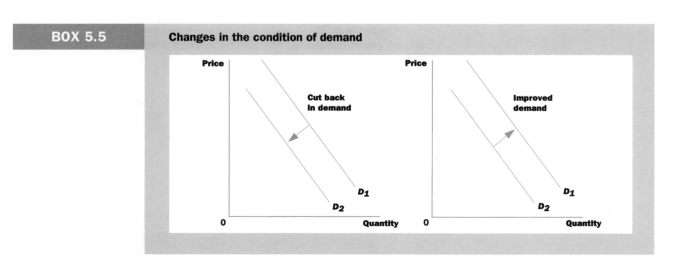

BOX 5.5   **Changes in the condition of demand**

The level of elasticity or inelasticity can be demonstrated in Box 5.6 through the gradient of the demand slope. A flatter slope shows greater elasticity, whilst a more vertical one means inelasticity.

Supply

Supply curves demonstrate the amount offered for sale at a certain price. It could be said that goods and services will always be sold at the market price, as this is the point at which supply and demand meet.

Supply is a response to demand. It is the role of the entrepreneur to create the supply for the market. Look at Box 5.7.

The movement along the curve is purely a response to price. This is again reflected in the price elasticity of supply:

$$\frac{\% \text{ Change in price}}{\% \text{ Change in supply}} = \text{Price elasticity of supply}$$

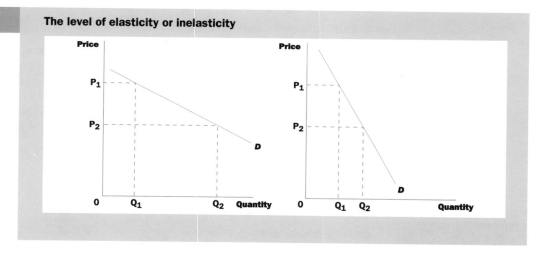

BOX 5.6

The level of elasticity or inelasticity

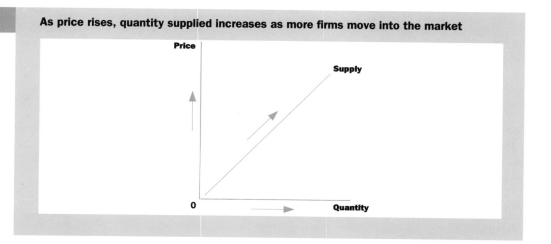

BOX 5.7

As price rises, quantity supplied increases as more firms move into the market

Other factors affecting supply

● Labour market shortage of skills and expertise to contribute to the creation of supply of a product – poor occupational and geographical mobility
● Shortage of other factors of production and again poor mobility
● Climatic factors affecting certain types of perishable products
● Output can be increased by an improvement in technology which will shift the supply curve to the right.

Box 5.8 demonstrates two of these responses.

Taxes and subsidies

There are two main types of tax, direct and indirect. Direct tax is a tax on income and is taken at source, i.e. income tax, corporation tax. Indirect tax is a levy on expenditure and is added onto things which are purchased, i.e. VAT and stamp duty.

The effect of direct tax has already been analysed in relation to income and demand. The impact of indirect tax on a good has the effect of reducing supply. If a tax of £1 is levied on a bottle of whisky the seller will want to charge £1 extra. This additional £1 will be charged on each bottle so the whole supply curve will shift upwards. The additional pound that the price has increased will mean there is a reduction in demand along the curve. Look at Box 5.9.

A subsidy is a grant given by the government to encourage the supply or demand for a particular item. The effect of a subsidy is to cause an increase in supply shifting the curve downwards to the right. Look at Box 5.10.

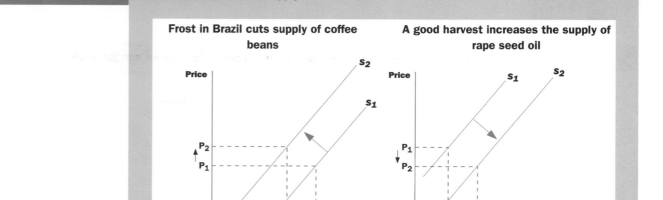

BOX 5.8 **Climatic factors and supply**

BOX 5.9   **Tax and demand**

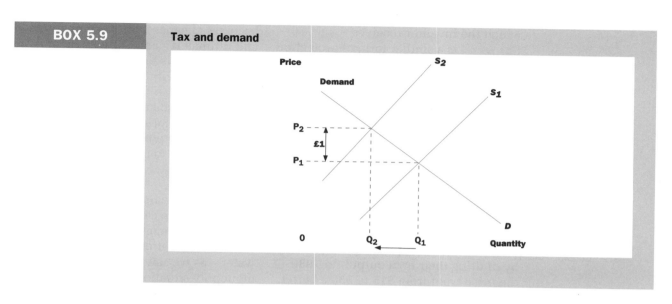

BOX 5.10   **Subsidy and supply**

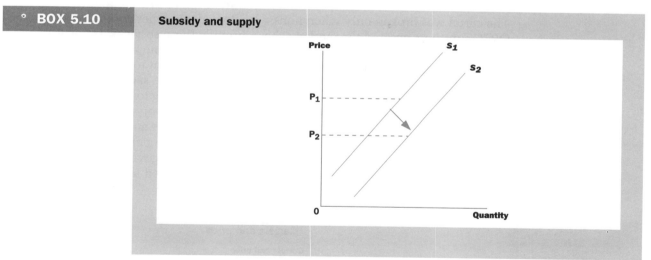

Barriers to competition

Anything which interferes with the concept of free market competition could be viewed as restricting the market and free marketeers may argue that this is not the role of governments. However, does the free market exist at all, and what barriers are there other than government intervention?

Patents

Individuals like Lasala Biro who invent a new type of product can obtain legal protection (a patent) which gives the inventor the sole right to produce the good. They, in turn, can issue licences to allow others to produce the good for which the inventor receives royalties. Copyright is a similar form of protection for the creators of the written word.

Cartels

Price fixing can occur when companies join together and agree to collude over pricing.

They can also limit the price by holding back their level of output. The Organisation of Petroleum Exporting Countries (OPEC) operated as a cartel throughout the 1970s. They managed to manipulate prices, pushing the price up by limiting their own output. In 1980 the price went from $15 to $30 a barrel. Box 5.11 demonstrates these pressures.

The cartel was broken only when non-OPEC suppliers entered the market. The North Sea fields and other sources of oil started making significant supply contributions in the early 1980s which disrupted the OPEC monopoly. OPEC's share of supply fell to around 43%.

Monopoly

A large monopolist can gain economies of scale and cut its unit costs so that it becomes cheaper than its competitors, and ultimately can eliminate them. Once it controls the market it can price fix and with the competition eliminated it can control the market. The power of the monopolist may depend on the price elasticity of demand. More power is held if the company sells to consumers with a less elastic demand.

In the past the large nationalised industries were called monopolies, particularly the major utilities – gas, telecommunications, electricity and water – as we saw in Chapter 1.3. The monopoly situation occurred because the Government controlled the industries and no competition was allowed. No other company could provide these services. Ironically the case of the monopoly provider was used in the argument to privatise them, and yet, as we have seen, the Government is still attempting to break down the now private monopoly situation by the use of the regulator and giving increased incentives for competition. There were other areas of government regulation which protected markets and these have

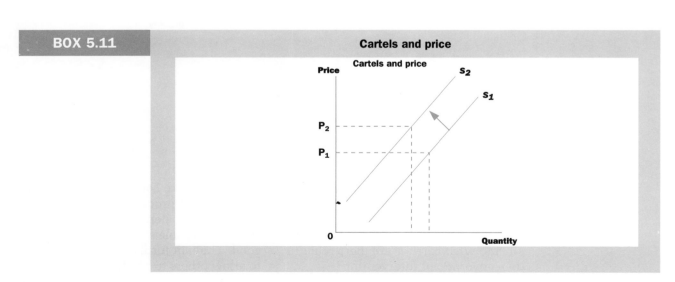

BOX 5.11

Cartels and price

Cartels and price

now been subjected to de-regulation. These areas include the *Radio Times* and *TV Times*, bus services and the sale of postage stamps in places other than post offices (remember Box 3.2).

The problem is that these public sector utilities have now become private sector monopolies. Because they are so large it is very difficult to compete with them. Whereas once they were accountable to Parliament now the control is left to the regulators (see Box 5.12). After British Gas and British Telecom were privatised the government were heavily criticised for not breaking up these two big utilities to make them small enough for other industries to compete in the same market. Therefore when water and electricity were privatised there were calls for the breaking up of the industries into smaller units. This meant that the structure of the water boards was made regional and the electricity industry was split into two generating companies with a separate Grid Company.

Oligopoly

Oligopoly is a situation where a few producers dominate the market. The dangers of oligopolists is that they can work together in forming a type of cartel, either fixing prices or collaborating to control supply. The two electricity generators, National Power and Power Gen, can be seen to be forming a duopoly as the only two suppliers of (non-nuclear) electricity. The danger in this particular duopoly is that where they have both come from the same camp (the Central Electricity Generating Board) they could be argued to be in danger of behaving in a similar way.

Multinational companies

A multinational company (MNC) has a legally identifiable base in one or more countries but produces in many different countries. This scale of operation gives them the power to switch production and capitalise on any advantages which are to be gained from operating in a particular location at any one time. Look at Box 5.13.

BOX 5.12	Monopolies and Mergers Commission

The power of the monopolist is a government concern. In 1948 the Monopolies and Mergers Commission (MMC) was set up to monitor the development of private sector monopolies. Public sector monopolies like the nationalised industries were not seen as a threat because the Government controlled them. They were called 'natural monopolies' and the benefits of their scale were believed to be beneficial to society.

In 1956 the Restrictive Practices Act set up a special court to take action against private sector monopolies. In the 1960s a considerable number of **mergers** took place in response to industrial concentration and in 1965 further regulations were passed allowing the Secretary of State to withhold permission from large companies. In 1973 the Office of Fair Trading was given powers to investigate practices that were operating against competition.

| BOX 5.13 | **Advantages of operating as an MNC** |

The MNC
- You can choose the most **cost effective area** for inputs to production
- You can gain advantages from **international specialist skills** in the labour market or climatic benefits
- by operating in a customs union like the EU **tariffs** can be avoided
- You can **reduce risk** by geographical diversity
- You can get the benefit of **preferential tax rates** in certain locations
- You can gain incentives provided by the **regional policy** of the government involved
- You can undermine collective labour bargaining by **switching production** at times of labour disputes.

Dangers of multi-national companies
- they tend to operate in oligopolist situations and can **control markets**
- if they operate in poor countries their power can **overwhelm** the national government
- although they provide a boost to the local economy providing employment and exports, if they move out because of poor demand or loss of benefits they can cause **economic destabilisation**.

The failure of the market

Experience shows that markets may function inadequately and in some cases completely fail to allocate resources effectively. The flaws in the perfect competition theory, which forms the basis of the laws of supply and demand, compound the dilemma.

Problems of mobility

For an economy to be allocatively efficient, as demand switches, businesses need to be able to create supply by utilising the redundant factors of production effectively. However, there are problems of mobility, in other words the restrictions which apply when switching resources from one type of production to another.

There are two types of mobility: geographical and occupational.

Geographical mobility is the movement of factors from one location to another, whilst occupational mobility is movement between one type of job and another.

There are many reasons why factors of production are immobile.

- If one looks at the labour market one person may have the capacity to be retrained in a type of skill for one job but to do another type of job may be beyond their capabilities.
- Again using labour as an example, if a factory is shut down in Wales there may be other jobs in London but there are many factors which could stop the worker from moving – house prices, children's schooling, family ties are a few examples.

The mobility of capital is largely dependent upon the form it takes – if the capital is in the form of money then mobility of use is flexible, but if it constitutes a machine, then switching use has severe limitations. The

Government can, and does, aid mobility of the factors.

- It intervenes in the market by providing retraining facilities for workers to increase occupational mobility of labour, and has a regional development policy which attempts to take 'work to the workers'
- The regional development schemes provide incentives for companies to set up their location in areas where there is 'structural unemployment' – in other words, areas where the structural changes in the economy have meant that regional unemployment has become intensified
- They can also provide schemes which help to direct capital for the purposes of production.

The EU now have their own schemes, to provide regional aid within the community. The EU will give grants to regions in the UK if they can prove a need for the allocation. However, there are so many different types of grants and the system of assessing them is so complex that regions are creating posts for 'European' officers. Their job is to seek and access any possible finance that may be available.

Merit and demerit goods

We can see that Governments, and indeed the collective EU, regularly intervene in an attempt to correct markets. In another context, governments may also regulate markets in line with what it sees as its own social objectives. As we have already noted, a business will provide a good or service all the while there is the incentive of profit, but we need only to look at the narcotics market to question the morality of an 'unchecked' free market. Merit goods are defined as those that the government feels society needs rather than what they would demand if left to the free market. These include public sector services like schools and health care. In a free market system there is likely to be an underprovision of merit goods. Demerit goods are those that the government feels individuals should not be able to purchase freely, even though the market would provide them if left unchecked. The narcotics industry is one example, whilst the health warnings on cigarettes is another; indeed, tobacco is obviously viewed as a demerit good but to totally ban tobacco would lose the Government considerable tax revenue.

Cost–benefit analysis

Cost–benefit analysis techniques are used to look into the **real costs and benefits** of each decision or scheme a government or firm undertakes.

It has been used particularly in the past by governments to analyse and appraise investment projects. In our increasingly environmentally aware society, businesses are being called upon to justify their decision-making, not just to

their shareholders as part of their projected profitability, but to society as a whole. Governments are increasingly taking an interest in the affairs of business which have an environmental implication and the 1992 Earth Summit in Rio was a reflection of this interest.

To be effective, cost–benefit analysis needs to investigate, not just the costs and benefits to the firm, but also the 'knock-on' effects to society and the economy.

When a business takes any action it will inevitably have external effects. These 'externalities', as we saw above, are the costs or benefits which occur as the result of any action a firm or government takes, which affect a third party.

The problem is that externalities cannot always be traced to the initiator, and also that they are inevitably difficult to cost:

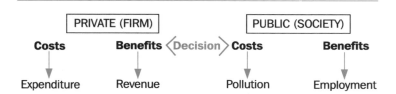

Attempts are made to put a cost on this type of externality, but the process is invariably problematic. Identifying, calculating and costing non-monetary factors will always be difficult and inevitably inaccurate. Look at Box 5.14.

BOX 5.14

Cost-benefit analysis of a major motorway link

If a private sector company built a major motorway link using a 'toll' or 'pay as you use' system, the private (firm's) costs and benefits are fairly straightforward.

Private

Costs
- Expenditure on materials, labour and other costs
- Interest payments on loans

Benefits
- Revenue earned
- Additional income from
- other developments, e.g. Service stations
- Advertising space

Examples of social implications can now be included.

Externalities

Costs
- Road accidents – effect on National Health Service
- Car pollution
- The cost could encourage traffic back onto other roads

Benefits
- Time saved on journeys
- Reduction in congestion
- Employment opportunities

Placing a social cost on accidents and deaths will always be difficult. A way of doing this could be to average out the income of an individual and assess the **financial loss over the years of life expectancy.**

The **value of time saved** could be calculated by assessing the average number of individuals who pass through the toll system and multiplying it by the average time saved. A value would then need to be placed on the time.

Social auditing

All production uses a mixture of the factors of production or natural resources. When the government argues for sustainable growth, it is aiming to ensure that our natural resources are not affected too adversely by our needs to develop industrially. Increasingly, the environment is being viewed by economists as a scarce resource which must be protected. With the current interest in green issues and environmental factors, society is demanding that firms account for their actions. It can be said that in cases of pollution, polluters take no account of the costs of their actions; if potential polluters were made to pay for this externality they would be forced to choose an alternative, less polluting method of production.

Because society is increasingly concerned about these issues it has become part of the political agenda – a potential vote winner rather than something to be ignored. Businesses are becoming more aware of the issues, not just because they may have a social conscience, but because the government is being pressurised to make businesses accountable.

There are two main ways in which the government could develop social accountability – taxation or legislation.

● It could tax businesses on the cost of the damage to the environment, or create laws to monitor their activity and make certain practices illegal
● The recent proposal to put VAT on domestic heating could be seen as an environmentally aware tax
● The expansion of the road building programme and the privatisation of other forms of public transport are moving ahead despite arguments to fund and improve the public transport system.
● An Organisation for Economic Cooperation and Development (OECD) report stated in 1994 that tax is more effective as a disincentive for pollution because it can be measured in monetary values and because it provides revenue to governments.
● In the USA they use a system called marketable pollution rights, whereby the government sets standards for pollution and issues licences allowing pollution up to a set standard. The problem with this system is that businesses may reduce pollution only down to the standards set.

Whilst consumer awareness of negative externalities is increasing, businesses are using consumer interest in green issues for their own benefit, increasingly marketing goods as environmentally friendly: even cars, possibly the biggest threat to the environment, are being promoted as being in tune with nature.

REVIEW

After reading this chapter you should understand the role of the market model in the allocation of resources, and the failure of market mechanisms. Also the need for businesses to be socially aware and the implications of their decision-making.

REVIEW TASK

PRACTICAL APPLICATION
Study the following data.

Quantity demanded (000 units)	Price	Supply (000 units)
20	19	60
30	16	50
40	12	40
50	8	30
60	4	20

- Plot a supply and demand curve for this data.
- If demand changes by 8000 at every price because of an increase in income, plot a new demand curve.
- Plot another demand curve to reflect a fall in incomes.

Study this data.

Original market		Changed market	
Demand	Price (£)	Demand	Price (£)
200	23	250	23
180	25	230	25
150	30	200	30
110	33	160	33
100	36	150	36

- *Draw demand curves for the original and changed market.*
- *Calculate the elasticity of demand for each market when the price moves from:*

  –£23 to £25
  –£25 to £30
  –£33 to £36.

- Give reasons why the market may have changed.

REVIEW TASK

CRITICAL ANALYSIS

Prickly time for Sonic
The computer games industry feels aggrieved that they are being referred to the Monopolies and Mergers Commission at a time when their sales and profits are sliding.

In the early 1990s, the industry doubled its size. In 3 successive years the UK market alone was worth £750 million and accounted for 40% of toy sales. In 1994 sales fell dramatically and looked set to go on declining.

The MMC investigation was prompted by a complaint that their products are much cheaper in the USA. This aroused suspicions of collusion pricing by the two market leaders, Sega and Nintendo. Sega argued that the price differentials internally are the result of higher VAT and retailer margins in the UK. It seems now that the computer games market has peaked and recent research shows an increase in sales of more traditional toys.

Source: National newspaper reports and author's research.

1. Explain what is meant by 'collusion pricing'. Demonstrate this manipulation of the market by the use of supply and demand graphs
2. What is the role of the MMC, and how effective can it be in market regulation?
3. Do some research on the market for computer games.
   - Conduct a survey on a cross-section of potential computer games buyers to find out what they would be prepared to spend on games.
   - Select a range of products on the market and do a survey across a number of retailers to compare prices charged.

QUESTIONS

Essay questions

1. Redwood Bros is a major local employer which processes low level toxic waste to make it safe. The directors of Redwood Bros are eager to expand the company and so they are considering investing in new plant and machinery to process high grade and therefore more dangerous waste products. On a computer or word processor if possible, write a report for the directors, outlining all the elements which should be considered before proceeding with the plan.

2. 'Monopolies are the natural outcome of a free market system.' Discuss this statement.

3. Explain the laws of supply and demand, and the factors which change market conditions.

CASE STUDY

Read the following article and the letter it evoked from a reader.

Who regulates the regulators?

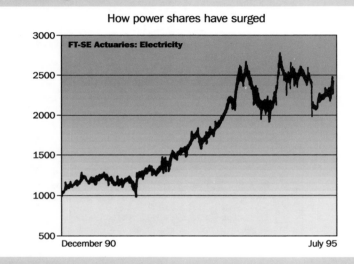

How power shares have surged

FT-SE Actuaries: Electricity

Source: Observer (July 1995).

Regulators were established to protect consumer interests from the power of the privatised public utilities. As the privatised public utilities report ever-increasing profits and higher pay to their top executives, the bills to consumers have kept rising whilst jobs in the industries disappear. The Government's White Paper on the future of the coal industry stated that a stable regulatory environment is essential to cultivate investors' confidence. British Gas, to its credit, has called for the Monopolies and Mergers Commission to look into the relationship between the privatised companies (many of which could be called private monopolies) and their regulators. Proposals put forward have called for greater parliamentary control over the system of regulation, possibly by creating a select committee of MPs.

British Gas is a prime example of a private monopoly, and following a Monopolies and Mergers Commission investigation into its monopoly of domestic gas supply, it is now involved in corporate divestment. The loss of British Gas's regulated monopoly on domestic supply means the largest corporate break-up in the UK.

Theoretically, the break-up of a monopoly could be seen as beneficial to the consumer, but in reality if new gas distributors are selling to the domestic market, this could lead to higher prices to take into account the lack of economies of scale of the smaller operators. The plan is that the North Sea pipelines could carry supplies of gas which would then be distributed by the new operators. The people who could suffer most would be the small-volume domestic consumers, who at present benefit from the advantage of cross-subsidy with larger-scale users supporting smaller ones.

Already companies are lining up to put in bids for the domestic supply business. Those companies interested include multi-nationals Esso, Mobil and Total – all foreign companies. British Gas's fear is that its Regulator, 'OFGAS', will allow competing companies a freer hand in the British market, in the name of increased competition. British Gas has called for all competitors in the market to be treated equally by the regulator, whilst widening its own horizon into overseas development with a view to becoming a multi-national company.

The privatised power industry is also under the spotlight. The media exposure of vast profits being made by senior executives from share options has led to the Regulator, Dr Stephen Littlechild, speaking out in favour of stricter regulations. A recent Electricity Regulator's price review has meant that bills are now coming down by 2–3%. This price review was also the topic of much criticism of the Regulator because 'price sensitive' information concerning the review was leaked to the Stock Exchange. This information then had an impact on share values. The Regulators of these large industries look set to increase their power at the instigation of public opinion and Government embarrassment.

Source: The Business Editor, Daily View, Business Comment page (1 October 1995).

Dear Sir,

I read your article of 1 October, 'Who Regulates the Regulators?', with interest. However, I do not usually read business pages and found some of the business terms you used, and the information you gave, rather puzzling. It would be most useful if you could explain these terms and give some background information on the issues involved in the article. This is obviously of interest to all householders who have to pay their fuel bills.

Yours faithfully,

CASE STUDY TASK

Write a reply explaining all the business terms and institutions addressed in the article above. You need also to explain the implication of 'price sensitive' information. Go through the text and write down all the business terms and organisations referred to, and then construct a reply giving detailed explanations. Lay this out clearly, preferably using a word processor or computer.

Integrated case study for Section 1: the transport debate

Introduction

The role of transportation in society is a hotly debated issue. Transport is a necessary part of the communication and distribution system of a business. It can also be a business in its own right. The question of whether the nation's system of transportation should be in the hands of the private or public sector is a central theme.

Whilst 'middle England' is uniting to protest about the social impact of increased road building, new phenomena like 'road rage' are making us question the social impact of the car.

Read the discussion that follows and use the data to answer the Case Study Tasks.

Car sick?

'Car dependency' could be called the latest social disease. The whole shape of towns and cities has changed, with shops, offices and hospitals planned around the car. New roads attract new developments which have added to traffic still further. Industry and shops have become hooked on heavier and larger lorries. Congestion gets worse, and the freedom that cars promise often means choosing your own traffic jam.

The pollution caused by cars is being linked to asthma in children, whilst new roads are devastating the countryside. Yet many places both in the UK and abroad are trying different approaches, reviving public transport and encouraging walking and cycling. It is all about giving people real choices in how they travel – but choices that do not involve so much environmental damage, risks and destruction.

The Dutch strategy

The Dutch Government has a coherent transport strategy which aims to halve the predicted growth in traffic from 1984 to 2010, and ultimately to cut it completely. The Dutch strategy also sets targets for cutting traffic pollution and noise while replanning towns and cities to reduce the need to travel. Elements in the strategy include:

- A Government funded rail development plan, 'Rail 21', to double the capacity of the rail network
- Tolls on some roads
- A car-free city centre for Amsterdam
- A convenient 'train–taxi' ticket, to help train travel compete with cars.

The British problem

British people use public transport less – and cars more – than almost any other country in Europe. Public transport could be a good alternative to a lot of car and lorry journeys, but it is not used enough. Government funding policies have not encouraged its use. Funding has gone to roads not rail or buses, and deregulation of the buses in 1986 (see Chapter 1.3) has led to services constantly changing, higher fares and less investment in new buses; partly

because of this, bus use has dropped by 25%. There are fears that the Government's rail privatisation plans and funding cuts will mean poorer rail services too: fewer through trains and through tickets, less investment, higher fares and closure of less profitable lines.

Efforts have been made in some regions of the UK. In Manchester, two rail lines have been converted to tram operation and linked together across the city centre. This 'metrolink' scheme, opened in 1992, has been very popular, and has attracted a lot of its passengers from cars. Sheffield has a 'Supertram', Croydon has a tramlink scheme, and other cities like Birmingham,

Nottingham and Glasgow also have plans to bring back the tram, funding permitting. In South Wales, local councils have re-opened rail lines closed to passengers during the 'Beeching' cuts 30 years ago. The response has been positive: extra trains have had to be laid on to cope with demand. Councils have opened stations and lines in many other areas – in all, over 100 new or rebuilt stations have reopened in the last 10 years, and councils concerned about traffic congestion plan many more. In York, Oxford and many other places there are 'park and ride' services, where drivers leave their cars at edge of town car parks and travel into the city centre by buses, which often have reserved lanes giving them priority over other traffic.

The national roads campaign

The battle against the national roads programme has moved centre-stage. As the bills – environmental and financial – for the biggest road programme in the nation's history come in, so protest has intensified and a constant stream of statistics which question the viability of the plans has made the Government rethink.

200 groups around the country are now waging intelligent focused campaigns against unnecessary and environmentally-damaging road schemes. Some schemes have now been dropped, among them the M1–M62 link road in West Yorkshire, much of the M25 widening, and perhaps most famously,

the plan to route an East London River Crossing through Oxleas Wood.

The environmental impact is colossal: 161 of our most important wildlife sites (Sites of Special Scientific Interest or SSIs), 844 important archaeological sites, and more than 40 National Trust protected properties are at risk. Many more roads will slice through communities, destroying homes and open spaces. The Government had planned to widen 600 miles of the motorway network, and develop many existing 'A' roads into fast, high-capacity expressways. The cost would be £3 billion a year, yet as surveys show that more roads will automatically be filled with traffic the Government now seeks an alternative strategy.

Source: Adapted from Transport 2000

Roads

Studies show that there can never be enough roads to satisfy the demand for their use. There are now plans to privatise Britain's motorways. This move has been encouraged by three factors:
- Government debt running at £50 billion
- The success of the Dartford River Crossing company, headed by construction giant Trafalgar House, which runs the Dartford Tunnel. The consortium is expected to break even by the year 2001, 7 years earlier than predicted. Trafalgar House also built the £86 million Queen Elizabeth II Bridge in return for receiving tolls.

- Britain leads the field in developing technology for high-speed toll roads. Development of a 'smart card' which is capable of recognising hundreds of vehicles per minute without making them slow down or stop was pioneered here.

The Government wanted the first private motorway to be in operation by 1996. Opponents of the privatisation programme warn of the dangers of driving traffic back on to minor roads. It is claimed that high tolls across the Severn Bridge (£3.80 for cars and £10.10 for lorries) has encouraged traffic on to country roads in Gloucestershire and Gwent.

The Department of Transport is inviting companies to bid to run Britain's proposed motorway toll system. Already 29 companies have declared an interest. Trials ran from March to November 1995 on a section of the M4, with trial results expected to be announced during 1996. The Government hopes that a toll road system will raise billions of pounds in revenue. The ultimate goal is to insert a toll-collecting system in every vehicle in the UK. The Department of Transport is investigating the use of overhead gantries to be erected across motorways, which will detect each vehicle and take its toll; this is known as the 'multi-lane free flow system'. Any bidder will need to have an 'enforcement' system to detect non-payers.

British Rail 1948–

'Evolution not revolution'
Prior to the privatisation plans of the mid-1990s, the publicly owned British Rail was a network of 6 operations:

- Intercity
- Network South East
- Parcels
- Trainload Freight
- Railfreight Distribution
- Regional

In 1992 the revenue earned was £3.7 billion, but a government subsidy of £1.15 billion was needed. The new structure does not involve a Stock Exchange flotation, but anticipates a gradual grooming of the system for the private sector sell-off.

The structure

Railtrack
This company controls the infrastructure of the railway system, including tracks, tunnels, signals and bridges. It was floated on 20 May 1996.

Passenger service
This will comprise 26 BR-owned shadow franchises. These 'shadow' franchises will be controlled by BR who will grant licences. Subsidies will be given to franchisees who run unprofitable lines.

Trains
These will be owned by 3 separate BR leasing companies.

Stations
Stations will be leased to private sector companies to exploit their market potential. The stations would be developed in a similar way to airports, with bars, shops and restaurants and other marketing opportunities.

The franchising process
Licences will be issued by the Franchise Director in the initial 'shadow franchises', but these licences will be gradually fully franchised out. At the moment BR itself can only make a bid for those franchise agreements that no-one else wants. This has proved a contentious issue for the Government in terms of free market opportunities being open to all.

The regulator
Standards and safety will be monitored through a Health and Safety Executive.

Problems?
- There is estimated to be £15 billion needed for investment
- The private sector have fears about running trains they do not own on track they do not control

- There has been a minimal response from the private sector so far
- There are fears over safety costs and risk assessments
- The block on BR bidding for viable licenses has been controversial.

Back to the future – canal development

Canal development reached its peak in 1793. Canals linked the centres of the industrial revolution with 4,250 miles of inland waterways carrying 30 million tonnes of freight a year.

In the mid-twentieth century, as roads and rail services developed, canals fell into disrepute and became largely used for leisure pursuits. Two centuries on from the height of the canal boom, plans are being considered to restore most disused canals owned by British Waterways. Business opportunities have been exposed and the possibility of factories hiring water for their cooling process is being investigated,

farmers are also looking at the possibility of canals being used for irrigation. Perhaps the biggest potential lies in the development of cable TV and fibre optic communication. Canal tow paths, and also British rail lines, provide the facility for running ducts for cable communication system. Similar opportunities are being exploited with the National Grid electricity cables. The offshoot of the National Grid Company, Energis, will soon be launched. Energis will use grid lines to transmit telecommunications and will no doubt be a force to be reckoned with.

Canals in the UK, 1995

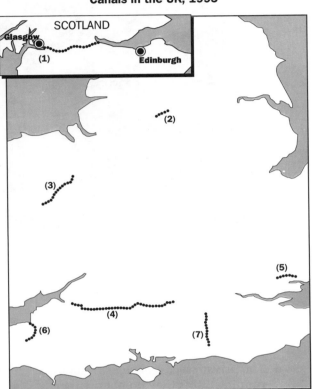

(1) Forth and Clyde Canal   (5) Chelmer and Blackwater Navigation
(2) Huddersfield Narrow Canal   (6) Bridgwater and Taunton Canal
(3) Montgomery Canal   (7) Wey and Arun canal
(4) Kennet and Avon Canal

INTEGRATED CASE STUDY TASK

In all cases use wordprocessor/computer spreadsheet/displayed-fonts facilities, if possible.

- Explain how a franchise structure operates and the possible implications of a business running a British Rail 'Shadow Franchise'. In all cases, use wordprocessor/computer spreadsheet/displayed-founts facilities, if possible.
- Construct a report analysing the potential business opportunities in leasing a railway station and the possible limitations. Structure the report in two sections:
  (i) Look at the general implications of leasing a railway station
  (ii) Choose a particular station and evaluate specific factors which relate to its location.
- Design a 'Business Opportunity' advertisement on behalf of the British Waterways Authority, setting out the business development potential of canals.

- 'A toll road system provides the answer to all our Transport problems.' Discuss this statement.
- What are the arguments for and against having a public sector integrated transport system?

Explain the process involved in:
- Registering a limited company
- Private and public cost-benefit analysis
- The use of supply and demand schedules
- Company integration.

Analyse and evaluate the implications of the following:
- A government moving from a planned to a market economy
- A private limited company going public
- The 'Tower Colliery' forming a workers cooperative

Compare and contrast:
- The private and public sectors
- Private sectors and cooperatives
- Perfect competition, oligopoly and monopoly
- Ordinary and preference shares
- Debentures and risk capital
- Economies and diseconomies of scale
- Elasticity and inelasticity of supply and demand.

TASK

Prepare a group debate with each individual representing different aspects of the transport controversy (pro-car, etc.). Ensure that each member of the group researches and analyses the implications from their own perspective. The debate should include:
- A car dealer
- A representative from the Transport 2000 group
- A company director interested in providing private toll roads
- A taxpayer
- A road commuter
- A representative of the British Waterways Authority
- A British Rail commuter
- A supermarket transport manager

ESSAY QUESTIONS
- 'The objective of all business is to maximise profits. This makes the idea of a profit making hospital in the private sector both unethical and potentially dangerous.' Critically examine this view.
- 'The most important asset a business must protect is its reputation.' Discuss this statement, with regard to cost-benefit analysis.
- Prepare a report from the Department of Transport to the CBI (Confederation of British Industry) analysing the business implications of the Channel Tunnel.

Some areas you should research include:
- The issue of the high-speed link to London
- Effect on ferry operators and their strategies for survival
- The consortiums involved
- Funding problems
- Impact on the local economy at Dover
- International/political dimension
- Cost–benefit analysis
- Impact on airlines.

In February 1986 the Greater London Council introduced a policy to control the movement of heavy lorries in the Greater London area.

Greater London Council Scheme

- Lorries over $16\frac{1}{2}$ tonnes banned from 9.00 pm to 7.00 am every weekday
- The ban operates all day at weekends
- Companies wishing to use heavy lorries during banned hours are required to fit 'hush kits'. Heavy lorries without such kits require a permit to enter the area
- What reasons might the GLC have for introducing these regulations?
- Briefly state the arguments which firms might make publicly against the introduction of these regulations.
- The 'hush kits' have been readily available for some time. Why have very few firms fitted them to their lorries?

Section 2
Finance and Business

2.6 Budgeting and Costing

The bottom line

The amount of profit made by a business is often called the 'bottom line' indicator of its success. However, it could be argued that the future performance of 'corporate UK', in a globally competitive market, relies on much wider indicators of efficiency.

If UK business philosophy is compared to that of our international competitors, our view of success may be judged to be blinkered. It could be said that it is a business's relationship with its 'stakeholders' that is the true measure of its efficiency. 'Stakeholders' is a term which defines those parties that are interested, and indeed involved with, the success of a business. Stakeholders include workers, shareholders, suppliers, customers and the wider community. Success could perhaps be measured by how effectively a company operates as a team.

A criticism of the UK equity market is that limited companies are too eager to please shareholders at the expense of the other team members. Shareholders are at the front of the queue for reward (dividend) yet take little responsibility for the wider implications of business decision-making. The 'push' for dividends could be the weakness of the UK business system. The training of the workforce, the relationship with suppliers, investment in research and development (R&D) and pleasing the customer, could all be seen as equally important and cost-effective.

The 'real' bottom line is that businesses are in the process of **adding value**. In simple terms, they aim to create an output worth more than the cost of the input. Yet ultimately it is important how this additional revenue is used. The company needs to analyse not just profit – this is an incomplete picture – but whether it invests in its workforce, creates training opportunities, keeps customers happy, cooperates with its suppliers, seizes investment opportunities, and works as a member of the larger community. This is the holistic approach to business success.

Source: National newspaper reports and author's research.

Preview

In this chapter we shall investigate the following key areas:
- sales and turnover
- measuring profit
- costs
- break-even analysis
- financial control
- cash flow analysis

Finance and the business

The aims and objectives of a business can be many and complex, but in order for any business to survive and prosper it needs to be financially stable.

Entrepreneurs are the initiators of enterprise, or the risk-takers. The reward for risk is profit. Profit occurs when there is an excess of income over expenditure. To calculate expenditure, costs need to be assessed, and to predict income **sales** need to be forecast. The need to budget is as true for a business or Government as it is for an individual. To achieve the most effective use of limited resources a budget needs to be established. Budgeting creates a forum for financial planning and decision-making. It also creates a structure within which to apply constraints to spending. Forecasting is inevitably problematic because it involves dealing with the unknown.

Whenever business objectives are established, the financial implications need to be assessed. Yet whatever financial plans a business makes there are factors which are beyond its control. The economic climate, both nationally and internationally, and Government legislation are two examples. We will look at these external forces in Chapter 6.15 on the economy.

The profit motive

The word profit arouses much debate throughout society. Many National Health Service staff would argue that profit is out of place in a public service industry. Slogans like 'profit before people' and 'costs before care' are powerful and emotive arguments against profit being used as the main measure of efficiency or success. However, some governments and most firms would argue they need measurable outcomes in order to gauge the efficiency of their operations. Profit, as we have seen, is simply the excess of income over expenditure; in public service organisations the measuring of costs and revenue can be much more complex. We have already explored the difficulties of measuring the costs and benefits to society from running, for example, a National Health Service.

However, profit is not the only motivation of the private sector. The objectives of a business will largely depend upon the individuals involved and the type of market in which it operates.

- The aims of a business will tend to be its longer-term policy goals
- The objectives explain more precisely the route by which the aims will be achieved
- The targets are the measurable units of achievement.

Whilst profit is not the only aim a business may have, its financial success can make other aims more achievable, whilst an awareness of financial limitations makes targets more realistic.

Aims (general policy statement)
Objectives (how aims will be achieved)

- Increase growth
- Increase productivity
- Diversify into new market areas
- Horizontal integration
- Increase loan capital
- Output levels to rise by 5%
- Staffing to increase by 2%, etc.

Targets (these would be set for each area of the company)

Aims of a business

Other aims of a business could include:

Survival
Some businesses may not operate to achieve any grand aspirations other than purely to **survive** – to stay in business. For some businesses this may be a short-term situation during difficult times. Yet for other businesses 'survival' may be accepted as a permanent target. This will usually be when the owners are motivated by an emotional or moral dedication to the business. This is sometimes true of family businesses which have an emotional or historical importance to members of the family, or businesses which are founded largely on an ethical or moral basis.

Growth
The motivations for 'growth' have already been analysed in Section 1. Growth can also run alongside a complementary objective, 'prestige'.

Prestige
Many companies see growth as prestigious and are keen to create an image of status that can be enhanced by size. Prestige may also be achieved by developing a positive public profile, by supporting popular charities or gaining national awards for efficiency or industrial achievement.

Satisficing
Whilst some businesses may constantly strive to raise their performance levels, others will set their sights on lower more easily obtainable goals. This is called 'satisficing': a satisfactory performance is enough. The danger of 'satisficing' is that if standards are set too low a business may not reach its full potential.

Social responsibility
Some businesses see their social responsibility as part of their reason for existing. Others may use the consumer's interest in social issues to their own advantage by directing their marketing strategy, for example, strategy towards creating a 'greener' image for the company.

Business sales

We need to understand some key terms here.

- Turnover is another term for net sales or sales *less* any returns.

    Sales *less* Returns = Turnover
- Average stock is an assessment of how much stock is being held
- Stock is money tied up in materials or goods, stock needs to be effectively monitored to ensure that only the most cost-efficient level is being held

The value of stock held can be calculated either at the cost price or the selling price. If you only know what the opening and closing stock figures are, you can calculate the average stock as follows:

Average stock held = Stock at start *plus*
$$\frac{\text{Stock at close}}{2}$$

- The rate of turnover or 'stockturn' shows the speed at which stock is sold:

    Cash = Stock = Sales = Cash

A business turnover rate can be calculated in two ways:

Rate of turnover =
$$\frac{\text{Turnover (net sales)}}{\text{Average stock at selling price}}$$

Rate of turnover =
$$\frac{\text{Turnover (net sales)}}{\text{Average stock at cost price}}$$

Measuring profit

The gross profit of a business is calculated by taking the sales, or turnover, of a business less the costs of the materials for making the goods. The net profit is the turnover less overheads (or expenses). Look at Box 6.2.

BOX 6.2	**Gross Profit**	
	The annual turnover (sales) of a company is	£
		990 000
	Costs of materials	356 000
	= Gross profit	634 000
	LESS	
	Expenses: Labour	100 000
	Light and rent	70 000
	Business rate	5000
	Sundry expenses	2500
	Therefore **gross profit** is £990 000 *less* £356 000 = £634 000	
	whilst **net profit** is £634 000 *less* £177 500 = £456 500	

Types of costs

The type of costs which are incurred during the business process varies. Fixed costs are the costs that do not change with increased output. In other words there are certain costs that have to be paid regardless of the level of output. For example, if you produce 30 000 units or 80 000 some costs will remain constant. Costs that come under this category include

- rent
- Business rate
- heating and lighting.

One can see here the relevance of economies of scale, in that once your fixed costs are covered the only additional costs are the ones that are involved with the actual production of each additional unit of output, your variable costs. An obvious example of variable costs is the raw materials involved in production.

Fixed costs *plus* variable costs = total costs

Look at Box 6.3.

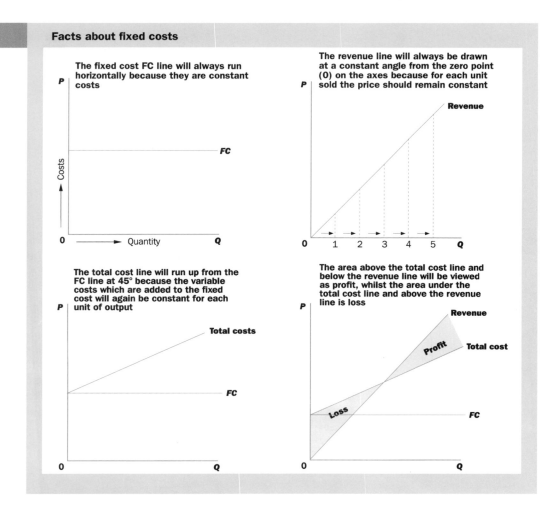

BOX 6.3

Facts about fixed costs

The fixed cost FC line will always run horizontally because they are constant costs

The revenue line will always be drawn at a constant angle from the zero point (0) on the axes because for each unit sold the price should remain constant

The total cost line will run up from the FC line at 45° because the variable costs which are added to the fixed cost will again be constant for each unit of output

The area above the total cost line and below the revenue line will be viewed as profit, whilst the area under the total cost line and above the revenue line is loss

The break-even point

The break-even point is used to see at what level of output a business is purely breaking even – no profit but no loss. This is also the guide to see at what level a profit or loss is being made. Look at Box 6.4.

Box 6.5 shows how costs, prices and profit are borne in a typical small business.

BOX 6.4 | **The break-even point**

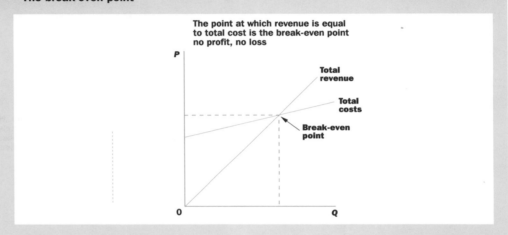

The point at which revenue is equal to total cost is the break-even point no profit, no loss

---

BOX 6.5 | **Break-even at the salon**

John Smith intends to start up in business as John Smith – Hair Design. He has been working for the last five years in a local salon and feels in a rut. He realises that before he can make this move he needs to work out the costs involved and decide at what level of pricing he would need to operate in order to make a profit.

He sees ideal premises to rent, and starts to calculate his costs. Some of the costs are known to him but others he has had to forecast, based on his knowledge of the trade. He decides he would need to take on another qualified hairdresser at £5500 p.a. and that he would be able to obtain a trainee from the local college for £40 per week. He feels the average price charged per client would be £11. He needs to take out a loan of £2000 to pay back over a year at 13.5%. His own salary would be £8000 p.a.

	£	
Rent	7800 p.a.	
Business rate	756 p.a.	
Lease equipment	15 p.w.	
Heat and light	309 p.q.	
Salaries	8000 p.a.	(John Smith)
	5500 p.a.	(Other hairdresser)
	£40 p.w.	(Trainee)
Payment on loan	? p.w.	

p.a. = per annum
p.w. = per year
p.q. = per quarter

Average cost per customer

	£
Shampoo	0.20
Other items	1.00
Water heating	0.15

TASK 6.1

A What will be the total **fixed costs** per annum?
B What will be the **average variable cost** per customer?

CALCULATIONS

A Fixed Costs (FC) (per annum)

Rent	7800
Business rate	756
Lease equipment	780
Heat and light £309 × 4	1236
Salaries £8000	8000
£5500	5500
Trainee £40 × 52	2080
Payment on loan £2000 @ 13.5%	270
	26 422

B Average variable cost (VC) per customer

	£
Shampoo	0.20
Water heating	1.00
Other	0.17
	1.37

C Now prepare a table to assess revenue and costs in relation to profit or loss per week (to the nearest whole number). Assume each hairdresser (not trainee) can do 10 haircuts a day maximum and works 300 days a year.

Assume each hairdresser (not trainee) can do 10 customers per day maximum and works 300 days a year.

Customer	FC	VC	TC	Revenue	Profit/loss
0					
1000					
2000					
3000					
4000					
5000					
6000					

D Plot a break-even graph using the information from the above table you have prepared.

E Is the price sensible, or does it need to be adjusted?

F Do you have any recommendations for John in his financial planning?

Limitations of break-even analysis

John's business is part of the **service sector** and, as it does not involve tangible output, it can be more difficult to link directly to output costs. In the secondary, or **manufacturing sector**, the process can be more straightforward because costs are often clearly linked to output. This type of analysis does show the relationship between costs and revenue and although many costs have to be forecast, especially when a new enterprise is being researched, forecasting is a fundamental business procedure.

Other costing classifications

Cost centres

Creating cost centres allows costs to be allocated back to a central point from which they can be accountable. With the emphasis on the costing approach not just in the private, but also in the public sector, cost centres allow for this more specific monitoring of financial resources. However, with some costs it may be difficult to allocate a proportion of the costing. For example, costs like raw materials may be straightforward to allocate to a cost centre but more general costs like insurance or maintenance may be more difficult.

Absorption costing

This looks at a product from a 'full cost' basis, FC and VC are absorbed into a unit cost. A percentage profit is added to TC in order to obtain a price level:

$$\frac{FC + VC = TC}{\text{Units of output}} = \text{Unit Cost}$$

Once the unit cost is decided, the percentage profit has to be added e.g.:

$$\frac{100\,000\ (FC) + 25\,000\ (VC)}{95\,000\ (\text{units})} = £125\,000\ (TC)$$

Cost per item = £1.31, profit is to be 41% therefore the selling price needs to be £1.85 per unit.

Marginal costing

This looks only at the VC of each unit of output and the difference between the VC and the price is called the contribution. A business needs to make a 'contribution' in excess of fixed costs in order to make a profit.

Direct costs

These are costs that can be clearly allocated to a particular product.

Indirect costs

These are similar to fixed costs because they cannot be clearly allocated to a specific item but are costs which go towards total output.

Average cost

This is cost divided by the total number of items produced.

Budgetary control

A budget is a financial constraint. It is a way of attempting to control limited resources by putting restrictions on spending and by providing a structure for resource allocation. Budgeting involves:

- Research – Assessing the finance needed to achieve the objectives across the company structure
- Planning – Forming a strategy to allocate resources in response to departmental needs
- **Research and planning** – The master budget

The budgetary process relies on sound information and effective forecasting. It puts the onus on each individual budget area to perform according to plan, monitoring the performance in each area. The performance figures from each budget area can also be used to forecast the final accounts of the business.

The departments or budget areas, though each is separate, in order to establish financial control, are in fact very dependent on each other for their financial needs and performance. We will examine this further when we look at organisational structures. The important point to grasp is that all components within an organisation are interrelated and interdependent. Assessing financial performance can be difficult, and a budgetary controller is sometimes appointed to coordinate budgetary activities across the functional areas.

The budgetary process

Rationalisation

In order to rationalise budget levels an analysis needs to be done to see how realistic it is to achieve the desired objectives within the financial constraints. If it is not feasible, the strategy needs to be reassessed.

Control

Once targets have been set there is a need to ensure that spending is within budget. The actual figures need to be monitored against forecast figures.

FINANCIAL AIMS OF THE BUSINESS

- SET OBJECTIVES
- ESTABLISH TARGETS
- APPORTION FUNDS
- COORDINATE ACROSS DEPARTMENTS (FUNCTIONAL HEADS)
- COMPARE ACTUAL FIGURES TO FORECAST

Variance analysis

A budget controller who monitors the financial activities of a particular area of a business will break down the activities into smaller periods over the year and compare the actual with the forecast. Variance analysis looks at how far the actual deviates from the forecast. If actual figures of expenditure are less than forecast this is a positive or favourable expenditure variance. If they are more than budgeted this is a negative or unfavourable variance. It is important that the 'standard' cost used is accurately forecast, and the materials advice would come from the purchasing department. For standard labour costs, the advice could come from the personnel department.

Variance analysis is a useful measure because performance is monitored over smaller units of time and therefore problems can be identified and more easily resolved. Look at Box 6.6.

BOX 6.6

Variance analysis

Look at the following typical variance analysis report.

Variance analysis report
for the month of May 1996   Production department

Output predicted 24 000   Actual 22 500   Variance 1 500

	Budget £	Actual £	Variance £
Salaries	15 000	15 000	–
Indirect labour (contract)	12 000	14 050	−2050
Materials	14 500	13 000	+1500

Several questions arise from the above figures.

- Why is contract labour costing more when output is down?
- Would direct labour be more effective than indirect?
- More has been budgeted for on materials than has been used. Is this directly related to the lower output?
- Or is too much stock being held than is cost-effective?

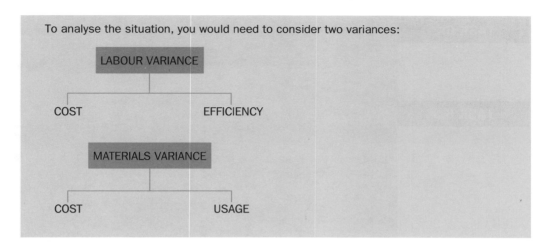

To analyse the situation, you would need to consider two variances:

LABOUR VARIANCE

COST   EFFICIENCY

MATERIALS VARIANCE

COST   USAGE

Cash flow forecast

Some businesses fail not because their order books are empty but because they do not control their cash flow. A cash flow is a record of predicted inflows and outflows of funds to a business. It is particularly useful when presenting a business plan to a bank in order to obtain support funds. Look at Box 6.7, again using John Smith's business as an example.

BOX 6.7							

John Smith – Hair Design: Cash flow forecast for Jan–Jun 1996

Receipts (amounts in)	Jan £	Feb £	Mar £	Apr £	May £	June £
Sales						
Others						
Total						
Payments (amounts out)						
Purchases						
Wages						
Rent						
Rates						
Bank						
Other						
Total						
Starting balance						
Add receipts						
Less payments						
Balance						

TASK 6.2

This format is an example of a cash flow forecast. Fill in the information for John Smith to give to his bank manager projecting his **flow of funds** based on the information in Box 6.5. Forecast John's figures for the first 6 months of trading, assuming he achieves 250 clients a month.

TASK 6.3

PRACTICAL APPLICATION

The costs of a limited company producing car sun roofs for wholesalers are as follows:

Manufacturing output	30 000 units p.a.
At a selling price of	£50 per unit
	(on past performance, all units have been sold)

Annual overheads

	£ p.a.
Rent	20 000
Administration	30 000
Rates	4000
Heating/lighting	6000
Wages	120 000
Total	180 000

Production costs (per unit of output)

	£
Frames	21.00
Glass	5.00
Catches and fittings	3.00
Total	29.00

- What is the gross profit and net profit per sun roof?
- Produce a table to demonstrate the costs and revenue at an output of 0 to 35 000 units, in a breakdown of levels of 5000 units.
- Plot a break-even graph to illustrate profit and loss.

REVIEW

After reading this chapter you should understand that profit is the reward for enterprise and one of the main, but not the sole, objectives of a business. You should also know how profit is measured and monitored.

REVIEW TASK

CRITICAL ANALYSIS

Using the information in Task 6.3:

A What is the profit or loss if only:
- 15 000 roofs are sold?
- 18 150 roofs are sold?
- 21 000 roofs are sold?

B Plot a further break-even graph to illustrate what happens to the profit or loss if:
- The price of glass increases by 2.5%
- The price of frames increases by 8.5%
- The company increases the selling price by £3.75 and demand drops by 4.5%.
- Draw a demand and supply schedule and calculate elasticity.

QUESTIONS

Essay questions

1 Analyse the usefulness of break-even analysis in financial decision-making. Outline any additional constraints which would need to be considered.

2 'Budgetary control is the major coordinating factor in any business.' Discuss this statement.

3 'Any business which measures its success only by its profit levels has a very narrow perspective.' Discuss this statement.

4 Identify the options available to a business if the level of expenditure deviates from the projected level. What factors could contribute to this deviation?

5 The following information relates to a company which produces a single product.

	£
Direct labour per unit	11
Direct materials per unit	6
Variable overheads per unit	3
Fixed costs	200 000
Selling price per unit	30

- Explain the term 'break-even'.
- Using these figures, produce a chart to show the minimum number of units which must be sold for the company to break even.
- Market research has indicated potential sales for the coming period of 30 000 units at the current price, or 37 500 units if the selling price were lowered to £28 per unit. Which strategy would you advise the company to adopt and why?
- Outline the factors which **any** business should take into consideration before using break-even analysis as a basis for decision-making. (AEB, November 1987)

Greenfinger gardens

Joe Green used to be a local authority gardener, but he decided to set up a business on his own and sets up a Garden Centre selling a variety of plants and fertilisers. A year after establishing the business he has asked you, as a business student, to look at his financial position. Attached are the figures for year 1 which you need to start by totalling, using a spreadsheet package if possible. Spreadsheets are computer programs which are used to do calculations. They are ideal for any financial costing exercise (refer to the section on data analysis).

The figures for the next few years are forecast in the following information:

Annual cost analysis for Greenfingers Garden Centre

	Year 1	Year 2	Year 3	Year 4	Year 5
Sales	120 000				
Fixed costs	60 000	62 500	63 000		
Variable costs	42 000				
Total costs					
Profit/loss from trading					
Cash at bank (start) B/F					
Cash at bank (end) C/F					

Greenfingers Garden Centre: cashflow analysis forecast for year 5

	Jan	Feb	Mar	Apr	May	June	July	Aug	Sep	Oct	Nov	Dec
Sales	11 249	12 600	11 115	12 800	10 919	11 860	12 350	12 250	12 819	11 986	12 515	12 010
Total receipts												
Fixed costs	5917	5917	5917	5917	5917	5917	5917	5917	5917	5917	5917	5917
Variable costs												
Loan repayment												
Total payments												
Profit/loss from Trading												
Cash at bank (start)												
Cash at bank (end)												

CASE STUDY TASKS

A   In year 2 the Government has announced cuts in income tax. Joe feels his trade should increase by approximately 8%. Assume variable costs alter by the same percentage as sales in calculations. Fill in the year 2 figures.

B   In year 3 bad weather results in a 7% fall in trade. Fill in the year 3 forecast.

C   In year 4 Joe anticipates a good year with sales rising by 12% due to a road diversion which will increase the flow of traffic past his business. He also takes on a helper at £8000 per annum so this will push up the fixed costs. Fill in the year 4 forecast.

D   Complete the cash flow forecast for year 5.

2.7 Financial record-keeping

Creative accounting

Accountants have thrived in a market place which has put an increasing emphasis on **financial monitoring**. As hospitals, schools and other public sector organisations joined the ranks of the profit chasers the power of the accountancy profession increased. Yet in a period of recession following a boom, a question mark was raised over the methods of some of the accountants in the boom period, and whether the optimism they presented was justified in a profession which is meant to preach prudence and caution. Creative accounting reflects the subjective interpretation of financial information in order to present the information in a way which supports the management objectives. How can this happen?

Accountancy not only has its own language, but its own mystique. Its esoteric process is open to interpretation. Many aspects of accounts are subjective valuations. The question is: what to conceal and what to reveal? What is the emphasis and who is the audience? The problem is that many interested bodies rely on the accountants' information, including shareholders and City analysts.

Some of the procedures carried out in the 1980s have led to an investigation by the Accounting Standards Authority.

The profit and loss account

Assets were sold and put into the profit and loss account as profit through sales. This would obviously devalue the assets in the balance sheet, but made the profit situation appear thriving.

Equity accounting

If a company owns 20% of equity in another company the purchaser of the shares can claim 20% of the profits as belonging to the initial company. It can therefore be added to the profit and loss account, as long as it can be stated that the purchaser has an influence on the policy decisions. This practice has been carried out by famous entrepreneurs like Robert Maxwell and Rupert Murdoch. Murdoch bought a 20% stake in the Pearsons Group (of Alton Towers and the *Financial Times* fame) for £350 million, but his plan to take 20% of their profit as his own failed when the Pearsons board refused to accept that he had any say in their policy decisions.

Valuation of assets

If the asset values are high this makes the company look healthy and improves the **gearing** (ratio of assets – what you **own**, to liability – what you **owe**). Assets comprise fixed and current assets but also intangibles. **Intangibles** are book values which are largely open to interpretation. Some examples include brand names, newspaper titles and franchise rights. All these items have a value, but how far can the value be established? And how quickly can the value fall if there is a change in consumer preferences? Yet to include these items is perfectly justifiable if it can be said that they could be sold separately as assets.

Cautious or prudent accounting means a business has something to fall back on in hard times. Creative accounting may have reflected the business optimism of the 1980s but when the boom slumped many companies, particularly the acquisitorial ones, had limited assets to fall back on and became extinct.

Source: National newspaper reports and author's research.

Preview

In this chapter we shall investigate the following key areas:

- the trading account
- the profit and loss account
- the balance sheet
- assets and liabilities
- double-entry bookkeeping
- trial balance
- valuation of assets

Financial control and decision-making

To monitor the financial position of any business records need to be kept, checked and analysed. These records form the basis of the financial control and decision-making of a business.

The day-to-day financial income and expenditure form part of the double-entry book-keeping system whereby transactions are logged as they 'flow' through the accounting process. All transactions start in one place and end up in another. What may start as cash could become purchases and ultimately sales. Each movement will have to be entered in the system in two accounts, the one which it left and the one which it enters. These are the two sides of the accounting equation. The trial balance is the accounting check which ensures that both sides of the equation tally.

The balance sheet summarises the way in which the business uses its resources in terms of assets (that which the business owns) and liabilities (that which the business owes). The profit and loss account is a record of the profit earned by a business over a period of time comparing income with expenditure.

In a limited company these records need to be kept, published and audited by law.

There are many interested 'stakeholders' (those who have a 'stake' in the business remember Chapter 2.6) who will monitor and evaluate the financial records of a business. Look at Box 7.1.

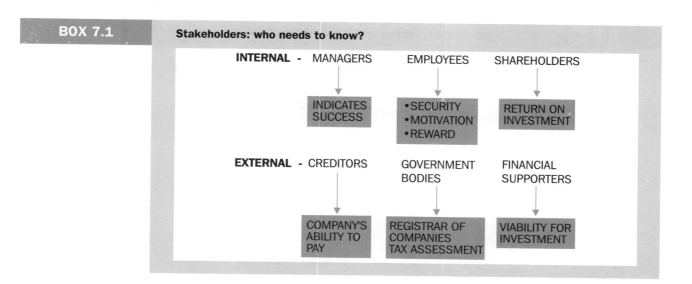

| BOX 7.1 | Stakeholders: who needs to know? |

The presentation and interpretation of accounts

- A financial accountant looks at the company's record-keeping process which is presented by the book-keeper from the double-entry system. The final accounts are then drawn up from the information given.
- A management accountant looks at the wider implications, interpreting the accounts and looking at the process of achieving the set financial objectives.

Because estimates have to be made about future events and projections of figures, it is not unusual to have varying opinions about the profitability of a company. This situation is known as 'varying practices'. Auditors are brought in as an independent body to check accounting records, but they are in effect employed by the company and receive their information from that company. Attempts have been made by accounting bodies to counteract this situation. However if you look at, for example, the balance sheet alone where an estimated value has to be placed on an asset, this can obviously be open to conjecture.

Trading and profit and loss account

For a business to establish whether or not it is making a profit, expenditure needs to be deducted from revenue. We need to be more specific in accounting terms, and we break this process down into two steps.

Step 1: Trading account

The trading account records the gross profit earned. Gross profit is sales *less* the cost of those sales.

Look at Box 7.2.

BOX 7.2	**Bigger burgers: trading account for the year ended . . .**			
			£	£
(Direct input into sales)	Purchases		32 000	Sales 161 000
(Stock held)	*Plus* Stock at Start		6 100	
			38 100	
(Stock left)	*Less* Stock at close		2 695	
=	Cost of goods sold		35 405	
(Difference between sales and cost of goods sold)	**Gross profit**		?	

The gross profit is £161 000 for sales less the cost of goods sold, £35 405, which would leave **£125 595**.

Step 2: Profit and loss account

The profit and loss account would then be added to the trading account. The profit and loss account assesses the net profit earned by deducting all the overheads from the gross profit figure.

Look at Box 7.3.

BOX 7.3	**Bigger Burgers: trading and profit and loss account for the year ended . . .**		
		£	£
Purchases	32 000	Sales	161 000
Plus Stock at start	6 100		
	38 100		
Less Stock at close	2 695		
Cost of goods sold	35 405		
Gross profit	125 595		
Less Overheads:			
Rent and rates	20 500		
Heat and lighting	6 921		
Wages	41 000		
Interest on loan	1 616		
Bad debts	3 962		
Net profit	51 596		
	161 000		161 000

Appropriation account

When the net profit is calculated, tax will need to be deducted. The amount which is left after tax has been taken from net profit is the concern of the appropriation account. This account shows how the business has used the net profit after tax and is usually added as a section in the profit and loss account.

For example, if Bigger Burgers were a limited company then the situation could be as in Box 7.4.

Bigger Burgers plc: appropriation account for the year ended . . .

	£
Net profit	51 596
Less Corporation tax	12 899
Profit after tax	38 697
Less Dividend for shareholders	22 690
	16 007
Add retained profit from the start of the account	15 495
Balance of retained profit at the year end	31 502

Balance sheet

The trading and profit and loss account show a flow of income and expenditure. In contrast, the balance sheet shows the balance of **assets** and **liabilities** at any one point in time. These two factors need defining.

Assets

A business's assets are its resources, those which it can utilise for production. Assets fall into two types, fixed and current. Fixed assets are assets which are relatively more fixed in form than other assets. Fixed assets are usually listed on the balance sheet in order of liquidity (how quickly their form can be changed into cash) with the most illiquid first and the most liquid last. An example of this type of asset would be buildings, plant, machinery and vehicles. If a business spends more and increases its fixed assets, this is defined as capital expenditure. Revenue expenditure is money spent on consumables (items more rapidly used).

Other assets

Trademarks and goodwill

These items are very difficult to value, but can be an important asset to a business. The goodwill that is built up by the use of a brand name or trademark for which consumers develop brand loyalty can form the basis of a business success. However, consumer preferences can change quite rapidly and therefore to overvalue this asset could cause misconceptions about the true valuation of the business. Patents, give a right for a company or individual to be the sole producer of an item over a given period of time, and hence also have an asset value. They may also receive royalties if they allow others to produce the item under licence. Copyrights have a similar value in the world of computer software, publishing, films and videos.

Investment

A business may buy stocks or shares in another business.

Current assets

Current assets change their form on a regular basis into output.

They are used up in the process of trade and comprise items like the cash book, bank balances and debtors (amount owed to the business). Reserves are also assets which belong to shareholders.

Liabilities

Capital is classed as a liability because it is the amount initially invested in the business.

The owner does not provide investment in the form of charity but as a loan to the business, which must be paid back in order to get the true picture of how financially effectively the business is operating. This figure therefore must be included in the accounts as a liability. Net profit is added to the capital sum, whilst if the owners have drawn out any funds for their own use, this is called drawings.

Current liabilities

These funds are due back within one year and are either short-term bank loans, overdrafts or amounts owed by the business to its suppliers (creditors – those who give credit). Look at Box 7.5, the balance sheet for the Mega Burger chain of factories who supply Bigger Burger's outlets.

BOX 7.5	**Mega Burger: Balance sheet as at . . .**		
	Fixed assets	£	£
	Building		90 000
	Machinery		12 560
			102 560
	Current assets		
	Stock	2 695	
	Debtors	16 550	
	Bank	1 000	
	Cash	25	
		20 270	
	Less Current liabilities		
	Creditors	3 230	
	Overdraft	1 600	
		4 830	
	(Working capital) – Current assets *less* current liabilities)	15 440	
		118 000	

	£	£
Financed by:		
Opening capital		60 100
Add net profit		52 999
		113 099
Less drawings		199
		112 900
Long-term liabilities		
Bank loan		5 100
		118 000

Note: Stock at close was £2 600.

The double-entry system

The recording of financial transactions takes place in the double-entry system. Each transaction has two entries:

- where the value came from
- where the value is going to

For example, if you buy a vehicle for £5000 then your bank account ledger would be debited (value taken away) by £5000, whilst your vehicle account would be credited (value added) by £5000.

There are always two sides to any transaction, and to test to see whether their are any omissions a trial balance is periodically created which lists all the credit and debit entries and tests the accuracy of the accounts. Box 7.6 shows Mega Burger's trial balance when it was last extracted.

Mega Burger: trial balance as at . . .

	Debit (in)	Credit (out)
	£	£
Stock at 5 April	18 902	
Purchases	112 000	
Sales		191 000
Heat and light	4 195	
Salaries	40 329	
Premises	15 100	
Bank	474	
	191 000	191 000

Note: Stock at the end of March was £600

Valuation of assets

Intangible assets

There are obvious difficulties in placing a value on intangible assets:

- Goodwill – the reputation a business earns
- Brand names – the consumer loyalty built up under the name of a good or service.

Tangible assets

There are also problems in valuing tangible items. The value of any item is only 'real' at any one point in time. The amount you pay for an asset may not be its current market price at the time of valuation, as markets fluctuate according to demand and supply.

Depreciation

Most fixed assets like machinery and vehicles, also have a limited life span and lose value with 'wear and tear'. An assessment needs to be made of the drop in value of any asset held by a business. It is usual to write off a proportion of the value of any asset on an annual basis. This is called depreciation'.

The fall in value of fixed assets, or depreciation, is shown in the profit and loss account as an expense and is therefore taken off the profit before tax is deducted. The business therefore saves tax by depreciating its fixed assets. Look at Box 7.7, showing how Mega Burger dealt with the depreciating value of its vehicles and equipment.

There are two main methods of estimating depreciation:

- The equal instalment method
- The diminishing balance method.

The equal instalment method (or straight-line method)

The same amount is written off each year, based on the initial cost of the asset, the expected life span and the residual or scrap value:

Annual depreciation cost (ADC) = Cost price less residual value Estimated life span

Box 7.8 shows a typical calculation.

The diminishing balance method

A fixed percentage is written off each year from the initial purchase value. Box 7.9 shows a typical calculation.

BOX 7.7

Mega Burger: Profit and loss account for the year ended . . .

	£	£
Gross profit	80 950	
Less		
Heat and light	10 000	
Salaries	29 500	
Rent and rates	16 902	
Provision for depreciation Vehicles	500	
Equipment	400	
		57 302
Net profit		23 648

BOX 7.8

Straight-line depreciation

A machine cost £12 500. The estimated working life of the machine is 10 years, whilst the expected scrap value in 10 years time is estimated to be £1500

$$ADC = \frac{£12\,500 - 1500}{10} = £1100 \text{ p.a.}$$

TASK 7.1

Work out the annual depreciation if the life span of the above machine were estimated to be 4 and the residual value £650.

BOX 7.9

Diminishing-balance depreciation

If a machine cost £12 500 and the depreciation is 20% over a 10 year period, the following calculation would be done:

		£
Year 1		12 500
	Depreciation	2 500
	New value	10 000
Year 2		10 000
	Depreciation	2 000
	New value	8 000
Year 3		8 000
	Depreciation	1 600
	New value	6 400
Year 4		6 400
	Depreciation	1 280
	New value	5 120
Year 5		5 120
	Depreciation	1 024
	New value	4 096
Year 6		4 096
	Depreciation	819.20
	New value	3 276.80
Year 7		3 276.80
	Depreciation	655.36
	New value	2 621.44
Year 8		2 621.44
	Depreciation	524.29
	New value	2 097.15
Year 9		2 097.15
	Depreciation	419.43
	New value	1 677.72
Year 10		1 677.72
	Depreciation	335.54
	New value	1 342.18

Unlike other aspects of the profit and loss account, depreciation is a 'non-cash' expenditure and is not an outflow of money, and is therefore open to wider interpretations of value. It is only when a fixed asset is sold that we get a true picture of its value. For example, if an asset costing £10 000 is depreciated by £500 over a year but the asset is then sold for £8000 there has been an underprovision of depreciation in the profit and loss account by £1500. This is called a 'loss' on sale. If this situation were the other way around and the depreciation allowed was £2500 then this would be an 'over' provision of depreciation by £500: a 'profit' on sale.

Valuation of stock

Stock = An asset = Money

Assessing the value of stock held

Stock could be referred to as 'money tied up'. The current tendency is for companies to hold minimum stock levels so that they can maintain their liquidity levels and possibly use the funds for some other purpose. It is felt by exponents of JIT (just in time – a stock control system) that too much stock tends to be held by businesses. This is unnecessary if there is an effective system for allocation of resources so that 'just enough' stock is held in order to keep output flowing if the stock inputs are ready 'just in time' for use. We will look at JIT in the section on production, but it is important here that we recognise the implications of stock being held, not only in terms of the acquisition cost but also in terms of storage space and security. The level and type of stock held will also depend on the type of business.

Because stock is 'money tied up' we need to be able to assess its value. There are two prices which could be used as a valuation

- the historic price: the price originally paid
- or the replacement cost of each item.

Methods of valuation

There are three main types of stock valuation:

- LIFO
- FIFO
- Weighted average

LIFO (Last In First Out)

- Stock is valued at the last price paid
- It is assumed that the last stock received is the first stock used, this is a more cautious approach when prices are rising.

FIFO (First In First Out)

- Stock is valued at the original price, and it is assumed that the first stock received is the first stock used.

Weighted average

- The average cost of items in stock is calculated and as new stock is purchased a new average evolves. This is usually worked out on a weighted average, based on the number of units acquired.

These systems of valuation are important not only to measure the value of stock held, but also to put a price on items which are inputs to the process of production.

Liquidity and the acid test

The liquidity of an asset is a measure of how quickly an asset can be converted to cash. The banks need to hold a proportion of their assets in a liquid or near-liquid form in order to be ready for any rush of withdrawals from customers; if they were not prepared it could undermine the whole banking system. Businesses, in a similar way, need to be able to have funds which they can call upon at short notice.

Working capital (current ratio)

The working capital of a business, which is needed to fund many day-to-day trading activities is defined as current assets minus current liabilities. The figures are taken from the balance sheet, demonstrating the liquidity of the assets. The survival of a business can depend upon the management of its working capital, because these funds can be vital in the running of 'everyday' business activities.

$$\frac{\text{Current assets}}{\text{Current liabilities}} = \text{Working capital ratio}$$

A safe working capital ratio is often considered to be 2:1 – £2 of current assets to £1 of current liabilities.

A business needs to monitor the make-up of its current assets and current liabilities to ensure, for example, that it is not holding too much stock which could make its ratio too high. In a retail business a lower ratio would be acceptable because the sales are predominantly for cash.

Liquid capital ratio (the acid test)

This test measures current assets against current liabilities but eliminates stock from the calculation. Stock is the most illiquid of current assets and some stock may be obsolete or unsellable. The ideal ratio of liquid assets and current liabilities is often said to be **1:1**.

$$\frac{\text{Ratio of current assets } minus \text{ stock}}{\text{Current liabilities}}$$
$$= \text{The acid test}$$

With both the working capital and liquid assets ratios, the best level will be dependent upon the type of business and the importance of liquidity in each situation. Businesses will need to monitor trends over the years in order to establish a clear picture.

REVIEW

After reading this chapter you should understand the importance of a business recording its financial transactions and the main records of account. You should also understand how financial records are interpreted.

TASK 7.2

PRACTICAL APPLICATION

From the trial balance information below, draw up a trading and profit and loss account and a balance.

A&B Co.: trial balance as at 31 December 1996

	£	£		£	£
Creditors		13 185	Rent	6 500	
Debtors	21 549		Other expenses	4 899	
Premises	98 100		Drawings	1 000	
Capital		74 000	Sales		250 000
Machinery	6 000		Purchases	170 000	
Bank	2 950		Bank loan		15 000
Cash	1 617		Stock at 1 Jan 1990	17 900	
Wages	21 670				

Note: The stock they were left with at 31 December was £21 400.

REVIEW TASK

CRITICAL ANALYSIS

Using the data for A&B Co. in Task 7.2:

1 Work out what the depreciation of furniture and fittings at cost would be using
- straight-line method
- diminishing balance method
- over a 3 year period with a residual value of £500.

2 Carry out an acid test on the company.

QUESTIONS

Essay questions

1 In what ways would accounting information, when prepared for internal management differ from that compiled for the use of other interested parties?
- What kind of information would a supplier require of a new customer ordering raw materials?

2 Accounting techniques are designed to present a true and fair picture of the activities of a business. Why is this essential
- for a sole trader
- for a public limited company?

CASE STUDY

When George Walker purchased William Hill and MECCA from Grand Metropolitan for a sum of £685 million he believed he was purchasing a valuable asset. However, the bookmakers' chain was later found not to be in a healthy financial condition and there was a large shortfall in profits. Walker believed his credibility was badly damaged when he refused to pay the final £50 million instalment for his purchase of the company. He believed that the City interpreted this move as Walker saying 'he can't pay rather than he won't pay'. His business reputation was put at risk.

The accountants had reflected the business optimism of the 1980s and the acquisitorial entrepreneurs were the ones to fall. John Ashcroft of Coloroll had won the Business Man of the Year award, but in 1988 he spent £217 million purchasing John Crowther Carpets. John Aschroft, like many others at the time, was lured by easy borrowing. Within a year, his business failed.

Men like Walker and Ashcroft may have over-rated the value of companies they were hoping to purchase in the boom period.

Source: National newspaper reports and author's research.

CASE STUDY TASKS

1. Write a report, on your computer or word processor if possible, entitled 'Final accounts and their anomalies'. Set it out as a report from yourself to your lecturer. In it:
   A explain the importance of financial record keeping to a business
   B describe the use and components of the profit and loss account and the balance sheets, drawing up a model layout of each (spreadsheet if possible)
   C explain how accounting figures can be 'massaged' to create a false impression of a company's 'health'.

2. Why do you think that 'acquisitorial entrepreneurs' were particularly at risk during the late 1980s and early 1990s?

3. Why do you think that George Walker's reputation was threatened by his refusal to pay? Explain the power of the City in this type of business reaction.

4. Explain what is meant by 'prudence and caution in accounts', and why this concept is so important for business stability.

2.8 Financial Decision-Making

FOCUS

Fools rush in where angels fear to tread

The Government is giving wealthy individuals, whom they call business 'angels', incentives to invest in small businesses. They believe that small firms are the key to economic regeneration. Small firms are continually struggling in a financial system which starves them of funds and they see external finance as the biggest obstacle to growth. Small firms, like large ones, need extra capital to fund expansion. This need has been reflected in recent years by the number of quoted companies putting out rights issues. Some small companies make the mistake of thinking they can expand without a capital injection. More than two-thirds of small-to-medium-sized companies rely on overdrafts as a cheap form of finance, but overdrafts are not an effective means of funding growth. The need for a structured approach to funding was the motivating force behind the Government's 'business angels' scheme. A similar initiative has worked well in the USA.

The UK scheme involves two types of investment, the EIS (Enterprise Investment Scheme) and Venture Capital Trusts. The EIS allows individuals to invest up to £100 000 each year in unquoted UK companies with income tax relief at 20%. Any subsequent profit would be free of capital gains tax. The Venture Capital Trusts are still in their formative stage but would operate in a similar way to investment trusts. Individuals would get the same form of tax relief as on a PEP (Personal Equity Plan) scheme. PEPs encourage individuals to invest their money in share capital, or equity funds. They receive tax exemption on dividends gained and on capital gains when the shares are sold. Venture Capital Trusts work on the same basis.

The problem with these initiatives is that the tax relief is not enough to encourage the level of investment needed. When venture capitalists take risks they expect a higher rate of return, and this would ultimately make this type of financial resource more expensive.

Another problem for small businesses could be the termination of the USM (see Chapter 1.2). It has been replaced by the alternative investment market (AIM). The uncertainty over this new market system has led to the City group for smaller companies (CISCO), made up of venture capitalists, merchant banks and stockbrokers, to look into setting up its own share trading system for non-listed smaller companies.

The fact that two additional sources of finance would be born through the present developments is a positive note. However, a more general question needs to be raised over the whole issue of business regeneration. The UK's policy of leaving businesses to market forces is in stark contrast to more successful business nations like Japan and Germany. The Japanese Government have a business and industrial strategy which is directed by MITI (Ministry for International Trade and Industry). Potential industrial growth areas are targeted and the business supported and funded. Business 'angels' may never get off the ground, whilst for British industry any commitment may be too little too late.

Source: National newspaper reports and author's research.

Preview

In this chapter we shall investigate the following key areas:

- sources of funds
- government grants and support
- investment decisions
- financial strategy
- the control of working capital

Business and the cost of money

Businesses, like individuals and economies, have scarce resources. They have to utilise their resources to gain maximum benefits. Decisions need to be taken and choices made. All resource allocation involves an opportunity cost.

- If you save, how much is it worth?
- If you spend, what assets are achieved, and how much do they contribute to output?

Finance is the fuel that drives a business, but money is only a measure of value. Money has a cost and a reward which is interest. If money is saved it earns interest and if it is borrowed, interest needs to be paid. Governments use the control of interest rates to manipulate the amount of money in circulation. Higher interest rates may encourage individuals to save rather than spend. The effect on businesses of high interest rates could mean that, not only will they have to pay more to borrow, but also demand for goods and services may diminish. If the government wanted to encourage business activity and stimulate the economy it may lower interest rates, thus reducing the cost of money. The level of interest rates will always have a direct impact on the business world. We will look at this again in Sections on 'The Economy' and 'The World Stage'.

The company's funds

Sources of finance

Businesses need finance in order to operate. Whatever profit or funds a business generates, it needs to be able to finance its trading in the short term and in the longer term its investment or capital expansion.

There are a number of ways a business can obtain finance:

Equity capital

Anyone going into business, whether as a sole trader or a limited company, will inject their own resources into the business. This is called equity or risk capital.

A sole trader will have limited resources to invest in the business, which is why becoming a partnership or a limited company is financially attractive. A private limited company can issue more shares to generate capital whilst a public limited company can sell their equity on the stock market and resort to new issues when additional funds are needed.

The profit and loss and appropriation accounts show that only a portion of profits are distributed to shareholders; the rest is kept as reserves. The reserves can be reinvested in the company. If a business is part of a larger group it may be possible to obtain inter-company loans to support financial projects. There are also organisations, mostly run by banks, who will provide funds in return for an equity stake in a company. Investors in Industry Group plc are an example of this type of organisation.

The money market

Virtually all businesses will need to call on external finance at some time in their cycle. To obtain funds a business must pay the cost of borrowing – interest – but also be able to convince the lender that it is a viable concern. Cash flow forecasts are an effective way of demonstrating the ability of a business to monitor and project its financial position. The forecast is therefore a useful tool in the quest for finance. The business plan (which we will look at in more depth later) is another way in which a business can show its ability to plan its development and project the funding needed.

Loans to business can be short term (1–3 years), medium term (3–10 years) and longer term (10–25 years). Whatever the time period, a loan is a source of money and the charge for money is interest. Whatever amount is borrowed must be paid back (the

principal) with interest (the payment for borrowing). The income generated from the financial input needs to be sufficient to at least cover the funding:

$$\text{Interest} = \text{amount borrowed} \times \text{interest rate} \times \text{years}$$

e.g. £15 000 borrowed at 11% over a 6 year period:

$$£15\,000 \times 11/100 \times 6 = £9900$$

The banks are the largest suppliers of business finance in the money market, but they are often criticised for inflexibility and an unwillingness to take risks on business ventures. Throughout the 1970s and 1980s the value of property was continually rising and many banks moved into the mortgage market believing the risk element to be minimal. Any difficulties over repayment meant the property could always be repossessed and sold. Property owners, seeing a rising market, put any extra funds they had into developing and improving the property, rather than putting funds into financial institutions. Therefore much capital investment which could have gone into industry went into fuelling the property boom.

Overdraft facilities

This is a service which allows an individual or a business the facility to draw out more than the funds available up to an agreed amount. For this privilege you pay interest on the overdraft plus a price for setting up the facility. This type of short-term borrowing is expensive but is often used to fund day-to-day transactions and emergency requirements. Medium-term loans are usually needed to fund capital purchases like machinery and equipment.

Longer-term loans

In a business context longer-term loans often need collateral or security to support their application. The risk in the business sector is much higher than, say, a mortgage where there is a tangible asset at the end of the period.

Other financial support

Hire purchase

A finance company pays for the item and remains the owner until the end of the payment period. The business would pay the cost of the item in instalments, plus the cost of borrowing the money.

Leasing

This facility is also provided by a finance house. The company can use assets bought by the finance house but ownership remains with the finance house whilst the business pays for the rental of the goods. Leasing is an effective replacement for capital purchasing and is becoming more widely used by businesses, particularly for buildings, equipment, machinery and vehicles.

Trade credit

Businesses which supply goods and services will usually allow a period of time before the debt needs to be repaid. In a recessionary period, businesses will often deliberately delay the payment of debts in order to protect their own cash flow. This delaying tactic can cause serious damage to the suppliers, particularly smaller businesses who do not have the resources to cope with the delay in obtaining funds. The government sees this as a serious threat to smaller businesses and is attempting to find ways of legislating against companies who do not pay their debts within a reasonable time. 'Cash discounts', or discount for prompt payment, may be given as encouragement, but at an obvious cost to the supplier. Again smaller companies do not have the spare resources to be able to support substantial discounts.

Factoring

Factoring out debts is a way of overcoming the financial difficulties caused by chasing invoices, or bills sent to customers. A factoring company will give a business funding for up to 80% of the debts owed to the business. For this service it will deduct a charge. The result of this facility is that the business achieves an immediately improved cash flow. The factoring firm pays the final 20% when the customer clears the debt. The factoring company is left to chase up late payers. A typical charge for this service is between 0.5 and 2.5% of turnover, often with 3% interest above the bank base rate on the payment advanced.

Bills of exchange

A bill of exchange is a promise to pay a bill at a future date. For example, if a business purchases goods from another company they can use a bill of exchange, which is an agreement that they pay for the goods in, for example, 3 months. This bill can then be taken to the bank by the seller who is able to cash in the bill, obviously at below the face value (the bank's profit is the difference between what it pays and the face value). At the end of the 3 month period the bank can claim the full face value of the bill.

Government resources

The Government has an impact on business finances in many ways. As already explained they compete for funds through the gilt-edged market.

Some governments have planned business or industrial and international trade strategies whilst others leave businesses to survive in the free market. Whatever policy is in operation it will either directly or indirectly affect businesses because they have to survive in the economic and social environment which is shaped by the Government. There is also the wider context of the EU and international markets.

Government grants

There are a variety of Government grants open to businesses, in particular small ones. Advice is available from local TECs (Training and Enterprise Councils) and other Government support bodies. Some of the grants available include:

- **Regional selective assistance** – This grant is related to the capital cost of a project and the jobs created. Companies need to prove the viability of the project, its contribution to the local and national economy and its relevance to the creation and maintenance of jobs.
- **Regional enterprise grants for investment projects** – These are available from the Department of Trade and Industry, mainly to the manufacturing sector, but some service sector businesses can apply. The project must be initiated in a Development Area with less than 25 employees. The Government will pay 15% of expenditure on fixed assets up to £15 000.

- **Regional enterprise grants for innovation** – These grants are available from the Department of Trade and Industry for schemes that involve the development of new products or ideas.
- **Small firms merit award for research and technology** – This is an annual competition for small firms (with up to 50 employees) with an interesting idea which is thought to have a good chance of commercial success.
- **Support for products under research** – This grant helps small firms develop products which involve technological advance. A fixed 30% grant towards the costs is available up to £150 000.
- **Small firms loan guarantee scheme** – The definition of a 'small' firm usually states an upper limit of 200 employees. This scheme can provide 70% of loans up to £100 000 to new businesses and 85% of loans between £5000 and £250 000 to ones that are already established.

The above are examples of the support available. The local TECs and the Department of Trade and Industry will have the relevant up-to-date information for businesses.

There are also Trusts which have been set up to encourage business activity. Supporters of these initiatives, like the Prince of Wales, are keen to help raise funds particularly in the area of new design and development.

The decisions

Investment appraisal

To appraise is to analyse a situation and decide a way forward. To invest is a risk which also involves an opportunity cost. The management of funds and the decision process involved are taking on an increasingly higher profile in the business sector. Some examples of questions a business should ask itself before making investment decisions include:

- Could the rate of interest be higher?
- What else could be done with the funds?
- Is the investment the right direction to take?
- Will it increase output?

ARR (average rate of return)

This is a fairly basic system of calculating the annual rate of return on an investment. It is a limited method because it uses the asset's 'book' value and does not consider fluctuating price levels, or the 'real' values. It gives a percentage accounting rate of return.

To calculate the ARR, the average annual profit (AAP) from the investment needs to be divided by the initial investment cost. Look at Box 8.1.

Payback

This system looks at the net cash flows returning to the company as a result of the investment and then judges how long it would take to pay back the initial investment. The quicker the payback, the more economical the investment. Payback is useful because it considers the time factor, but its weakness is that it fails to analyse specific cash receipts, concentrating on the payback period. Look at Box 8.2.

The weakness of this system is that it looks at income on a simple level, ignoring the comparison between future returns and net present values. Also, if two projects were to achieve payback over the same period of time, cash flows for individual periods would be ignored.

BOX 8.1	**Average rate of return**								
		Outlay	Year 1	Year 2	Year 3	Year 4	Year 5	Receipts	Profit over period	Annual average profit
		£	£	£	£	£	£	£	£	£
	Project 1	28 000	9 500	8 150	9 260	10 230	9 600	46 740	18 740	3 748
	Project 2	30 000	8 900	9 560	10 100	11 200	10 860	50 620	20 620	4 124

Project 1
  ARR = AAP/Initial investment = 3748/28 000 × 100 = 13.4%

Project 2
  ARR = AAP/Initial investment = 4124/30 000 × 100 = 13.7%

BOX 8.2	**Payback**		
		Machine A	*Machine B*
		£	£
	Initial cost	32 000	34 000
	Cash flow		
	Year 1	9 600	10 100
	Year 2	15 800	11 900
	Year 3	10 700	10 100
	Year 4	11 600	12 900

If a company were using the 'payback' system to analyse which machine they should choose for their investment, they would choose machine A. Machine A had achieved payback by year 3, whilst machine B did not achieve this until year 4.

Discounted cash flow (net present value)

The level of interest rate levied on an investment will depend on the risk involved, the period of the loan and the demand and supply for money. The opportunity cost of any investment will need to be related to what could otherwise have been achieved with the funds:

£10 000

Possible options?

- Invest in a bank at 7% interest rate p.a. for 3 years
- Purchase a machine which will increase output by **20%** over 3 years

Before any business makes an investment decision it needs to take account of the real value of the future flow of income from the investment, in relation to the present value.

To find out the comparative present values of future income flows, instead of calculating forward to find out how much would be earned if the amount was invested for a set period, a reverse process is used. The starting point for the calculation is the future sum which needs to be reduced by an annually agreed percentage for each year of the investment. Instead of starting with the principal and ending with the interest earned (compound interest) you would need to start with the interest and work back to the principal. Look at Box 8.3.

This process does not look into other cost factor, but only return on investment. No expenses have been taken into account. To put this process into perspective a discounted cash flow (DCF) would need to be drawn up which took into account production costs and operating expenses. This appraisal system would show whether the total of the DCF (discounted cash flow) over the life of the machine was greater than the proposed investment, and therefore more profitable.

BOX 8.3

Present values of future income flows

In the example above, the investment of £10 000 on machinery would generate the following income over a 3 year period:

Year 1	£50 000
Year 2	£53 000
Year 3	£60 000

To find the present value of the above income flows when we discount by 7%

£1 discounted at 7% = 0.93
Therefore for year 1 – £50 000 × 0.93 = 46 500

For year 2 the money earned would be discounted over a 2 year period so the value of each £1 would be lowered to 0.86

Year 2 – £53 000 × 0.86 = £45 580
Year 3 – £60 000 × 0.80 = £48 000

This process may seem long-winded, but this can be done easily on a computer spreadsheet by setting up a formula. Also there are tables available which show £1 discounted at various interest rates over different periods of time.

The company's financial strategy

Investment ratios provide information on the profitability and growth of a business and are important to investors and managers. There are four main types of ratios which can be used:

- Return on equity
- Dividend yield
- Price/earnings
- Gearing.

Return on equity

$$= \frac{\text{Net profit after tax}}{\text{Shareholder's funds (equity capital)}}$$

Equity is the term used for capital investment by ordinary shareholders. Prospective shareholders may look at the ratio in order to compare the return on equity of a number of companies, before making an investment decision.

Dividend yield

$$= \frac{\text{Dividend per share}}{\text{Share price}}$$

As we have already discovered, not all net profit after tax is distributed to shareholders. Directors may decide to retain profits to fund further growth. This ratio will be important for investors to decide whether they want high income over a short period, or their investment to grow over a longer period of time.

Price earnings

$$= \frac{\text{Market price of shares}}{\text{Earnings per share}}$$

Assessing the risk involved in an investment can be done by measuring the time it takes to pay back the initial cost of the investment. This is similar to the 'payback' approach to investment appraisal.

Gearing

$$= \frac{\text{Loans and preference shares}}{\text{Equity}}$$

The assets of a business are funded by the owners' capital investment and other borrowed funds.

The relationship between equity (owners' capital) and borrowed funds is expressed by the gearing ratio. Equity capital necessitates a return to shareholders based on profit distributed. However, borrowed funds must be paid back at a fixed rate of interest. If profits are rising this cost can be small compared to the volume of profit, but if profits are falling, the sum becomes relatively greater and liquidity can be affected.

Control of working capital

Working capital is vital to any business because it is the difference between current assets and current liabilities. It reflects the liquidity of a business and is known as the acid test (see Chapter 2.7). Working capital is also used to finance daily trading activities and presents a picture of possible cash flow movements.

Working capital ratio =
Current assets: Current liabilities

A prudent ratio is considered to be **2:1** but many businesses never achieve this target.

How a business could improve the ratio

- Operate a minimum cash operating cycle by holding cash as long as possible and collecting cash from debtors as quickly as possible
- Assets could be sold and then leased back; businesses are increasingly leasing vehicles and equipment because it allows them to hold onto their cash reserves
- Debt factoring (discussed further in the Case Study to this chapter.
- Some businesses delay payments to their creditors. This obviously helps their cashflow situation, but can mean the downfall of suppliers, particularly the smaller companies.

The government sees this latter tactic as very damaging to the business sector and is looking at ways of counteracting this practice.

REVIEW

After reading this chapter you should be aware of various sources of funds available to a business, the importance of financial decision-making and the techniques which can be used.

TASK 8.1

PRACTICAL APPLICATION

Consider the two investment projects set out below:

	Project 1 £	Project 2 £
Outlay in Year 0	51 900	62 800
Cash receipts Year 1	25 000	11 600
2	30 000	20 100
3	12 000	18 000
4	10 500	19 000
5	9 000	22 000
6	8 100	10 000

The cost of capital over 6 years is estimated to be 11% per annum.
- Carry out an analysis of the discounted cash flow.
- Draw up an appraisal of the above two projects, using
- Payback
- ARR
- NPV

REVIEW TASK

CRITICAL ANALYSIS

Explain in detail how the following methods of increasing cash flow can be put into operation. Also analyse the implications of each of them to the business.
1 Reducing the cash operating cycle.
2 Increased credit control.
3 Cutting investment.
4 Use of lease back.
5 Raising capital.
6 Stock control.

QUESTIONS

Essay questions

1 How useful is ratio analysis for the decision monitoring and control of a business?

2 Explain the importance of cash flow to a business.

The facts of factoring

Debt factoring is a method of selling off the book debts of a firm to a specialist company which operates a system of collecting debts. The company will usually immediately pay the firm with the debts, up to 80% of the value owed with the rest following when it is collected. The fees for the service are taken off the final amount, and can total as much as 5% of the debts.

A Confederation of British Industry (CBI) survey in 1990 reported that around 4% of firms use the factoring system. In 1993 the Association of British Factorers and Discounters reported a 23.3% increase in turnover. The association found that factoring is under-utilised as a financial tool, primarily, they say, because businesses are unaware of its potential.

Factorers find it difficult to offer a service in certain sectors, for example the construction industry. The problem is that within this industry there are often disputes over work done and prices paid. Also factorers do not like dealing with businesses who invoice for small amounts, or those who buy and sell to each other and cancel out the debts.

Factoring is not for those who find difficulty obtaining finance through the banks. It is also not for those whose credit rating is dubious. Factoring is ideal for businesses who are expanding rapidly and who do not want to keep going to the clearing banks for funds. The service could prove valuable for exporters who could factor out their export debts leaving them free to manage their home trade. This could be a major advantage in an international market place which is often fraught with language problems, complex documentation and currency fluctuations. It could be left to a factorer specialising in this type of market. Ultimately the important advantage of factoring is that it allows the generation of **extra working capital**.

Source: National newspaper reports and author's research.

1. Explain the advantages and disadvantages of factoring.
2. What type of businesses do you think are suitable for debt factoring?
3. Explain what is meant by 'working capital', and its importance to a business.
4. How could debt factoring be useful in an international market?

Integrated case study for Section 2: Gourmet Garlic

'Gourmet Garlic' has been formed by two brothers living on the Isle of Wight working in a partnership. They decided to develop this specialist crop and have been very successful. They now feel it is time to expand. To do this they will need to obtain a loan from their bank. They are aware that you are a business student and have asked you to have a look at their financial situation first. Opposite is their trial balance for the year ended 31 March 1990.

	£	£
Sales		93 870
Opening stock	289	
Purchases	5 500	
Machinery	5 600	
Depreciation	200	
Rent	10 000	
Wages	59 505	
Sundries	1 236	
Bank	9 528	
Debtors	1 850	
Capital		61 000
Creditors		250
Drawings	1 000	
Cash	412	
Premises	60 000	

Note: closing stock £210

INTEGRATED CASE STUDY TASK 1

A Complete Gourmet Garlic's profit and loss account.

B Explain the term 'depreciation' and demonstrate the different types of methods used to calculate this.

Look at the value of the machinery and calculate:

(i) the annual depreciation if the life span of the machine was estimated at 4 years and the residual value £650. Use the equal instalment method;

(ii) the annual depreciation given the above data using the diminishing balance method.

INTEGRATED CASE STUDY TASK 2

Compile a new Profit and Loss Account for Gourmet Garlic taking the factors below into consideration:

A They have planned to give the workforce a rise of 4.4%

B The rent may be increased by 16%.

INTEGRATED CASE STUDY TASK 3

Draw up a balance sheet based on the information in the trial balance using the framework below.

Gourmet Garlic: balance sheet as at . . .

	£	£
Fixed assets		
Premises		
Machinery		

	£	£
Current assets		
Stock		
Debtors		
Cash at bank		
Less		
Current liabilities		
Trade creditors		
Capital		
Add Profit		
Less Drawings		

INTEGRATED CASE STUDY TASK 4

In order for the brothers to obtain a bank loan, they need to present a cash flow forecast to the bank on estimated income and expenditure for the forthcoming year.

A   Produce a cash flow forecast from the predicted information given below, if possible using a spreadsheet programme. Use the specimen layout below as a guide.

Example layout of cash flow forecast

	Apr	May	Jun	Jul	Aug	Sep, etc
Receipts						
Total						
Payments						
Total						
Inflow/outflow						
Bank balance b/forward						
Bank balance c/forward						

B   Prepare a report, on a word processor or computer, if possible, giving your own views on how you see the financial standing of the business, given the financial records now in your possession and the forecast figures.

C   Include a copy of the cash flow forecast with this report, stating if there are any changes to the cash flow situation that you would want to implement – i.e. increase sales, cut certain costs, make the necessary amendments to the cash flow forecast, recalculate the forecast and, if you have used a spreadsheet program, print a hard copy.

Information for cash flow forecast – receipts
Revenue of sales for the forthcoming year is estimated at £122 000

	£		£
April	10 000	**October**	10 600
May	11 000	**November**	10 980
June	10 500	**December**	11 640
July	10 100	**January**	9 890
August	9 680	**February**	9 610
September	8 900	**March**	9 100

In November and December some machinery is hired out and the company receives an income from this of £500 per month.

Payments

Cost of materials for the year is estimated to be £8500

	£	
April	Purchase	3500
July	Purchase	3000
November	Purchase	2000

Wages for the year are now estimated to rise by 2.4%. Total rent of £10000 paid monthly.

Sundries and depreciation will also remain the same.

INTEGRATED CASE STUDY TASK 5

The brothers have given you some other problems to tackle for them. Present your recommendations in the form of a report with main headings for each of the 3 areas below, and relevant subheadings:

A They have noticed a general trend in late payments of invoices, and fear that this could jeopardise their cash flow situation. Explain the ways that they could get around this problem.

B They see the way forward as being to expand, but are unsure about the best method of expansion. Explain the options available to them.

C In the course of your research, you uncover the fact that they have never drawn up a partnership agreement. Explain the importance of the agreement and do a draft outline setting out the important factors to be included.

INTEGRATED CASE STUDY TASK 6

The brothers have just received their Uniform Business Rate assessment, and are concerned because under the old system the rate levied was 35p in the pound and the uniform rate is 48p. Their old rateable value was £56000 whereas their new one is £72000. Work out for them how much they will have to pay, deducting transitional relief at 7%. Use the current rate of inflation.

INTEGRATED CASE STUDY TASK 7

Gourmet Garlic see their expansion opportunities in developing a food processing plant. To do this they need to:

A lease the land next to their present site including a concrete building;

B buy plant and equipment.

They will start by processing only a limited range:
    (i) Gourmet Lasagne

   (ii)   Gourmet Korma
   (iii) Gourmet Cod

Costs

	£
Lease building	8 000
Lease land	10 000 p.a.
Lease machinery	5 000 p.a.
Labour costs	35 000
Ingredients	45p (lasagne) 55p (korma) 85p per item (cod)
Packing	15p per item

Carry out a break-even analysis to see how much they need to sell, and at what price, to make a profit for each product.

ACTIVE LEARNING TASK
The expansion of the garlic company
Local residents are 'up in arms' today as news has been leaked that the local garlic company is looking at expanding into the food processing business.

A petition was being gathered by local resident, Mr Nimby, which was to be lodged with the local Planning Committee, because of fears of increased traffic and noise, to name but a few concerns.

The local Planning Committee was unavailable for comment.

Source: Local Echo, comment column.

1. Write a letter to Mr Nimby from yourself, as Management Consultant to Gourmet Garlic, putting forward the positive aspects of the development and inviting him and any other interested parties to have a meeting with the company.
2. Prepare your own debate in your 'Learning Group' with individuals representing each of the interested parties:
   Yourself : Management Consultant
   The brothers
   Mr Nimby
   A prospective employee
   A local resident with young children

QUESTIONS
Essay questions
1. Explain what is meant by 'working capital', and its importance to the business.
2. Outline the function of the trading and profit and loss account and the balance sheet. Explain their importance to a business.

Section 3
Marketing the Business

FOCUS

The campaign for the real male

The marketeers have been exploring the female consumer psyche for decades. They created a series of female stereotypes from the image of the home maker to the modern emancipated woman. The male consumer model was fairly neglected. Yet in the car market the male had reigned dominant. It was felt that to drape a few scantily dressed females over a new car would be enough to give it 'man appeal'. Things are changing. Car dealers Cowies did a recent survey of car showrooms which demonstrated the chauvinistic attitude of the predominately male staff and the effect this has had on the female customer. It showed that females had been largely seen as peripheral to the market. With women now forming 40% of the new car market and having a deciding vote in 80% of all car sales, things have had to change.

Ford has launched its own women's 'car marketing panel' to advise on all aspects of car marketing, from design to methods of selling. 'Kiddies' corners' are planned in many showrooms and the staff are being re-trained to be 'female friendly'. As the modern female of advertising campaigns drives into the sunset or to pick up her divorce papers, modern man is left along the wayside. The car has become the symbol of freedom and independence.

As another male bastion topples, what is to be made of the modern male? Extensive research has been done on the female as consumer, but it is a challenge to marketing departments to understand what motivates the modern male, and what are his aspirations, in order to enable their marketing to be targeted at him.

Understanding the modern man involves a complex form of gender analysis. The 'new man' that the brands are seeking has a muddled role in a society which has become far more female dominated. Females are set to form 55% of the workforce by the year 2001. The male has become disenfranchised, losing his role as the provider and unsure about his new function, caught between advertising images of the lager lout and the househusband.

Guinness attempted to solve this problem in an unusual advertising campaign which was aimed at the 'individual male'. They decided that the 1980s male was motivated by the need to be an 'individualist'. The problem was: how do you produce an advertising campaign which targets individualists, as by definition any image created can become a stereotype? They came up with the idea of using the pint of Guinness as the alter-ego of Rutger Hauer, who himself symbolised a pint of Guinness with his black suit and white hair. He fitted into no marketing stereotype and remained his own man. The advertising campaign became so intricate that only an individual or those who felt they were, could understand the symbolism, or at least pretend they did. The esoteric promotion was aimed at not disenfranchising the traditional Guinness drinker whilst encapsulating the aspirations of the modern male. The later 1990s Guinness campaign features a celebratory tribal dance around a pint of Guinness.

A similar 'modern man' campaign was used by John Smith bitter. Beer is still largely a male dominated product so marketing is more clear cut – at least for the moment.

Source: National newspaper reports and author's research.

Preview

In this chapter we shall investigate the following key areas:
- the marketing function
- the 'four Ps'

The concept of marketing

Marketing is the management process responsible for identifying, anticipating and satisfying consumer demand. It involves deciding on the right product, setting the best market price, effectively promoting the goods or service to the consumer and deciding on the correct distribution outlet. It is inextricably linked with production because the two areas rely on each other to justify their existence.

If financial control is the key business objective in a recession, marketing is the high profile function in a boom period. The consumerism of the 1980s was fuelled by easy credit and materialistic aspirations and the marketing executives were only too keen to ensure that it was their brand that led the field. Marketing is not exclusive to the business world. A modern election is likely to cost the political parties in excess of £20 million in focused direct mail marketing and extensive market research. The creative skills of advertising men and professional public relations consultants can be used to trap the affections of the voters who are after all political consumers. It could be argued that marketing pervades everything a business does because its motivating force is consumer satisfaction: the 'total' marketing concept.

The concept of marketing developed historically from the need to direct consumer demand and control supply. In a subsistence economy supply and demand function in a very crude and automatic way. The industrial revolution in the UK, with its increased population, created a need to satisfy an ever-increasing demand with supply. Increased capitalisation, or investment in production, was necessary in order to increase output. In an enterprise culture the free market approach increases the emphasis on competition and accentuates the role of marketing.

The marketing function

The marketing function is the process of linking the flow of goods from the producer to the consumer. It identifies consumer demand, and takes on the role of ensuring customer creation and customer satisfaction.

The objectives of marketing
- Identify needs/wants of consumers
- Provide the best product/service
- Introduce the product/service to consumers

- Persuade consumers to buy
- Determine the best price
- Find the most effective distribution channels.

The process of marketing

Starting from the general aims of the company:

- Formulate marketing objectives
- Set targets to achieve objectives
- Decide strategy.

Typical company marketing aims might be:

- Formulate an advertising campaign?
- Implement a price change?
- Have a distribution rethink?

Planning a marketing strategy

To plan a marketing strategy it is necessary to analyse what is termed the marketing mix. These are the factors which form part of a marketing policy and are otherwise known as the four Ps:

- The product – what good/service should be created?
- The price – at what price should the good/service be put on the market?
- The promotion – how should the product be promoted to the consumer?
- The place – where should the good/service be sold?

Analysing the four Ps

The product

The type of product involved will determine the type of market: industrial or consumer. Industrial goods and consumer goods operate in two separate markets, but some goods will operate in both markets – for example, computers and cars may be supplied for industrial and consumer use. Some companies have a limited production range, others are multi-product firms. Conglomerates produce a diverse range of non-related products.

Product diversification needs to involve a risk analysis. To update or re-package a product is less risky than to manufacture a completely new range and to look for new markets. We have already demonstrated that to merge with a company producing a successfully branded product is a safer bet as consumer loyalty is already established. The reasons a company could want to diversify their products is to spread risks. Monitoring what is called the product life cycle is a vital element in planning the production strategy of a business.

The product life cycle
No product has a definite life.

Changing consumer preferences, economic forces, the structure of the population and social attitudes all have an impact on demand.

The normal life cycle of a product has five stages – a natural life cycle:

- Introduction
- Growth
- Maturity
- Saturation
- Decline.

Box 9.1 demonstrates a product's life cycle.

BOX 9.1	The life cycle of a product

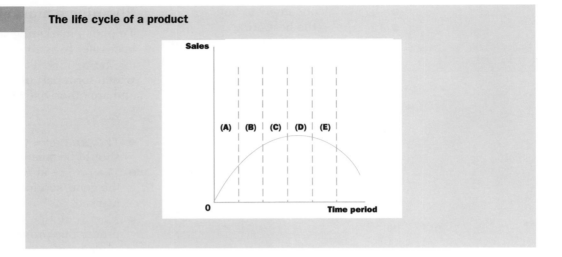

We can now analyse periods (A)–(E) in more detail.

- introduction – this is the most expensive stage, high-cost and high-risk
- growth – a period of expansion with increasing sales
- maturity – as the market is fully exploited, competition increases
- saturation – too many firms are competing in the market
- decline – therefore sales decrease.

The time scale of a product life cycle can vary from a few years to decades, depending on the type of product. The constant factor is the cycle of events. The role of monitoring the product life cycle is vital in planning an effective marketing mix. A business will need to assess the stage at which, for example, life extension policies would be effective. The possibilities could include:

- a drop in price
- a change in the distribution outlet
- launch of a promotion campaign
- termination of the product.

Product portfolio

The product portfolio of a business represents a range of products, each with their own life cycle. The range is monitored to ensure that as one life fades, another comes into force. Look at Box 9.2.

This method is particularly useful in markets which fluctuate, in particular, seasonal ones.

Product utility

Consumers will usually purchase products if the utility (benefit) gained is greater than the price.

When marketing departments assess the price of the products they need to relate this to demand.

Economists assume that consumers will maximise the utility value of the product. The law of diminishing marginal utility states that as consumption of a product increases, each additional unit of that product will be less valuable and therefore give less utility than the previous unit purchased.

The product portfolio

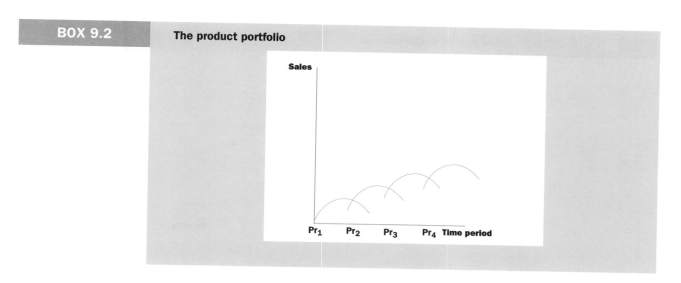

Pricing strategy

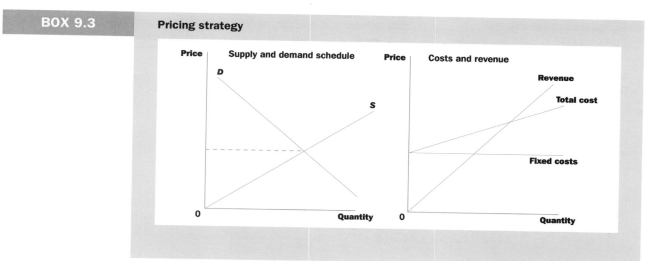

Price

To an economist, in a perfect market, price is decided by the interaction of supply and demand for the product. For the accountant price is dependent on the pattern of costs.

In reality, a pricing strategy is a much more complex procedure. Box 9.3 shows the interaction between supply and demand, and costs and revenue, for a company's product.

As we have already seen, a normal demand curve will illustrate that as a product becomes cheaper, consumption should increase, as Box 9.4 demonstrates.

A shift in the actual demand curve for the product will mean that rather than just a change in demand due to a price change, actual market conditions have changed and the whole curve moves to the right or the left (see Box 9.5).

BOX 9.4   **The normal demand curve**

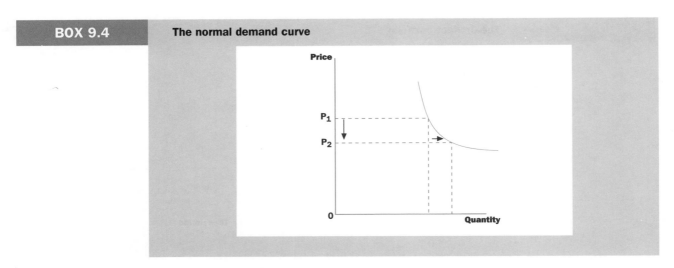

BOX 9.5   **Change in market conditions**

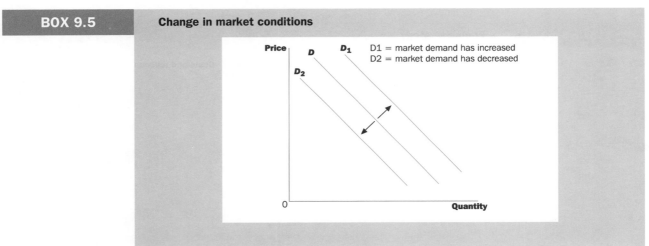

Changes in the conditions of demand will depend on:

- the level of disposable income held by consumers (income available for spending after direct deductions like income tax)
- climatic conditions in certain types of markets
- changes in taste or fashion
- effective advertising/promotion.

Elasticity of demand

As previously explained, the price sensitivity of a product is measured by elasticity of demand. The products which are highly sensitive to price changes are elastic. Those that are not are inelastic.

The elasticity may be based on competition in the market or purely on the type of good in question. If a good is classed as a necessity, then by definition the price may be a secondary factor, whereas luxury goods, or non-necessity items are ones that can be done without and left on the shelf if a price rise occurs. Other factors affecting elasticity may be whether the good is habit-forming or the availability of substitutes in the market. The proportion of disposable income spent on the good also has a role to play. If an item only takes up a small proportion of total disposable income, then this will have less impact on the total consumer spending.

Price elasticity of demand is measured by:

$$\frac{\% \text{ change in quantity demanded}}{\% \text{ change in price}}$$

In reality, businesses do not know exactly what these percentage changes would be, but through market research and data collection they can gain an idea of likely demand fluctuations.

The level of elasticity or inelasticity can be demonstrated through the gradient of the demand slope. A flatter slope shows greater elasticity whilst a more vertical one means an inelastic demand. Look at Box 9.6.

Consumer perception of price

A consumer's perception of price may vary according to their own social status, an awareness of the product, or its relative utility value.

A high price strategy could win over consumers in the interests of quality, whilst a lower price may prove less attractive for the status of certain types of goods. If a good is marketed as being environmentally friendly, it may be that price is a secondary factor to social concern. The perceived utility, or benefit, gained by the consumer will also be a deciding factor.

Effectiveness of price competition

Price competition depends very much on the availability of substitute products and other available brands.

A product in a highly competitive market with direct competition will find it difficult to raise its price without losing market share. In 1994 a price war evolved between the major national newspapers which resulted in large price cuts as each newspaper fought to increase its circulation. The readers have benefited from the large price cuts, but in the process, some of the papers have become financially vulnerable. In

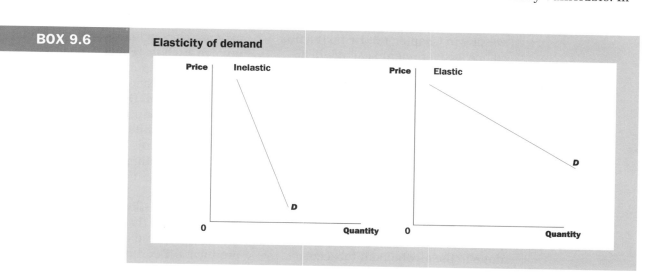

BOX 9.6

Elasticity of demand

the longer term, if the price cuts result in the elimination of some of the suppliers, consumer choice will be limited. Price rises may also return once the competition is rationalised. In this type of price war there may be no 'real winners', only some losers.

Firms in direct competition can also offer other non-price incentives to gain sales over a competitor. They may invest in a promotional campaign to develop brand differentiation. This type of competition is in direct contrast to the price fixing of cartels and the market control of monopolies (see Chapter 1.5). The level of competition in the market will often dictate the degree to which a company can control price.

Government policies and price

Governments intervene in business markets either directly or indirectly. They may have a policy which is designed to create a direct impact on businesses, or the business sector may suffer indirectly from a government policy which has an impact on their market.

Merit and demerit goods

A government may define some goods or services as merit or demerit goods, as we saw in Chapter 1.5. By taking this stance a government is acting in a paternalistic role deciding which goods the consumer should be encouraged to buy or be discouraged from buying. To carry out this policy the government may intervene in the private sector markets, or provide the good or service through the public sector.

Demerit goods   Demerit goods may have a tax levied on them which will make them more expensive and potentially less attractive. This has been done to the alcohol and tobacco

industries by successive governments. More recently, leaded petrol has been targeted for a higher tax levy than unleaded petrol. However, the net effect on consumption will depend on the elasticity of demand and supply (see Box 9.7). In 1988 the government raised the tax on leaded petrol by 10p, leaving the tax on unleaded unaltered. After one year sales of leaded petrol had fallen by nearly 25%. Unleaded petrol has become an effective substitute for leaded petrol as more cars are being converted and manufactured to use unleaded.

The government may wish to be seen discouraging the consumption of tobacco and alcohol but if demand is inelastic consumption may not be affected, though tax revenue will certainly rise. The revenue lost by not increasing the tax on unleaded petrol may be an opportunity cost the government is willing to bear for the environmental impact and the popularity of the voters.

Those opposed to government intervention in the market would argue that this direct interference can distort the market. Some would also argue that the real value of unleaded petrol is a complex environmental issue which may not be conclusive and which may involve a whole range of other issues. Questions have now arisen over the carcinogenic (cancer-causing) content of unleaded petrol. Diesel may appear to be more environmentally friendly because more miles can be achieved per gallon, but its role in the increased incidence of asthma is another debate. The research continues.

The British whisky industry has argued for many years that it has been unfairly treated compared to European wine producers. Tax duty on a measure of

BOX 9.7

The effects of an indirect tax on demand

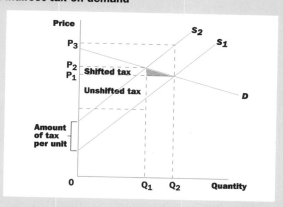

A supplier's ability to raise the price and shift the incidence of an expenditure tax such as VAT depends on **the price elasticity of demand**. When demand is relatively elastic only a small proportion of the tax levy can be shifted onto the consumer. The imposition of a tax raises a supplier's costs so that at each price they are prepared to supply less. If the tax is changed at a set rate, irrespective of price, the supply curve should shift upwards from S_1 to S_2. In order to shift the tax onto the consumer, demand will need to be completely inelastic and in this situation the price would rise to P_3.

If demand is not completely inelastic some consumers will reduce their demand as the price rises so the price will go from P_1 to P_2. The shaded area represents the 'lost' consumer surplus.

whisky in the UK is 23p, whilst wine with the same alcoholic content has a tax of only 14p. The European Commission ordered an investigation into the anomalies of alcohol taxation. The study looked at the impact of taxation on competition in the market, in particular, whether wine and whisky were competing in the same market. The study supported the case of the UK whisky producers, which is good news for one of the UK's major exporters.

Merit goods   Merit goods will either be encouraged by the government through the private sector, in the way unleaded petrol was, or provided through the public sector. The public sector provides education for all and a National Health Service. When these services were established, governments felt that the education and health of the population were vital to economic success. This is still true but more emphasis is being placed now on private sector provision. In the future government provision of other welfare services, in particular old age pensions, could be handed over to the private sector who would provide this service through private pension schemes, and other personal insurance plans.

Pricing policy

Another factor which will affect the price of a good is the policy of the business in relation to each item produced.

- Market skimming

    When a new product is developed there may be an initial period before competition develops, in which a company can capitalise on a monopolistic market (skimming the cream off the market!).

- Market penetration

    The objective is to penetrate a section of the market in a short space of time. This may result initially in lower or no profit, but once market share is established the producer can secure greater control of the market. 'Loss leaders' can be offered to attract an initial interest, in order to form a basis for promoting other products in the range or market. Retailers may advertise bargain items in order to attract consumers into their market place, believing that they will be tempted to buy many other items. Cross-subsidy can also occur, where a more successful product can cross-fund an initially less successful item until the market is established. Promotional pricing is also an effective way of gaining market access. Once brand loyalty has been established consumers are less likely to switch to other products.

Competitive tendering and price

As already stated, a growing trend in the business world is that of increasing indirect labour through competitive tendering. Increasingly companies are sub-contracting much of their work out into the tendering market (see Box 9.8). Large contracts are being put out by the

---

BOX 9.8

The process of tendering

The process of tendering starts with the company specifying the work it wants to be completed. It will then invite **tenders** or **quotes** for the work. The tendering company will have to calculate a **set price** for the work, justifying their costing figures. They will need to state a **completion date** if relevant, and a **quality** specification.

There have been problems with this system. The promise of quality can be difficult to judge, unless the contractor has a sound reputation. Quality can also be compromised in the interests of the cheapest price for the job. In order to win bids firms may put in unrealistic figures, and then find they cannot fulfil their obligations. There are usually **penalty clauses** for work unfinished by the agreed time, but many smaller firms have been unable to survive in this very competitive market.

The question of quality control has led to the development of systems of 'quality standards'; the quality management system called BS5750 (now replaced by an international standard IS9000) is being widely used.

This system is a measure which sets quality standards by laying down procedures and processes which are to be used in a production context. In order to achieve this British Standard, the company needs to establish its quality systems process and be assessed by an external body. This validating body then makes regular checks to ensure the systems are operating. Setting up and administering these systems can be costly and involve so much paperwork that smaller companies often do not have the resources. These standards have also been much criticised by the business world as each business sets its own standard, which may not be as high as some would wish. However, for all their faults, carrying the 'quality standard' mark may be the ticket to winning a contract.

privatised utilities who have made vast cuts in their own labour force. Competitive tendering is all around us – on a local basis, in our schools (cleaning, dinner service), hospitals (cleaning, canteen facilities) and local councils (refuse collection). Security contracts for defence establishments have also been put out to tender. The army catering corps is to be replaced with private contract catering companies.

Types of pricing

Cost plus pricing This is also called full cost or absorption pricing. Businesses will work out the price to charge based on their costing assessment. The total costs are merged and a margin of profit is added to set a price level. A firm's pricing decision will be established by dividing total costs by units of output and adding a margin:

$$\text{Price} = \frac{\text{Total costs}}{\text{Output}} + \text{Profit margin}$$

$$\frac{£500\,000}{2000} = £250 \text{ plus a profit margin}$$

A firm may decide what price they think the market will bear of the desired profit, and then decide if the good can be produced for the price.

Contribution pricing This method is used to establish an individual price for each product in a company's portfolio. Each item would be assessed for the share they would be expected to contribute to the indirect costs of the business. This amount would be their 'contribution':

- Indirect costs – the costs which are not directly related to each unit of output (fixed costs)

- Direct costs – the costs which are directly related to each additional unit of output (variable costs)

Revenue from product *x* *Less* direct costs of *x* = Contribution of *x* to indirect costs.

The total indirect costs are then taken from the total contribution to see what profit level is left.

Promotion

Promotion is a collective term for a series of activities designed to draw the consumer's attention to a product. Advertising describes only one aspect of promotional activity. Other types of promotion include sponsorship and creating a positive public relations profile for the company. Anita Roddick of The Body Shop has proved that products can be effectively promoted without advertising. The Body Shop's need to create consumer interest, and indeed loyalty, to its brands have been helped by its environmental campaigns. The campaigns have proved to be a way of enhancing the company's image as a caring concern, tapping into the motivations of the modern consumer.

Not all promotion is aimed at consumers. In-store displays and demonstrations provide an effective support system from the supplier to the retailer. Merchandising has become an important part of the manufacturer's service to the retailer. It involves elaborate display techniques provided by the supplier including selling and stock control specialists. Promotion in industrial markets, for example the selling of machinery to a producer, would need to include a detailed analysis of the product and its specifications, with demonstrations and after-sales support systems.

Quality assurance kite marks are now being used by companies as an effective form of self-promotion. To obtain a 'quality' kite mark is to gain accreditation for having achieved a specified standard of operation: a very useful marketing tool.

The promotion strategy

In order to achieve a successful promotion, a structured approach needs to be taken:

● Is the product aimed at a national or local market?
● Who are the target audience?
● What is the right promotional vehicle?
● What resources are available?
● What resources are needed?
● How can the results be effectively measured?

Advertising terminology

● Classified – small advertisements set out under different headings.
● Corporate – the promotion of a product by a group of companies in the same industry. Two examples of this in the early 1990s were: the campaign by the sugar industry, and the campaign by the butter producers.

The markets for both these products were threatened by public concern over health and fitness so they collaborated to develop a campaign which promoted the product, not the brands.

● Generic – advertising aimed at building up the reputation of the company, not the individual products it manufactures. An example of this is an advertisement that was designed to promote the achievements of ICI.
● Point of sale – advertising by displays at the point of sale terminals (check outs).

Other types of promotion

Product placement is a practice which is used in the USA but outlawed on British TV and films. Products are placed within films and television programmes to gain valuable advertising space.

Film	Product
ET	Reese's pieces (American sweets) – 300% jump in sales
Wall Street	Nino Cerruti suits
Baby Boom	Huggies nappies
Back to the Future, Part 2	Toyota, Texaco, Millers beer, Nike trainers
Top Gun	Ray Ban aviator shades – 40% boost in sales

This can be a highly effective form of promotion, particularly if the film turns out to be a box-office success.

Whilst this form of promotion is banned in the UK, with budgets becoming tighter, regulations may well be loosened and it could prove to be a strategy for the future.

Direct marketing Direct marketing, sometimes branded as junk mail, is a growing industry. In the USA the volume of direct mail entering people's letter boxes has been detrimental to its image, since it can be viewed as highly intrusive and a waste of natural resources. It is important for companies to reach those individuals it has attempted to target directly. Therefore marketing departments are constantly seeking to find new ways of stopping their marketing material being put straight into the bin. Personalised material, including the individual's name, competitions and prizes are all ways of making the householder think twice before destroying the information. Other methods – for example, attaching coins or samples – are also used.

Sponsorship Sponsorship is the support of a group or event in order to promote the sponsor's name or image in the market place. It is used widely in sport and is increasingly being used in commercial television. By giving its name to a football league or cricket championship, a company can gain valuable advertising space whilst the sport benefits from the additional resources. It could be said that snooker was transformed from a back-room bar game into a nationally covered event through its sponsorship publicity. Many of the tobacco companies use this type of sponsorship to get around laws which regulate their advertising activity.

Company	Sport
Benson and Hedges	Cricket
Rothmans	Cricket
Embassy	Snooker world championships
Benson and Hedges	Snooker Classic
Mirror Group	Boxing

Yet sponsors can suffer if the sport has bad publicity. The tragic incidents that have occurred in the boxing ring or hooligans at football matches could have a negative effect on the sponsors.

Increasingly sponsorship is being used to subsidise TV productions.

Programme	Company
Weather Forecast	Powergen
This is Your Life	Konica
Darling Buds of May	Tetley tea
Inspector Morse	Beamish Stout
Film Première	Coca Cola
Peak Practice	PPP

Box 9.9 examines one of the issues raised.

BOX 9.9

Sponsorship on the box
This television subsidy is an expanding aspect of sponsorship. Beamish Stout boosted their sales by 150% as a result of their successful linking with *Inspector Morse*. However, there has been controversy. When *Peak Practice* (a programme about the National Health Service) was sponsored by PPP (a private medical company), it was seen as ironic, and an ITC investigation was held.

Direct response advertising A growing and effective development has been that of direct response advertising. Increasingly you will notice that phone numbers are being placed in advertisements, requesting those interested to call the number. This is an effective way of monitoring the response.

Promotion and image There are many other ways in which companies promote their goods. When you carry your goods home from the shop in a plastic carrier bag bearing the name of the company you are presenting them with a free advertising opportunity; you may even have to pay for the privilege. When a company wraps its goods much care is taken to ensure that a promotional opportunity is not missed. Portraying the correct image in terms of the wrapping paper, colour and name are important.

It may seem ironical but some manufacturers compete against themselves for market share. The reason for this is that they are aiming to create a unique selling proposition (USP) and may aim several brands at different market segments. Van den Berghs margarine producers promote their own brands of Stork, Blue Band, Echo and Flora, but each has a USP.

Exhibitions and events are also effective in promoting not only the product but its image. National events like 'ice cream week' raise the profile of the product and create consumer interest.

Targeting promotion   The type of promotion will depend on the target audience and what appeals to them. Classifying the market into consumer segments allows marketing to be targeted at a specific area of the population. This is a much more cost-effective approach. It is sometimes called the 'rifle or shot gun' approach, as opposed to the scatter-gun effect. The problem is: how can consumers be separated into specific market segments? Market researchers gather information which allows consumers to be put into certain socio-economic groupings which relate to incomes, profession, age and other personal and social factors. Companies can then target different sectors of the population designing their promotional material to

appeal to the relevant group. However, this whole area is becoming more complex. Psychologists are being used in marketing to try and enter the minds of the consumer to assess their motivations and their aspirations. It could be argued that it is consumers' aspirations which motivate them and shape the way they perceive a product.

If a consumer group can be targeted, the product and the way it is promoted will need to inspire the consumer, making them identify with the product (see Box 9.10). Market research may allow consumers to be categorised into distinct groupings but what producers really need to know is what individuals actually buy. With the use of a computer database this ideal is not so futuristic as one might think.

US stores have developed a system whereby any shopper can join the retailers 'club'. Each member gets a store card which allows discount on purchases. As goods are passed through itemised checkout systems, a name is put to the purchases and consumers can be targeted for any promotional campaigns. The main problem with this system is the vast amount of information which needs to be held on computer.

These loyalty card systems are now being used in the UK. Data information companies can be used to hold the large quantities of information on purchases but questions are being asked about the potential exploitation of this information. The market in information is an expanding one and the protection for the consumer, in the form of the Data Protection Act, may be ineffective.

The strapline is a term used to describe a short saying that identifies a product

Promotional soaps and sex

The Gold Blend advertisement has used drama to catch the imagination of consumers. Its episodic approach creates a drama around the product. With the popularity of soap operas, it is understandable that people watch with interest.

Sex is another big seller. Hägen Das has used sex in its advertising to secure an upmarket niche in Britain's £400 million ice cream market. An American company using a Danish name, it has pioneered luxury ice cream catering for a new market – adults.

Source: National newspaper reports and author's research.

without mentioning its name, for example, 'Vorsprung dürch technik' (Audi cars). Other popular straplines of the past include 'Gotta lotta bottle' (milk), and 'Schh you know who' (Schweppes drinks).

Place

Businesses need to decide upon the most effective way to present the product to the consumer. The traditional channel of distribution was usually:

THE MANUFACTURER

(the producer)

↓

THE WHOLESALER

(buys goods from the producer and breaks them down into sellable units)

↓

THE RETAILER

(sells directly to the consumer)

↓

THE CONSUMER

(the purchaser of the product)

The increase in the scale of firms has led to the breakdown of the traditional distribution structure. Increasingly, the 'middlemen', often the wholesalers, are being eliminated. The emergence of large retail outlets has resulted in a simplified chain. The large retailers may produce their own goods, hold their own stock, and then supply them through their distribution outlets to the consumer. Direct selling is also increasing, with producers selling their goods directly to the public. Direct order catalogues enable the consumer to buy direct from the producer, eliminating the role of the wholesaler and retailer.

Franchising is another method of distribution because it devolves the responsibility of selling the goods away from the manufacturer.

The appropriate distribution outlet for the product will need to match its image. Some items may have 'exclusivity' value, so they would need to have an 'upmarket' outlet. Lower-priced goods would have a very different distribution network. Some goods are 'specialist' products which are only relevant to specific individualistic markets.

The most appropriate method for the transportation of the goods to the consumer outlet will depend on the type of goods – their bulk, perishability and value.

Controls over marketing

The British Code of Advertising Practice

A voluntary Code of Practice has been established by firms operating in the market. The industry attempts to ensure that advertisers fulfil a certain standard of practice. It requires advertising to be:

- legal
- decent
- honest
- truthful

1. There are detailed rules in the Code of Practice concerning the promotion of some products. These products include health and medical care, slimming, alcohol and tobacco. There are also regulations concerning advertisements aimed at children.

2. There are other laws which affect the control of advertising. For example the Trade Descriptions Act 1968 makes it a criminal offence for a trader to falsely describe the goods for sale.

3. Other bodies like the SIB (Securities and Investment Board) control the advertising of financial services and pension plans. Consumer dissatisfaction with the level of protection they have been receiving from SIB has led to pressure to tighten up the financial services regulations. However, with competition increasing in the market of financial services and communication technology becoming more sophisticated, controls are becoming harder to implement.

The ITC (Independent TV Commission)

Television sponsors can only use the name and logo of the product; they cannot make statements about the qualities of the product, and are unable to influence the content or scheduling of the programme. However, there is no doubt that programme sponsorship is a growing area of marketing for the large companies. The Beamish Stout sponsorship of *Inspector Morse* resulted in a 150% increase in sales, as we have seen. However, there are dangers in this type of marketing. A newspaper carried out research about the way consumers felt about the PPP sponsorship of *Peak Practice*. The outcome of this was an ITC investigation.

Market research

The objective of market research is to gather the necessary information to allow the development of a company's marketing strategy. In order for a business to target its promotion at the right audience, assess demand, set a price at which it will sell and choose the most effective distribution outlet, it needs to assess consumer needs and wants. Accurate research information involves collecting, recording and processing information on the potential market.

Types of market research

Field research

Field research is the gathering of information from market sampling:

Questionnaires
- postal
- in person
- telephone

Interviews
- postal
- in person
- telephone

Panels
- assessing the response of a target group, e.g. female drivers in the Ford panel

Desk research

Desk research involves the collection, analysis and evaluation of data from journals, Government statistics and other business information.

Desk research is usually a development from field research. Field research is carried out and then logged for future use as desk research.

Purpose of market research

There is a thriving business in the processing of market information, as already illustrated. Knowledge about the potential market allows targeting

and therefore a more effective use of resources

The information contained in (for example) the Government Census of the UK population, gives sex distribution, occupations, housing, vehicular use and much more. This data can give businesses an idea of the total UK market in relation to the types of products that may be demanded, either nationally or locally. The 1991 results are being extensively used by market analysis firms.

Geodemographics is the process of matching an address to the lifestyle of the residents. By looking at a specific postal area the marketing men can assess the type of individuals who are likely to live there, their status and hence ambitions and aspirations. Assessing the likely lifestyle of the residents of a certain area can allow the marketing specialists to predict their spending patterns.

REVIEW

After reading this section you should understand the role of marketing in deciding on the right product, the right distribution, setting the most competitive price and effectively promoting the goods or service.

TASK 9.1

PRACTICAL APPLICATION

Draw a pie chart to represent the average weekly spending of a family in a week, given the following data.

	£
Housing	100
Fuel, light and power	30
Food	80
Drink and tobacco	20
Clothing, footwear and personal services	20
Motoring and fares	30
Leisure and services	30
TOTAL	310

REVIEW TASK

CRITICAL ANALYSIS

'Junk mail' arouses hostility because it is personally intrusive. On entering our letter boxes it demonstrates not only that we have been market 'targeted' but it represents a vast waste of natural resources. The bad news is that the amount of junk mail delivered is actually worse in most parts of the EU. The danger is that once pan-European barriers are fully dismantled the UK could also be receiving 'Euro junk mail'.

The larger UK direct marketing groups are seizing the opportunity to move in on this trade rather than be flooded with a host of foreign competitors. It would certainly be more convenient for European companies to use British direct marketing sources with their access to extensive UK database lists.

Yet given the consumer response to junk mail one could ask: Why do companies bother? The problem seems to be that this form of direct marketing is not quite as direct as it should be. If the targeting was more accurate they would not be seen by consumers as so intrusive.

So how did they get your name?

There are list brokers who collect names and information on consumers to define social groups and hence spending patterns. Companies can use these lists to promote their products. For example, a list would be available to enable companies to target the subscribers to a certain magazine. It is a straightforward process to construct a 'consumer profile' of the type of people who read certain magazines.

The industry has certainly been given a bad name by some dubious operators. For example, some time-share companies have received a particularly bad press. The 'green' issue is also a factor, as much of the direct mail ends up in rubbish bins. Many companies have tried to improve their image by using recycled paper.

The market in the UK is estimated to be worth approximately £758 million. With that sort of market share at stake the direct marketers will be doing all they can to get it right.

Source: National newspaper reports and author's research.

1. How can direct marketing be made effective?
2. What are the implications for personal privacy, particularly with the increased use of information technology?
3. Describe the role of list brokers.
4. Why is this type of market research valuable?
5. Explain the different types of market research used by businesses.

Exam questions

Read the attached extract on marketing of the Cadbury Wispa and answer the questions that follow.

MARKETING THE CADBURY WISPA

The gigantic brands in the 'pure' chocolate market had, without exception, origins dating back to before the Second World War. Cadbury's Dairy Milk was launched in 1905 and has sold prodigiously ever since. Some 20 years later Cadbury launched Flake, which was discovered as a by-product of manufacturing milk chocolate.
These two products set the pace in the market for 80 years. There have been many attempts to launch a product to stand alongside CDM and Flake. None succeeded until the late 1970s when Cadbury started a secret R&D project.

It was found that the latest technology applied to chocolate manufacturing could confer a different texture and new eating characteristics on the classic milk chocolate product.

All the pre-launch research suggested that the product was a winner. However, as years of bitter experience have taught many manufacturers in this market, having a product the public likes its not always enough. The complete marketing package is just as critical.

Nothing new under the sun

This was the attitude of most consumers to chocolate products. They simply didn't believe you could produce anything new. Reversing this belief was the problem facing the Young and Rubicam advertising agency when Cadbury brought them the product, now named 'Wispa', in 1980.

(AEB, November 1987)

Source: Adapted from a Cadbury advertisement, The Economist (March 1986).

A Give 3 examples of what would be included in 'the complete marketing package' (referred to in the extract).

B The initial launch may well have been accompanied by special pricing deals. What factors might the company have taken into consideration when setting the long-term price?

C Cadbury now have 3 major confectionery products instead of 2. What advantages does this give the company?

D Outline the factors that the company might take into consideration, before embarking upon a European launch of the product?

(AEB, November 1989)

CASE STUDY

The Body Stop

Scenario

Alan Jones is an army physical training instructor who has served his time and is leaving the army with a lump sum of £48 000. He wants to use the money to set up in business and feels that the fitness industry is an expanding field and one in which he is suitably qualified and experienced. He has decided to explore the possibility of setting up a gym calling it 'The Body Stop'.

He would like you to analyse the figures he has estimated and do some market research and analysis for him in order to establish whether he is making the right decision.

He provides you with the following information:
- I am thinking of investing the lump sum in obtaining premises on the edge of town which I feel are ideal for my use. This would leave me with a mortgage on the business of about £500 per month.
- To lease the equipment I will need about £6000 per annum.
- The estimated cost of heating and lighting is £2000 per quarter.
- For staff, I will need a receptionist and a full-time female instructor. I estimate the receptionist will cost approximately £6000 per annum whilst the instructor will cost £12 000 per annum. I would pay myself £16 000.

I would initially like to start by offering facilities and classes in:

- Weight training
- Circuit training
- Aerobics
- Reebok step
- Karate
- Tumble tots

My programme would be as follows:

Mornings	Afternoons	Evenings
3 hours	3 hours	3 hours
(1 hr) Reebok Step	(1 hr) Circuits	(1 hr) Aerobics
(1 hr) Weights	(1 hr) Weights	(1 hr) Aerobics
(1 hr) Tumble Tots	(1 hr) Karate	(1 hr) Weights

CASE STUDY TASKS

You would need to undertake the following tasks:

1 Design a **questionnaire** extracting the following information from potential consumers:
   A. Sex and age group.
   B. Would they be interested in the facilities offered?
   C. If so, which specific area would they be interested in and what price would they be willing to pay for each?

Here is a sample of a layout you could adopt:

Would you be interested in: *Yes   No*   *Price per hour*
                                      (You need to insert a
                                      range of prices)

■ Weight training

■ Circuit training
Other facilities, i.e. sauna
                    refreshments

1 Would they be interested in annual membership?
   ● Would they be interested in other possible ways of paying (e.g. season ticket)?
2 **Test this questionnaire** on people you know, selecting a cross-sample of the population by sex and age group. You will need to choose a minimum of 20 individuals.
3 Present a **report** summarising your findings.
4 For each leisure area, fill in a **consumer profile** (example attached) from the information obtained and include with this report.
5 Decide on a **promotion campaign**.
6 Decide on **advertising** – how, where?
7 Decide on other **promotional initiatives** and activities – leaflets, tee shirts, competition, free sessions, etc.
8 Decide on your marketing strategy for this campaign, i.e. design your advertising, decide on the appropriate media. If you go in for leaflet distribution, design the leaflet and indicate where you would circulate the information – using the techniques of 'geodemographics' in your local area.

There are many factors to consider. When you have finished your research you should send to Mr Jones:

1 The questionnaire (preferably in the form of a computer print-out).
2 A report on your findings from your own market research cross-sampling.
3 A consumer profile for each fitness area.
4 A report on your promotion strategy – the chosen methods and the target audience, and enclose some sample promotional material you have designed.
5 Given the cost figure Mr Jones has already worked out, decide on how much he would need to charge on average per hour in order just to break even if he were to be open 9 hours a day, 7 days a week and how many customers he would need. Calculate these figures and do a break-even analysis.
6 Decide on a price for each facility based on your market research, and justify your pricing levels in a wider context.
7 If Mr Jones were to achieve an average of 12 customers per hour at the **average** price (over all other facilities) for the first month, increasing by an additional 5% demand in each subsequent month at the same price, do a cash flow analysis for the first year on a spreadsheet.

CASE STUDY QUESTIONS

1 If a product is good enough, it shouldn't need marketing. All marketing does is to mask poor quality products. Assess the arguments for and against these statements, and say why you agree or disagree. (AEB)
2 Discuss the impact of the findings of market research on the marketing and production strategies of a business (AEB).
3 An enterprise invests a large sum of money in promoting its corporate image, with particular emphasis on the contribution it makes to the community. Comment on the reasons for such an expenditure.

Statistical Analysis for Business

'Lies, damn lies and statistics' (Disraeli)

The paradox of the written word is that we are often able to read between the lines: 'the said and the unsaid'. Figures have their own mystique. They are actuals, solid reality that we do not question, only digest. It is therefore predictable that statistics are often read as fact. But when reading statistics, apart from allowing for any irregularities in data collection, we need to question not so much the figures or facts that are shown but those which are left out – the empty spaces.

Politicians use statistics to prove whatever they want to prove by choosing the figures that represent their own view of reality. By pronouncing figures they can support their argument until another bunch of figures are thrown back at them. With the 'marketisation' of the public sector and the absence of a clear profit indicator the government has been struggling to find some form of measurable output by which to assess performance and achievement. One outcome has been the use of statistics to form league tables of performance for schools and hospitals.

The question must arise: what is being measured? In a non-profit-making non-competitive organisation how do you illustrate performance and measure success, and can this be done numerically? In response to the league tables of hospitals, the British Medical Association has accused the Government of failing to reflect the quality of care through the use of statistics. Quantitative techniques may be able to log the time it takes in a waiting room but not the quality of care received. The danger in any system like this is that it is the easily measurable facets which take the highest profile. This type of measuring could lead to the 'ghettoisation' of many inner city schools and hospitals who operate with limited funds in difficult circumstances with high priority demands.

Schools and hospitals should be accountable for their performance, but it must always be realised that users of hospitals and schools are not customers – they are patients and students, their needs are wider and often immeasurable.

The service they receive reflects social need not consumer demand and to measure performance is a much more complex process which the simple use of statistics is unable to encompass.

Source: National newspaper reports and author's research.

Preview

In this chapter we shall investigate the following key areas:
- the role of statistics
- statistical representation

Statistical analysis: an introduction

Statistics are a form of communication by numbers. They are representations, of a numerically quantifiable picture. From the Domesday book and before statistics have been gathered to help planning in all aspects of life. In many situations we refer to statistics to increase our ability to look into the future. Statistics are important to a business because the data they represent enable a situation to be analysed and evaluated and form a base for decision-making. They are also used to present and analyse an organisation's own performance. The process of statistical analysis involves **three** key functions – the collection, analysis and presentation of data.

A business will use its own primary data, which it may collect to demonstrate a particular situation, but it will also use the data gathered by the government and other bodies including other businesses. These figures prove an important reference base. Many statistics gathered by the government are reflections of the structure of the populace or the economic climate. The population represent potential market whilst the economic indicators are a good gauge to the external factors which may affect the business operation.

The problems with statistics is that they are really quantitative measures which give a snapshot of a situation at a particular point in time. They often need to be viewed alongside other qualitative factors which are not so easy to judge numerically. Nevertheless, for the purposes of businesses they are a vital indicator of performance and provider of information.

Statistical analysis in marketing

Gathering data
Figures are gathered by governments on all types of data. The UK Government collects information on the population via the Census so it can plan its needs and resources. It also collects a range of various other data topics as diverse as economic performance indicators and accident rates. Businesses collect data to aid their own decision-making. They also use data collected by other organisations. Government statistics are

an important aid to businesses because the 'statistical snapshot' the data portrays can reflect the business market and prove to be an important point of reference for business analysis. Figures are also collected by independent market research agencies.

Types of data

Primary and secondary data
Box 10.1 shows how marketing data is categorised.

Types of secondary data
Data information and statistical analysis can be gathered through many sources

from newspapers and journals to the UK Census. Newspapers, magazines and trade journals produce information over a wide range of topics which can influence a business's views on its market. Firms can also gain information from other firms who have produced their own primary data.

Some data is published and needs to be purchased, whilst other data may be obtainable at no cost. Data from other companies may be particularly useful if they are operating in the same market area, using the same type of equipment or labour supply.

BOX 10.1

Marketing data

PRIMARY DATA
Information collected by the firm for its own use.
This is collected for a specific purpose and use, so it is part of marketing's own decision-making and planning process.

SECONDARY DATA
Secondary data is that which is collected for a purpose other than that for which it is being used.
It may not always be totally appropriate to the business needs, but it is an economic way of gaining information.

Government data

The Government produces many forms of statistics which are useful for business analysis. Look at Box 10.2.

Business use of secondary data
Businesses operate in the market. The types of information a government seeks are just as relevant to business. The Government needs to know the make-up of the population to project and forecast its needs in relation to the social context. A business needs to

know for its own decision-making and market planning.

● Because the economy and its forces are possibly the most significant external factor on a business, economic indicators allow the business to view the climate in which it is operating. It needs to be able to judge the implications of an interest rate rise, an increase in the rate of inflation and general economic

BOX 10.2

Government statistical sources

Bank of England
The *Bank of England Quarterly Review* presents figures on the economy known as 'Economic Indicators'. It also gives figures on the money supply and interest rates which are an important indicator for a business on the potential market, and the cost of investment. It also gives a firm a good idea about the way the economy is performing and the confidence in the market. Data also illustrate trends in terms of the population, the market and the business environment.

Census office
A census is produced every 10 years and has been since 1801. The last census was in 1991. The Government requires by law that each household must complete the census form. On the form there are 5 questions about housing and 19 about people. It is used to provide a 'statistical snapshot' of each region of the nation so that regional comparisons can be made on aspects like population, housing and employment. This enables the Government to plan for land use, employment creation and social development.

Central Statistical Office
This is the Government office for producing statistical information on the UK. The type of information collected is on law and order, population, social services, agriculture, industry and the weather. Certain financial and economic data are also collected and presented.

Local reference libraries
Much of the information collected by Government statistical services is held in local reference libraries. Details of the Census are available plus other data on 'Social' and 'Regional' trends for individual areas. There are also copies of *Britain – An Official Handbook*, which creates a profile of the UK economy and social trends, and other similar information on the EU.

Department of Trade and Industry
This department produces an industrial magazine in which it publishes information on types of producers and volume of output. It also gives information on imports and export which are ultimately presented in the balance of trade and balance of payments figures which we will look at in 'The World Stage'.

Department of Education and Employment
The Education and Employment Department produces and publishes figures on the levels of employment and unemployment, wage rates, levels of deductions and overtime. These figures can be used to compare wage rates with the Retail Price Index (RPI) which looks at how prices are rising.

Much of the information produced by the Government can be obtained direct from their own publishing department, but many of the statistics can also be obtained from public reference libraries. Figures produced by companies are sometimes published for sale, or they may be produced for their own publicity and be presented in trade magazines. There are also international and European data sources. Organisations like the OECD (The Organisation for Economic Cooperation and Development) produce special project studies on particular economic areas which can be used as a guide to economic performance internationally.

Some statistics and information produced are purely self-publicising. Many Eastern bloc states and newly industrialised countries (NICs) produce information about themselves in the hope of receiving investment funds and luring multi-national corporations to their sites.

trends. It also needs to be aware of the European dimension.

- The cost of living index is also an important indicator in wage negotiations and pricing, as it reflects the general trend in prices which is often used as a bargaining point in pay settlements.
- The population represents the demand the business needs. The structure of the population and current trends allow a business to plan its marketing strategy. It is important to know not just what the population is, but who they are – what the age structure is, and the regional spread. These do not just answer demand questions but also location ones.

- The Census is estimated to cost the government approximately £135 million over the 10 year period. The individual forms collected are confidential for 100 years but the actual figures are published and the information can prove invaluable to a business. This information is particularly useful to the Marketing and Production departments and their inter-related functions.

Business use of primary data

Each department of a firm will produce statistical performance figures for its own functional area. Departments will also seek statistical information which will enhance its own decision-making. Look at Box 10.3.

BOX 10.3

The information-gathering process in business

- **WHAT** DO YOU WANT TO KNOW? ⟶ OBJECTIVES
- **WHO** IS IT BEST TO ASK? ⟶ TARGET GROUP
- **HOW** CAN THIS BE DONE MOST EFFECTIVELY? ⟶ IN-HOUSE/AGENCY
- **WHAT** STRUCTURE SHOULD BE USED? ⟶ FORMAT

Objectives of business information-gathering

To enable data to be gathered effectively it needs to be decided exactly what information is sought and from whom. Look at Box 10.4.

In-house vs agencies for data-gathering

The tendency to sub-contract out certain 'stand alone' projects is as prevalent in statistical collection and analysis as it is elsewhere in business. Statistical collection is a specialist area from which certain economies of scale can be achieved by private agencies. It can also be very time-consuming and expensive for firms to do themselves, and is therefore suitable for contracting out. As in all of these types of decisions, the opportunity cost needs to be assessed.

Structure and the format of data-gathering

Questionnaires

Research-based methods of gathering information are usually in the form of questions. The questionnaire is a common form of response-driven research:

- The input, or format of the questions will largely dictate the effectiveness of the responses
- The way the questions are phrased should be clear for all to understand: ambiguous questions will lead to ambiguous answers
- Questionnaires should also not be too onerous for the respondent or they will not be completed
- Questionnaires can be either postal or

BOX 10.4 **Getting the data**

- **The customer**
  Increasingly companies are seeking **feedback** from customers about their level of satisfaction with the product or service provided.
  The 'consumer sovereignty' approach means that for many companies the only ultimate objective is consumer satisfaction.

- **The market**
  Companies can look at Government statistics on population figures and social structure in order to identify and satisfy potential consumer demand.
  Market research needs to be done to ensure effective decision-making in relation to the Marketing 4 Ps.

- **The competition**
  It is useful for companies to be aware of the activities of their **competitors**; it is only by increasing this awareness that they can stay 'one step ahead'.
  Companies can gain information about the consumers' perception of the competition from their own research; they can also monitor their performance from published figures.

- **The economy**
  Government statistics can be used for this type of analysis, but many of the larger companies have their own economists who forecast market and economic trends

on a one-to-one basis; the latter would be the more efficient but also more costly.

Sampling

In order to gain responses from a cross-section of the audience it is possible to use sampling methods rather than attempting to reach the whole market, which is, in most cases, an impossible aim. By sampling a cross-section of the market it should be possible to gain a fairly accurate picture of what all the responses would be.

- The selection of a **representative group** can be done by random

sampling, which involves the selection of any member of the target group
- A systematic method would be a specific selection of, say, every 50th person in the group
- Cluster sampling is done on a regional basis whereby a certain target type is selected
- Quota sampling can be less effective, because it is based on a set number of responses rather than a target group, so ultimately there needs to be a group breakdown in order to analyse the responses.

Presenting and analysing data

The gathering of statistical information is only the first step in the process; the information needs to be effectively presented and analysed. There are many ways of presenting figures, but ultimately the format needs to suit the content and the objectives.

We need to look in detail at four statistical concepts:

- The range
- Measures of central tendency
- Dispersion
- Deviation.

The range

The range is the difference in extreme values in a series of figures.

It is a measure of numerical dispersion but can give a misleading view as it does not show the distribution within the range. Look at Box 10.5, showing the output of 100 workers on piecework over a week.

The range is the highest number *minus*

the lowest number. Find the range of the workers' data.

The mean is the average value of the variates. It is the sum of the figures divided by the number of times they occur. Calculating the mean of a large set of data can be done by grouping the data. Raw data can be split into classes of a set size. Once a class width is determined data can be formed into common arithmetical groupings. The mid value of each class is taken to be representative of the class. To calculate the arithmetic mean, (i) multiply each mid-value by the class frequency, (ii) find the total of these results, and (iii) divide by the total frequency. Look at Box 10.6.

The advantages of using the mean value are:

- It is a widely understood value
- Each value is incorporated into calculating the mean; none is ignored.

BOX 10.5	**Output of 100 workers on piecework over 1 week**									
	22	11	23	41	23	31	47	27	49	39
	7	18	27	36	24	44	53	41	22	41
	25	13	30	48	35	52	41	46	32	46
	31	48	26	34	42	32	52	29	36	58
	37	41	43	59	45	68	28	40	42	37
	48	56	38	32	53	47	71	53	41	49
	56	47	68	41	42	35	62	47	57	33
	31	59	47	38	57	48	52	69	43	42
	49	66	64	41	63	37	32	41	54	64
	58	61	50	63	47	42	51	38	42	51

BOX 10.6	**Arithmetic mean: grouped frequency distribution**

A sample of the ages of 100 citizens:

Age	Frequency
1–10	10
11–20	12
21–30	18
31–40	18
41–50	9
51–60	16
61–70	9
71–80	6
81–90	2
91–100	0
	100

Age	Mid-point (x)	Frequency (f)	(xf)
1–10	5.5	10	55
11–20	15.5	12	186
21–30	25.5	18	459
31–40	35.5	18	639
41–50	45.5	9	409.5
51–60	55.5	16	888
61–70	65.5	9	589.5
71–80	75.5	6	453
81–90	85.5	2	171
91–100	95.5	0	0
	Totals	100	3850

$$\frac{3850}{100}$$

Arithmetic mean = 38.5 years

TASK 10.1   For our piecework example, find the most frequent output figure.

The disadvantages of using the mean value are:

- The mean value stated may not correspond to any real value, e.g. 2.3 children
- It can also be distorted by high or low values.

Mode or modal value

The highest frequency value is called the mode or modal value. This is the value which occurs more frequently than the other values.

If more than one frequency value or mode occurs, it is termed multi-modal.

The advantages of using the mode are:

- Where it is useful to know the most common value, the mode is more useful than the mean.
- It can be useful to demonstrate common demand patterns.

The disadvantages of using the mode are:

- Every value is not taken into account, unlike the mean value
- Values may be multi-modal, which can confuse the issue
- The dispersion of variates around the mode is ignored.

Median value

The median is another useful measure of central tendency. It can be defined as the value of the middle item of a distribution when the items are arranged in ascending order of size. If the data is ungrouped the process of calculation is simple. The figures should be organised into an array – from the smallest to the largest. Then find the middle item using the following formula:

$$\frac{\text{number of items} + 1}{2}$$

If there were 19 items, the calculation would be

$$\frac{19 + 1}{2} = 10$$

Therefore the value of the tenth item would be the median value. When the number of items is even the middle value cannot be found so simply:

$$\frac{22 + 1}{2} = 11.5$$

The middle value will be the 11.5th item. In this situation, it is necessary to find the average value of the 11th and 12th items:

$$\frac{11\text{th} + 12\text{th items}}{2} = \text{Median}$$

Cumulative frequency

The cumulative frequency (or **cf**) of a variate value is:

the frequency of that value plus the frequency of all lesser values.

Box 10.7 is an example using business data.

| BOX 10.7 | **Demand for product A by a cross-sample of 100 consumers over a week** |

Product 'A' units class	Sample of 100 consumers frequency
0–10	2
11–20	8
21–30	13
31–40	34
41–50	16
51–60	15
61–70	10
71–80	2

Class	Cumulative frequencies
0–10	2
0–20	2 + 8 = 10
0–30	10 + 13 = 23
0–40	23 + 34 = 57
0–50	57 + 16 = 73
0–60	73 + 15 = 88
0–70	88 + 10 = 98
0–80	98 + 2 = 100

From the cumulative frequency calculation we can see that from our sample two consumers demand between 0 and 10 units whilst ten consumers demand 20 or less units.

Measuring dispersion

The measures of dispersion shows how values are scattered or dispersed in statistical data.

The range is a simplistic measure of dispersion from the highest to lowest value. The median represents the middle number or 50% value. A quartile represents 25% and 75% or three quarters:

25% = lower quartile
75% = upper quartile

Look at Box 10.9.

Measuring deviation

The variate deviation is the value of the variate **minus** the mean or the average value of the cumulative variate.

Each variate will have its own deviation. The ways of measuring deviation are through the mean deviation or the variance or standard deviation.

BOX 10.8

Measuring dispersion

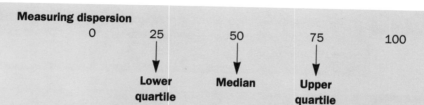

Upper quartile less lower quartile = interquartile range

In the sample of 100 consumers and their demand for Product A in Box 10.7, the 25th consumer is 1/4 of the way up the cumulative frequency axis. If we plot cumulative frequency against demand, we get the graph shown below.

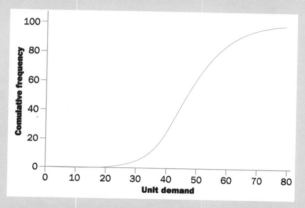

We can find the median, the quartile and the interquartile range.

Mean deviation

The mean deviation represents the average deviation of all the values from the mean value. To do this we need to take the numeric value ignoring any negative signs:

Data: **10, 28, 40, 12**

Mean $\dfrac{10 + 28 + 40 + 12}{4} = \dfrac{90}{4} = 22.5$

The mean is 22.5.

To find the mean deviation we need to find the difference between the value of the variate and the mean value of 22.5:

$10 - 22.5 \quad 28 - 22.5 \quad 40 - 22.5 \quad 12 - 22.5$

Ignoring the negative signs, the mean deviation will be calculated as follows:

$\dfrac{12.5 + 5.5 + 17.5 + 10.5}{4} = 11.5$

Variance and standard deviation

Because of the need to ignore the distinction between positive and negative values in the mean deviation, for statistical analysis the more effective measure of dispersion is considered to be the variance and standard deviation.

To eliminate the negative factors the variance and standard deviation square the difference. The squared differences are then averaged. This creates the variance. The square root of this deviation provides the standard deviation.

REVIEW

After reading this chapter you should understand the role and limitations of statistical analysis in predicting market demand and forecasting business activity with its use in presenting business data.

REVIEW TASK

PRACTICAL APPLICATION

1 The daily demand for a product unit over 40 days was:

4	5	5	7	8	3	2	4	9	7
7	3	5	5	4	2	9	10	3	6
8	2	3	2	6	5	5	6	7	6
9	3	5	6	5	5	6	6	9	5

A Calculate the arithmetic mean.
B Find the median.
C Identify the mode.
D Which is the most useful measure of dispersion in this case?

2 Output of 100 workers on piecework over 1 week:

22	11	23	41	23	31	47	27	49	39
7	18	27	36	24	44	53	41	22	41
25	13	30	48	35	52	41	46	32	46
31	48	26	34	42	32	52	29	36	58
37	41	43	59	45	68	28	40	42	37
48	56	38	32	53	47	71	53	41	49
56	47	68	41	42	35	62	47	57	33
31	59	47	38	57	48	52	69	43	42
49	66	64	41	63	37	32	41	54	64
58	61	50	63	47	42	51	38	42	51

A Draw the cumulative frequency graph.
B Use the graph to find the median.

3 A Study the attached questionnaire and then make a list of comments on how well you think it will help to give the bank the information they need.
B Why does the bank include a box on the Data Protection Act 1984 in its questionnaire?

TASK

CRITICAL ANALYSIS

Bankonit plc

At Bankonit we have some of the information we need to deliver a banking service that really meets our customers' needs. But, we would be the first to concede, not enough. And partial information inevitably results in partial solutions. That's why we would be grateful if you would help us, by giving us the information we need to get a clearer picture of you as an individual with individual needs, rather than as a number on an account.

Fifteen minutes of your time will make a real contribution to our ability to offer you an appropriate banking service. By filling in gaps in our knowledge of you, you'll be helping us fill in the gaps in our service to you.

Any information will be treated in the strictest confidence.

Data Protection Act 1984
This form asks you to provide information, which may be used to update and enhance our records. An important purpose of this exercise is to obtain improved customer information. This should enable us to advise you more efficiently of other Services provided by our Group of Companies in which you might be interested

Personal Data

1. Age: ☐ <30 ☐ 30–35 ☐ 36–40 ☐ 41–45 ☐ 46–50 ☐ 51–55 ☐ 56–60 ☐ 60+
2. Occupation ....
3. Employment Status: ☐ Full Time ☐ Part Time ☐ Self-Employed ☐ Retired ☐ Other
4. Home Telephone: .... Office Telephone: ....

Financial Profile

5. Individual Gross Income: ☐ Up to 20K ☐ 20-35K ☐ 35-50K ☐ 50-60K ☐ 65-75K ☐ 75K+
6. Household Gross Income: ☐ 25-40K ☐ 40-55K ☐ 55-75K ☐ 75-100K ☐ 100K+
7. Do you have funds in:
   ☐ Building Society account ☐ Bank Savings account ☐ Current account.
8. What is the total approximate value of your assets in cash, i.e. Bank and Building Society accounts, Unit Trusts, Stocks and Shares, and Gilts?
   ☐ 5-20K ☐ 20-75K ☐ 75-150K ☐ 150K+
9. If you have occasional large balances in your current account, would you want to be advised about short term money management to increase your return on those funds?
   ☐ yes ☐ no

Investments

10. What is the approximate market value of your main residence?
    ☐ Up to 70K ☐ 71-120K ☐ 121-200K ☐ 201-500K ☐ 501K+
    Do you have a second property? ☐ yes ☐ no
    What is the amount of mortgage you have currently outstanding?
    ☐ Up to 30K ☐ 31-50K ☐ 51-100K ☐ 101K+
11. Do you get financial advice from: ☐ Accountant ☐ Financial Adviser ☐ Stockbroker
    ☐ Bank ☐ Building Society ☐ Press ☐ Other

If you have any comments or suggestions we would be pleased to hear from you.

Thank you for completing this questionnaire. If you prefer **not** to receive further questionnaires, please tick this box. ☐

Signature ....

Filling in this questionnaire will enable you to enter our prize draw for a new Rover car

Essay questions

1 State and discuss the criteria on which a statistical layout should be based. Comment on the extent to which the presentation of data is as important as accuracy. (AEB 1984)

2 The collection of statistics is expensive in terms of time and money. It is not really cost-effective. Discuss.

3 State the importance and the techniques of analysing statistical data to illustrate business objectives.

An endangered species

The milkman, as a breed, is becoming dangerously close to extinction. The old system of the Milk Marketing Board, which had been fixing the price of milk since 1933 in order to stabilise a market that was threatening to put many farmers out of business, was overturned with the reform of the dairy industry. From November 1994 the UK's 30 000 milk producers have been free to sell their product on the open market. So far 65 per cent have signed up with the new Cooperative replacing the Milk Marketing Board and called 'Milk Marque'. Unigate have estimated that the new selling system will cost them £40 million in a full year. It will therefore be forced to establish price increases. As most of the milkrounds are now franchise contracts, the rounds will inevitably become less viable.

Figures show that supermarkets are charging much less for a pint of milk than the milkman providing doorstep delivery. This is partly because supermarkets can afford to sell milk as a 'loss leader'.

But it could be argued that the milkman offers more than the daily pinta. In many situations they offer a much needed community service for elderly or disabled people. With the milkman priced out of the market the supermarkets will hold a monopolistic position and be able to set their own prices.

In the quest for free market choice, factors other than supply and demand are often ignored. In the production of figures, unquantifiable values can undoubtedly be lost.

Source: National newspaper reports and author's research.

CASE STUDY TASKS

1 Make a survey in your local area, comparing prices charged for milk in a range of different retail outlets:
   - Milkman
   - Corner shop
   - Chain store
   - Supermarket
   - Restaurant/café.

A. Collect and present the data in the form of a table.

B. Analyse the data and find the
   - mode
   - mean, and
   - median

   price for each type of outlet.

C. Do a cost–benefit analysis based on the average price in each outlet and the value to the consumer and society at large.

   Dear Customer

   I have just taken out an agreement with your supplier to continue to operate my round on a franchise basis.

   I can assure you that this should not affect your service in any way. I would, however, be grateful if you could pay your weekly bill as soon as possible. I would also appreciate any advice you could give about the type of service you require. Also any ideas about other types of produce you would find it useful to have delivered by me.

   Many thanks
   Yours

A. Describe a franchise agreement and its benefits and drawbacks to this milkman.

B. Explain his concerns about 'prompt' payment and ways of getting around this problem.

ACTIVE LEARNING TASK

This is based on the case study following Chapter 3.10 – you may need to refer to it again.

A comparison of the price of milk delivery to your door and the price in supermarkets

5p = Milkman's margin

9p = Milkman's costs

9p = Processing and dairy
     company's margin

1p = Milk Marque's costs

13p = Farmer's price

UK doorstep price 37p

Supermarket price 25p

Approximate percentage share of household milk purchases, 1986–93						
Year	1986	1989	1990	1991	1992	1993
Doorstep	80	70	68	65	61	59
Shop	20	30	32	35	39	41

Present the information above in graphical form to demonstrate the market shares of doorstep delivery and supermarket sales.

QUESTIONS

Essay questions

1 What is the role of the average rate of return when evaluating investment projects? What other techniques might be better? Why?

2 Study the graph below and answer the questions that follow.
Total sales of sports equipment by UK manufacturers for the period 1961–77:
(a) Sales at current prices.
(b) Sales deflated by sports equipment price index.

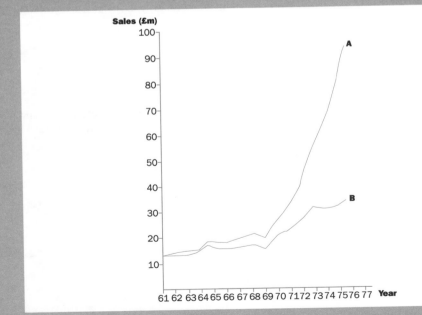

Exports and imports of sports equipment

	Exports (£ thousand)	As proportion of total UK manufacturers' sales	Imports (£ thousand)	As proportion of total UK manufacturers' sales
1970	9888	50.99	3105	15.99
1971	13562	48.47	4285	15.31
1972	15209	46.01	5775	17.47
1973	20393	48.76	8981	21.47
1974	25935	47.05	13850	25.12
1975	32184	50.42	18168	28.46
1976	36187	47.30	20500	26.80

Source: Business Monitor, PQ 494.3

A. Briefly explain why the two lines on the graph diverged between 1971 and 1977.
B. On graph paper, construct a bar chart to compare Exports and Imports for the years 1971, 1973 and 1975.
C. (i) Calculate the relative increase in both Exports and Imports between the years 1970 and 1976.
   (ii) Identify **four** economic and social factors which might have led to these changes.

(AEB, June 1986)

Integrated case study for Section 3: *The News*

The background

Two partners are in a business which produces a free local newspaper. It earns revenue from local advertising. The paper is circulated over a 10-mile radius and is distributed free to local shops and offices. It is also delivered to local areas of dense population.

One partner is a printer by trade and actually produces the paper, whilst the other is in charge of the administration and canvasses for advertising revenue.

The business is located in a small industrial unit; it has been established for 3 years and is making a reasonable profit for its owners.

The proposal

The partners feel it is time to expand their operation. They would like to set up a local newspaper providing a range of articles with a local interest. The business will be funded by both advertising revenue and a charge for the paper.

Distribution

In order to achieve this goal they feel they will need to:

1 Gain additional capital
2 Move to larger premises
3 Recruit more staff
4 Promote their advertising space
5 Extend their circulation to a 20-mile radius
6 Decide on what articles would attract buyers
7 Select potential outlets
8 Do some market research to find out whether there would be sufficient demand (using your own area).

INTEGRATED CASE STUDY TASK 1

Prepare a feasibility study, advising them on whether this is a viable project, using the projected figures as set out below.

Fixed Costs

£15 000 salary per present partner with 3 additional journalists at £14 000 per annum each and 4 print workers at £11 000 each. One is already employed at £17 000. New equipment will be leased for £20 000 per annum. Two vans will be leased at £1200 each per annum.

Variable costs

Materials will cost 6p per newspaper.

Revenue

Advertising revenue is estimated to be £22 000 per annum, paid monthly based on sales of 18 000 per week. It is felt that once the 20 000 threshold is reached, the advertising revenue will rise by 8%.

Location

There are 3 potential sites available – refer to map.

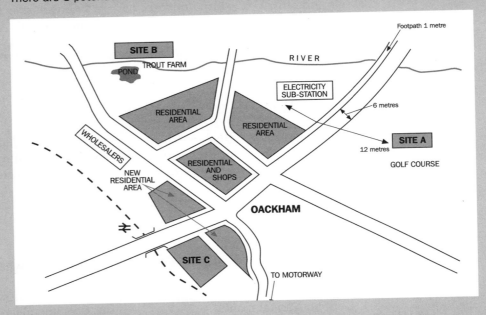

Site A

The lease will be £19 000 per annum but additional heavy electricity feed will need to be installed from the electricity sub-station.

The Electricity Board have 3 rates for laying new cables

	£ per metre
A Carriageway/roadways	40
B Footways	15
C Soft surfaces, i.e. grass	9

Site B

The owners of the trout farm are concerned that printer's dye and oil may get into the stream. There is also a local pressure group fighting for local environmental issues who may cause problems.

The cost of this lease is £15 000 per annum. It is a smaller building than Site A but there is sufficient land to extend the operation.

Site C
This is near to a residential area and the partners fear local opposition to the siting. It is an ideal building and near to the wholesalers.

The cost of the lease is £16 000.

TASKS

1 Construct a break-even analysis for each site, assessing the profit/loss per annum at a selling price to the wholesaler of:
   (i)   20p –   30 000 per week
   (ii)   25p –   25 000 per week
   (iii) 30p –   20 000 per week
2 Plot a demand curve for the above figures.
3 Do a cost-benefit analysis on each locational option, and decide on the best site.
4 Having decided on a site, create a cash flow forecast (using a spreadsheet if possible) based on 2 years:
   ● *Year 1* – Sales of 24 000 copies per week at 25p
   ● *Year 2* – Sales of 28 000 copies per week at 21p
5 Use your local library to gather statistics on your local population. Create a consumer profile based on the potential socio-economic market mix of the area. Use this as a base for your recommendations on articles to run and types of advertising to promote. Present this as a report.
6 Make a further report setting out your marketing strategy for the business based on the headings of the '4 Ps'.

Section 4
Strategies for
the Business

Notes towards an industrial strategy

Manufacturing industry represents the making of tangible products. To have an effective industrial policy there needs to be a marriage of inventive or creative activity with entrepeneurial vision. A government's industrial policy needs to nurture inventiveness and encourage creativity, in the process benefiting the whole economy by increasing output. To merge the creative with the productive to form an idea into a reality a 'hands on' approach is needed by government – an industrial strategy.

British industrial history presents a catalogue of missed opportunities. The lack of integrated industrial strategy has meant that many great inventions and designs have not become great products of UK industries. History speaks for itself. In the 1920s Frank Whittle invented the jet engine, which could have become a major UK industry. Rolls Royce made the first prototype but with war looming funds were short and there were insufficient resources to develop the engine. The idea was given to the Americans with the intention that they should develop the engine and help the war effort.

In 1949 a Manchester University research team invented the first electronic brain – in effect the first computer memory. This breakthrough happened not in a boom era but in an impoverished economic and social climate. The National Research Development Council (NRDC) had been set up by the post-war Labour government to help develop, research and support new product ideas. However, it found that industry was not keen to share its ideas. Limited funds meant that, in most cases, the NRDC failed to achieve its objectives. In the case of the electronic brain, the NRDC held the patent but there was no UK computer company to whom to issue licences. The US response was very different, with IBM just waiting to exploit a new opportunity.

In the 1970s the situation deteriorated further. The prevailing free market philosophy meant that companies were expected to stand alone and respond to market forces. The privatisation programme took large areas of industry out of the hands of the government and into the private sector. Much potential research and development was sacrificed for short-term profit. Inventors were told they had to find their own market and the NRDC was rendered redundant. Yet inventors are inevitably scientists or engineers with little interest in market forces, product portfolios or balance sheets. They need to be part of a chain of production which fosters their ideas and interests towards the ultimate goal of effective output. It was this lack of foresight which was the demise of the Hovertrain. British Rail were understandably concerned that the development of the Hovertrain necessitated ripping up their standard track and massive reinvestment. An innovative concept got stuck in the sidings of bureaucracy.

Complacency by UK companies over product portfolios is another negative factor. When an EMI researcher invented the CT Scanner it was a major breakthrough in medical science but UK hospitals were not initially responsive. The idea was taken to America and demand soon outstripped supply. Because EMI had control of the market they did not develop the product further, becoming a one-product company. General Electric entered the market, did further research and produced a better machine. Thorn took over EMI and closed production down.

In contrast the Japanese market economy incorporates a planned industrial strategy which is integrated with an international trade policy. The Ministry of International Trade and Industry (MITI) is the body that plans that strategy. The Ministry makes decisions which direct and shape its industrial structure, working together with the business sector. The weakness of an unplanned industrial sector is that it responds to market events rather than seizing market opportunities: a re-active rather than pro-active approach. A British inventor, Des Maps, recently developed a glass computer disc which can make a lap-top as powerful as a mainframe computer. He is now working in Japan.

Source: National newspaper reports and author's research.

Preview

In this chapter we shall investigate the following key areas:

- types of production
- the production factor
- the product
- the relationship between marketing and production
- materials
- stock control
- lean production
- quality control

The production process

Production, in an economic context, is anything for which someone is prepared to pay. It involves a combination of the factors of production (inputs) and the product (output) has a price. A bank provides a service, for which it is paid. Through the public sector governments provide, for example, education, defence and health services, which also contribute to what is termed 'production'.

Operations management involves effective decision-making which includes analysing what to produce,

where, how and when. All these decisions have marketing implications, and the links between the two need to be emphasised and identified. Many factors will influence these decisions, the type of product, the market, the inputs and the costing implications. The government can also influence the decision-making process by providing regional development incentives, training schemes, information services and financial support.

Technological development is another factor which has had a major impact, making production much more capital-intensive. This has also led to a loss of specialised skills and an increase in 'repetitive task' labour. The UK employment structure has increasingly become 'part-time female', rather than 'full-time male', in response to the type of work evolving. However, new EU employment legislation has given part-time workers new rights, in particular with regard to pensions. This may mean an ultimate reversal in this process as part-time workers become more expensive.

The UK has been called a screwdriver economy, meaning that our manufacturing output mainly involves assembling component parts, often from other nations. The changes in the structure of production has meant a massive loss of jobs in manufacturing and a switch of emphasis to the service sector.

The expansion of the service sector in the 1980s was initially welcomed by the government. However, its contraction in the late 1980s led to even more unemployment. The UK economy is suffering from de-industrialisation. De-industrialisation describes the decline in manufacturing industry, with falling output and increased unemployment. In the 1980s employment in manufacturing fell throughout the developed world, although the UK suffered one of the largest declines. The UK has de-industrialised faster than its major competitors and workers have not been redeployed. The decline in manufacturing has also meant that the UK is not selling so many goods abroad and this has been detrimental to our balance of trade.

Whilst the UK has been de-industrialising, successful economies like Germany and Japan have been exploiting marketing opportunities by exporting their own manufactured goods to the UK.

Types of production

The production process is not purely the creation of a tangible good but can also be the provision of a service: in economic terms, anything for which someone is prepared to pay. The process is not always as clear cut as 'product' or 'service': most forms of production also incorporate a service element.

Many forms of production are easier to track by categorising them into primary, secondary and tertiary production:

Primary	Secondary	Tertiary
Oil/coal	Produce electricity	Supply to consumer
Tobacco	Produce cigarettes	Supply to consumer

Operations management

Operations management is the organisation of the processes and decision making needed to achieve output.

The four key questions that need to be posed are:

- What to produce (the product)?
- Where to produce (location)?
- How to produce (methods of production)?
- When to produce (demand and product life cycle)?

The questions of 'what' and 'when' are dependent upon advice from the marketing department – there needs to be a demand before a supply will be initiated. However, it is not only the potential market for the output which is vital but also the availability of the inputs. The correct site or location (where) needs to be found and the right process or method of production (how) needs to be decided upon.

In the service sector these questions are not always as relevant, and neither are they for some parts of the primary or secondary sectors. The decisions will depend on the type of business and the product or service involved.

What to produce?

Design of the product

The responsibility of product designers can be defined as interpreting the needs or wants of the customer into a suitable form, in the most cost-effective way.

The role of the designers and other individuals in the production department will depend upon the size of the company and the type of output. A large company will include most of the sub-sections shown in Box 11.1, whilst a smaller one may buy in expertise in areas like design and development.

The design function concerns the designing of new products or modifications to existing ones in response to market demands. In some areas, for example the fashion industry, design has a high profile whilst in other types of product its profile is much lower.

The design process

The standard stages in product development are:

- The idea – this could be an original idea or one that has evolved from a response to market research.

- The test – at this point the idea is tested for viability. This could be done by scaled models, computer simulations and mock ups. If the product is not seen as valid it is cancelled.
- Construct a prototype – a full-scale model can be developed if the test is seen as successful.
- Set out a specification – in products like consumer durables – cars, TVs washing machines, etc. – there should be specifications drawn up from the product and laid down as a consistent standard to which all of the products will adhere. In the past within the EC each member state has had its own standard specifications for certain goods (i.e. computers). If another EC country did not produce goods to the same specification it was unable to export the goods. The 1992 Single European Act aimed to stop this anomaly and to set up standard European specifications in terms of safety and standard regulations for products.

Marketing and production

There are close links between marketing and production, as Box 11.2 shows:

BOX 11.1

The role of production and design

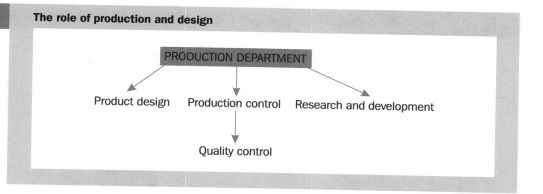

BOX 11.2

How marketing and production relate

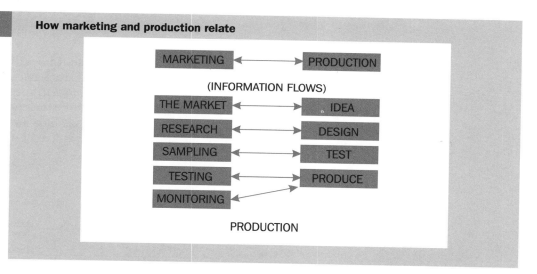

Materials input

Stock and stock levels

Stock (or inventory) in its simplest terms is money tied up. The type of business will dictate the levels of stock investment, whilst the management policy on stock will also have a direct impact on the levels held. Some of the factors considered will be:

- the opportunity cost – what else could have been done with the money
- the use of storage space
- the liability in terms of security and insurance

- the working capital tied up and the reduced liquidity.

In a manufacturing context there are two main types of inventories

- Raw materials and work in progress
- Finished goods.

Stock control and lead times

It is important to establish a balance between holding enough stock so that there are no production hold-ups, and holding the minimum level so that money is not tied up unnecessarily. Look at Box 11.3.

| **BOX 11.3** | **Output, lead time and stock receipt** |

MATERIALS OUTPUTS

DECIDE NEED STOCK? ⟶ RECEIVE STOCK

LEAD TIME

We can show this on a stock control graph (see below).

The lead time is the time it takes to make a decision about the need for stock and the actual arrival of the stock.

The lead time will dictate the minimum level of stock needed to be held. A long lead time will result in a higher minimum stock level than might otherwise have been needed. A stock card (see Box 11.4) will usually be held

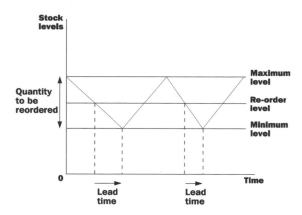

| **BOX 11.4** | **A stock card** |

ITEM . . . .

MINIMUM LEVEL . . . . MAXIMUM LEVEL . . . .

RE-ORDER LEVEL . . . .

for each item of stock. This will usually be computerised but it may be a paper record.

Other factors which will have an impact on stock levels held include the life expectancy of the stock. Holding perishables can be a significant liability as their value may deteriorate to zero before they have been processed.

Stock control is increasingly being computerised. The large retail stores have their stock control tied in with bar codes which are logged at the point of sale. New stock can then automatically be reordered.

Lean production and JIT

Modern production control systems are based on the importance of planning material inputs to involve minimum costs. These systems necessitate the use of computer integrated manufacturing, such as JIT. Look at Box 11.5.

The use of JIT puts an increasing emphasis on suppliers to get the stock to the production line on demand. Increasing pressures are being applied to suppliers, often resulting in contracts being drawn up with penalty clauses if the delivery cannot be fulfilled. The success of JIT depends largely on management systems which support its philosophy. There need to be regular team meetings of all those involved in the production process in order to ensure the effective flow of production. JIT relies on the computerisation of stock control procedure and also the increased use of computer integrated production.

Computer integrated production

The use of computers in production is a rapidly expanding field and is particularly well developed in the area of design and production control. Computers are opening up new freedom from repetitive processes. This has also brought negative aspects, particularly in the switch from labour- to capital-intensive production, causing unemployment.

Walk into an engineering company design room: the days are long past when you would see rulers, pencils and drawing boards. The room will now be filled with computers running design programs. Today's designers call up stock measurements and patterns from computer memory and create their designs. A two dimensional drawing can be transformed into a 3D model. It can be twisted and turned and even subjected to stresses and strains. Products as diverse as power boats and nuclear power stations can be designed on computers.

BOX 11.5	**JIT (Just In Time)**

JIT (Just In Time)

The Japanese system of JIT, or Just In Time stock control, is increasingly being used by UK manufacturing companies. Rover Cars are reported to have saved £50 million by implementing JIT. The philosophy is that instead of holding raw material or component inputs stock, the stock arrives on the production line 'just in time'. The use of JIT means that:

● Money is not tied up in stock
● Storage space is not necessary
● Insurance and security procedures are of limited necessity.

Computer aided manufacturing means that designs can be produced using computer technology. The direct path flow production system makes this a straightforward process. An American aerospace company uses a system called 'place' which allows the creation of an entire production cell using computer simulations. The computer shows assembly lines using machinery and robots. The robots can be programmed to perform set tasks and the whole process can be viewed on screen from every angle.

The Department of Trade and Industry has invested funds to promote the use of computer technology in manufacturing. They believe the key to future success is AMT (advanced manufacturing technology) which incorporates computer aided design (CAD), computer aided manufacturing (CAM) and computer aided engineering (CAE). This also involves the use of advanced robotics. Systems like JIT also link into this type of model.

Value analysis

Value analysis applies constraints and accountability to the factors involved in the production process. A budgetary model can be established which sets parameters of spending on each stage of production. A team of specialists can then be set up to ensure that costs are assessed in each area and continually evaluated.

Quality standards and control

Quality standards have as much importance to marketing as to production.

Quality control has two main forms:

● Legal – legislation protecting consumers must be complied with
● Commercial – consumer satisfaction must be met.

The process will involve checking the standards of:

● Inputs
● Process function
● Quality of workforce
● Goods in process
● Finished goods.

Quality standards have become increasingly important as a measurable objective. The British Standards Institute (BSI) is the largest of the bodies awarding set standards of specification. There are now an increasing number of quality standard procedures.

BS5750

BS5750 (IS 9000) is probably the most widely used production system standard. It is actually meant to be a standardised management system but is most widely used in areas of manufacturing, although it has been much criticised for the way in which it has been implemented (see below). The process involved takes four stages, as shown in Box 11.6.

BOX 11.6	**BS5750**
	1. The company seeking the certification prepares a 'quality manual' setting out the policy and procedures of the company in agreement with the consultation body
	2. An assessor visits the company to check that procedures are being followed
	3. The certification is issued and can be shown on letterheads and in marketing information
	4. Continuous assessment takes place with follow-up regular visits.

By January 1993 the BSI had issued approximately 14 000 certificates to companies which formed 70% of the market. An example of another quality standard for non-manufacturing industries is the IIP (investors in people); this is used more widely in the service sector.

BS5750 has been much criticised. The main area of contention is that it monitors the procedures by which standards are met: it does not actually establish the standards. Therefore if the standards are consistently low, they may comply with BS5750.

One of the problems could be that the standard had its origins in sophisticated industries like defence, where standards are well established, yet it has been applied to industries where such standards have traditionally not been established.

Many companies are adopting the standard for marketing reasons – for many, it is the fear of losing contracts from large industries and government contracts. Many smaller companies are struggling to afford the amount of set-up costs required and the increased administrative burden.

Where to produce?

The choice about where a business locates will primarily depend upon the type of business. Each type of good or service will have different inputs or resource needs whilst other factors, for example access to the market, will also need to be considered.

The factors which will need to be analysed before deciding on a location will not apply to all businesses but will generally include those outlined in Box 11.7.

Management policy

The location of a business will be a management decision dependent upon the perceived balance between the costs and benefits of each possible site option. There could also be a longer-term policy decision to link with other aims and objectives of the business. On a simple level the immediate needs will dictate the type of site specification. A service sector business will require a central market position whilst an industry creating, for instance, a toxic by-product will need to be sited as far

away from the public as possible. The size of the site will depend on the scale and type of output involved, and therefore the space required. Cost is also a primary consideration. Some types of businesses are called 'footloose' – in other words, their location is not restricted by these considerations and cost may be the deciding factor. Other businesses may suffer from what is known as industrial inertia, meaning that they locate in an area purely because it has traditionally been their base.

Available staff

The type of staff input to production again depends on the type of output and the balance of the factors of production in the business. Some industries are capital-intensive, which means that funds are directed to machinery and other capital items. Other firms are labour-intensive, meaning that they have a higher concentration of workforce. The quality of the workforce and the type of skills needed are other considerations. Some areas have large concentrations of skilled workers that

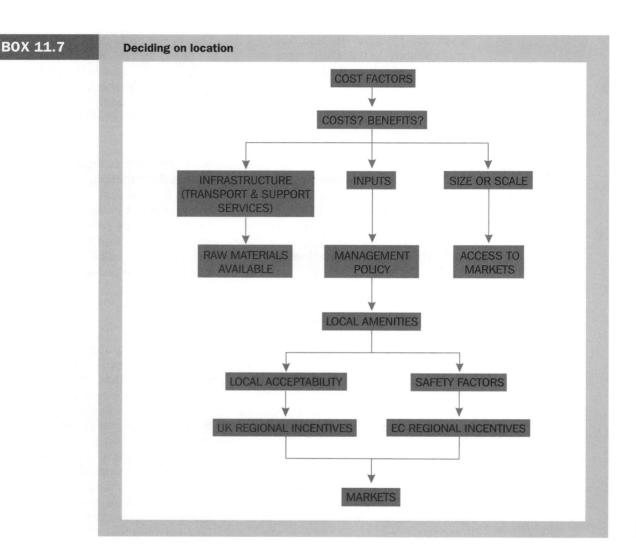

BOX 11.7 **Deciding on location**

have been built up over the past because of the localisation of industry, which evolved because large industries like steel, shipbuilding and coal mining needed to be near their sources of power and raw materials. These industries have been seriously undermined, and in some cases destroyed, by a changing economic structure which has meant increased foreign competition and a changing pattern of world demand.

The large pools of skilled labour left unemployed in these areas has caused what is called structural unemployment. Government retraining schemes and regional development incentives are designed to combat the historical effects of industrial concentration.

Local support services, including staff training courses and financial services, could be important to some businesses. Businesses that need to take on highly skilled personnel, who may be in short supply, could locate in areas with good schools and other amenities in order to attract quality staff. However, the increased development of the transport system (see below) has made the location of a business much more flexible: as the scale of national communications has become increasingly developed, countries are becoming 'smaller'.

The increased use of information technology has meant that there is a rise in the number of people working from home on computer terminals. A personal computer linked to a modem (telephone line) can gain access to a network of information, which means that increasingly the need to travel to the office is eliminated. Computer banking, information and telephone-based financial services are not only displacing jobs in the service sector but also allow flexibility of location.

Raw materials

Some businesses need access to raw materials which may be bulky in format. If the raw materials are bulky it is sensible to be sited near their source of supply whilst if the finished goods are bulky it may be more economical to be sited nearer the market.

Climatic conditions may be important for businesses involved in the holiday trade, whilst agricultural firms will not only have the climate to consider but also the suitability of the soil or the location of minerals and ores.

Infrastructure

An important factor in considering location is the transportation facilities and other support services available in the area. The importance of transportation will again depend on the type of business. The success of a production firm may depend on getting its output as economically as possible to

the market place. A service industry, on the other hand, needs to attract the consumers to the service it is providing.

Transport facilities will be a mixture of road, rail, air and sea access. For a company expecting to export to the rest of the EU the sea route could be paramount whilst a company transporting goods between UK cities could be dependent on motorway access.

The amount of freight which is carried via the rail network has diminished considerably, and road freight is increasing. In response, Green campaigners have called for a policy of rail subsidies to get freight back on the railways and off the roads. The phased privatisation of British Rail, and what has been called the rising up of 'Middle England' against the concept of 10-lane motorways, could both have significant impact on the shape of freight transportation in the future. The development of toll roads could also contribute to pushing up the price of road freight.

Government incentives

Businesses need factors of production to be readily available and therefore mobile. Regional development schemes are a way of taking the work to the workforce. In other words, companies are given incentives to locate in areas of high structural unemployment (see map overleaf). Grants, loans and preferential planning procedures are given as inducements for firms to locate where there are problems in the local economy.

EU funding

The EU also has a regional funding role and British regions are eligible to apply for grants and aid if they can prove a case for support. This funding will become increasingly important as the UK moves

UK Regional Development Areas

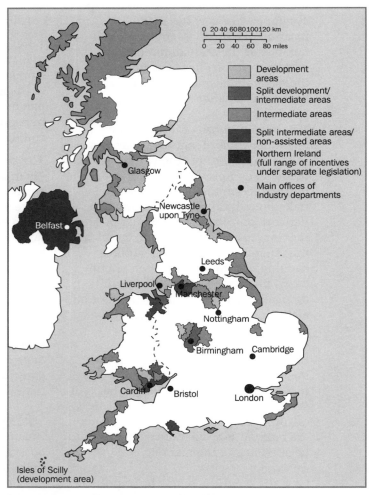

Source: Britain: An Official Handbook (HMSO, 1995)

towards becoming a region of Europe, since it is the local region who applies for the aid and who obtains the funding.

There are two criteria that have to be satisfied in order for British regions to obtain funds for development projects in depressed areas:

● The UK government must match the amount provided
● The firm must be able to prove that without funding the project would not otherwise take place.

As the government has been reducing the power of local authorities, such direct regional aid is at odds with government policy. This has caused conflict and the holding back of EU funds from some UK regions.

The local community

The type of business will usually dictate its acceptability to the local community. A nuclear power station with obvious safety and health risks will of necessity be located away from centres of population, whilst a service industry will need to be located near to a populated area. However, with increased car ownership, out of town sites are a cheaper option. The increased emphasis on 'out of town' sites has meant that many towns have lost much trade and this has resulted in many shops having to shut down. This situation has led to the government and local authorities beginning to discourage 'out of town' developments through their planning procedures.

A noisy night club or public house, which needs to be located near its market, could soon become unpopular with local residents and risk losing its trading licence which is issued by the local authority. Pressure groups can be formed and act as powerful lobbies against businesses which are deemed unacceptable to them. A business which is likely to cause an increase in traffic, and which could prove hazardous to children, is also likely to be opposed.

Those opposed to the locating of a business will need to weigh up the advantages to the local economy that accrue through the creation of jobs, against the negative aspects caused by the company conducting its business.

How to produce?

The organisation of production

A company which is producing a good, rather than providing a service, will need to decide whether to initiate a single product item, a product line or groups of similar products, or a product mix with various different products. The company will need to balance its product portfolio to take account of the product life cycle. Product development may mean that cross-subsidisation takes place. Some products, termed 'cash cows' by the Boston Consulting Group, are high-volume, high-sales products and can help to fund newly developed products. Look at Box 11.8

Ways of carrying out production

Job production

Here a single product is created by a person or group. The advantage to the workforce is that they see a completed product, which may improve their motivation. For the consumer, goods can be tailored to meet a specific market. For the producer it is easier to isolate any faults in the process of production and maintain flexibility of output. The disadvantages of this type of production is the higher costs involved when compared with batch, or flow production (see below). The process necessitates a wide range of tools and machinery, which are used on a random basis, and a flexible workforce, which needs to master a number of skills.

Batch production

Here a group of products undergoes production at the same time. It is a way of organising production work so that a number of operations can be completed for a group of products or batch. Examples of items suitable for this are bread (bakeries) and china (potteries).

Flow production

This is based on the principles of division of labour and specialisation. Here each part of the production process is broken down into specific

Product portfolio and marketing strategy

The range of products a company supplies, or its 'product portfolio', will depend primarily on its marketing strategy. The strategy may be for:

● **Concentrated** – focus on one market segment
● **Segmented** – many different products targeted at various markets
● **Differentiated** – What is in reality the same product differentiated in some way to achieve a USP (unique selling proposition)
● **Undifferentiated** – production consists of the same standard product

tasks. One product flows through a number of production processes. This eliminates waiting time for tooling up or tooling down – that is, the physical organisation of each worker using a number of tools consecutively. Hence it allows for increased automation and mechanisation. It increases specialisation, as only the skills necessary for each part of the process need to be developed by each worker. Economies of scale can be achieved with a lower unit cost, and less stock has to be held. The use of stock can be tied in with the flow and therefore organised to maximum efficiency. The level of skills per worker required are minimal. At its extreme level, as has been seen in the car industry, robots can take over the production process, making the process capital- rather than labour-intensive.

Flow production does, however, involve large amounts of capital investment. It can be inflexible in terms of switching or amending output because of its direct flow process and commitment to automation. Workers can become disenfranchised, seeing themselves as just a number in the process: the sense of 'ownership' of production can be lost. Faults can be more difficult to identify and because of the repetitive nature of the process can be repeated without anyone noticing. This necessitates a very effective quality control system.

When to produce?

In order for a business to decide when to produce an item or service they would need to monitor market demand: the links with the marketing department are vital in understanding consumer demand patterns. The product life cycle will also be a vital factor in deciding when new products should be developed in order to enhance the product portfolio of a business.

Production decision-making

The costs and benefits of each aspect of production need to be balanced against the type of market demand. Some initial decisions which need to be made are to assess the:

● Type of product
● Scale of production
● Balance of factor inputs
● Type of production process
● Use of technology.

The production department, like all other departments of a business, has its objectives broken down into measurable targets. Quality factors will be an important element in target-setting, and quality control minimises the rate of failure. There may also be safety standards which a producer needs to meet – for example, the British Standard Kite Mark is applied to products like crash helmets where safety considerations are vital.

The quality control system will often be applied by sampling output, sometimes using statistical techniques to test performance. Poor quality control can result in the destruction of a company's reputation – the poor quality control standards in the British car industry in the 1970s, together with poor workforce relations, contributed to its virtual destruction.

REVIEW

You should now understand the meaning of the term 'production' and its many forms. You should also be able to analyse the processes involved and understand the importance of technology.

REVIEW TASK

PRACTICAL APPLICATION

A manufacturer making hand saws uses 50 sheets of metal a day and its main factory produces an output of approximately 2000 saws a day. A new contract agreement has recently been signed with a large 'do it yourself' retailer which means sales should increase by 23%. Output is to be increased by the same proportion but there is another smaller factory which is already producing 1000 per day.

1 Decide on what you feel should be the stock levels held, before and after the new deal, at the larger factory. Base your assessment on
   A. operating a JIT system
   B. operating a conventional system.
2 Construct two stock control graphs illustrating what you feel the minimum, maximum and re-order levels of the sheets of metal should be at both factories before and after the deal. Base your decision on A and B above and justify the type of system you choose. Note any other information which would be useful to you and any ideas you may have as to how this form of production could be improved in relation to the type of stock control.

BOX 11.9

CRITICAL ANALYSIS
Patently obvious?
Many individuals may have brilliant ideas but they never put them into practice, thinking that it must have all been done before. It is always worth checking to see if your idea is unique.

An inventor can save a good deal of money by checking at the British Library Science Reference and Information Service, or at any of the 13 public libraries in the UK patent's information network. Staff will also carry out the search for you for a fee.

To actually get an invention patented in the UK costs £3000–£5000. However, if you need international patent protection the price is nearer £10 000. In increasingly global markets it could be argued that international patent protection is a must, but even then small adaptations can be used to overcome patent protection. Industrial espionage is also a major problem.

TASKS

1. Explain the value of the patent system to a company with a new idea.
2. Do you think that cost implications are a deterrent to creative design and development? If so, what could be an alternative procedure?
3. Relate this critical analysis to the Focus on industrial strategy. What type of industrial structure could best harness UK creative potential?

QUESTIONS

Essay questions

1 Explain the interdependence of marketing and production.

2 'Nothing effective was ever designed by a team' (Sir Alec Issigonis, the designer of the Morris 1000 and Mini car). Discuss this statement.

3 What are the objectives of product portfolios in relation to the product life cycle?

4 The following extract is part of a document sent to Trafalgar House shareholders informing them, among other things, of a proposed acquisition. Read the article and answer the questions which follow.

> **Trafalgar House and its activities**
> Trafalgar House was incorporated in England on 22 December 1965 as a private limited company under the Companies Act 1948 with registered number 867281 and was re-registered on 20 January 1982 as a public
> 5 limited company pursuant to the Companies Act 1980. The Company now operates under the Companies Act 1985. The registered office of the Company, which is also its principal place of business, is at 1 Berkeley Street, London W1A 1BY. The principal objects of Trafalgar House, as set out in clause 4 of its Memorandum of Association, are to act as a holding
> 10 company and to invest in and develop property and to enter into financial and commercial transactions of all kinds.
>
> Trafalgar House is the holding company of a group whose principal activities include property and investment, construction and engineering, shipping, aviation and hotels, and oil and gas.

A. What distinguishes a public limited company from a private limited company?
B. Explain the main purpose of the Memorandum of Association (line 9).

C. List **two** pieces of information, other than the Memorandum of Association, required by the Registrar of Companies when forming a public limited company.

D. Explain the term 'holding company' (lines 9–10).

E. Suggest and explain **three** factors that might be considered by Trafalgar House when assessing whether to go ahead with any acquisition.

AEB June 1993

5 Read the article and answer the questions which follow.

PRIME MOVERS

Stocklin Limited is the wholly owned UK subsidiary of the Swiss materials handling specialist company, Walter Stocklin AG. It is one of a number of European based organisations that has chosen to locate its UK operation at Aston Science Park, Birmingham.

Two years ago, under the direction of Bill Strickland, Stocklin Limited was formed. The company has installed materials handling systems across a wide range of manufacturing, distributive and service industries, including numerous companies, such as the Nationwide Building Society, Walkers Crisps and Proctor and Gamble.

Stocklin Limited works in close collaboration with another Swiss company which also has its UK headquarters at Aston Science Park. In fact, Bill Strickland reports that the decision to start-up from Aston was largely influenced by the presence of Sprecher & Schuh Automation Limited – specialists in complementary computer control and software for warehouse applications.

"There were also a number of other factors that we considered important to Stocklin", explains Bill Strickland. "We appreciate the range of facilities offered by Aston – and the big city environment with its tradition of engineering means that we can draw on a specialist engineering labour pool."

Through its 2 divisions, Stocklin Limited covers all aspects of factory and warehousing materials handling – conveyors, cranes, lift trucks, trailers – equipment for moving anything from pallets through fluids to granules in bulk carrying containers.

The company specialises in designing complete warehousing systems. However, all Stocklin equipment will interface with that of other suppliers – and conforms to European and UK standards.

Increasingly Stocklin Limited is being commissioned to install systems in banks and building societies, to store property deeds, stocks and share certificates and wills for clients. "Many such institutions are centralising their deed stores – which can amount to some 6 million items under one roof. Such facilities need to be fully automated – and that means total accuracy." Without that assurance you could end up with complete chaos, Bill Strickland points out.

Source: Adapted from Aston Science Park, Venture, 2 (6) (Autumn 1990).

A. What is meant by the term 'a wholly owned subsidiary'?

B. Consider three reasons why Walter Stocklin AG decided to locate its UK operation at Aston Science Park.

C. Why is it important to the success of Stocklin Limited that its equipment 'conforms to European and UK standards' (line 32).

D. Explain two advantages and two disadvantages to 'companies such as the Nationwide Building Society. . .' (line 6) of centralising and automating their document stores.

AEB June 1993

6 Read the article below and answer the questions which follow.

Information systems

The momentum established by ICL, our computing subsidiary, last year continued despite the market growing at a slower rate. ICL's business strategy proved to be a correct estimation of the direction the market

5 would take, and the results, shown below, justify their judgements.

Industry Standard Operating Systems are becoming more plentiful and popular, and this will reduce growth rates and margins for hardware. The company will therefore continue to shift its emphasis from hardware to software and services. The 1988 results already reflect such a shift.

10 Growth in ICL's International Retail Systems business continued. It is now the number one supplier of checkout machinery and software for French hypermarkets. In 1988 ICL entered the North American supermarket business with a range of specially designed hi-tech products. The net result was a 50% growth in retail systems revenue in the USA over the

15 past year. The year ended with the acquisition of Datachecker Systems Inc. which, when merged with ICL's Retail Systems organisation, creates the third largest in-store retail systems business in the world.

RESULTS	1987 (£m)	1988 (£m)
Turnover	1299	1363
Operating profit	111	129

Source: Adapted from STC plc, Employee Report 1989.

A. Explain the phrase 'the market growing at a slower rate' (line 2).
B. (i) Calculate the percentage change in turnover and the percentage change in operating profit between 1987 and 1988.
(ii) Should the firm be satisfied with these results? Justify your answer.
C. The information suggests that ICL has altered its product policy (lines 7–9). Explain two external pressures that may have influenced this change.
D. Outline an appropriate promotional strategy for the firm's products and services.

AEB June 1990

7 A. What are the principal types of production system?
B. How would the management of a catering establishment choose between them?
C. What problems might occur in moving from one system of production to another? (CLES)

8 A. What are the objectives of stock management systems?
B. How might each of these objectives be achieved by the stock control staff and systems? (CLES)

CASE STUDY

Falcon Cars: 1

The Falcon Car Company are producers of exclusive sports cars. The cars have traditionally been hand-built by teams of craftsmen on a small scale of production. However, demand has outstripped supply to such an extent that they are now investigating increasing their output by the mechanisation of their production process. They will also have to either expand their present site or move to a new one.

They will, therefore, have to:-
A   choose the best site;
B   implement the right production process.

Site 1 is in the South West and is in a regional development area (refer to the map on p. 196).

Site 2 is not in a regional development area but is much nearer to the UK main market area and is nearer to the European ports.

The present site is near to site 2 but would need to be extended.

The company has a new production manager who has been given the brief to look into both the locational aspects and the production process and report on the implications of each option.

CASE STUDY TASKS

1   Create a report (if possible, on a computer or word processor) putting yourself in the position of the new production manager analysing and evaluating each possibility for A and B above.
2   You are also a JIT enthusiast and feel that the new automated production process would suit the implementation of JIT. However, the marketing manager is not impressed by the plans for automation and he feels this could damage the exclusive 'hand-built' image of the Falcon; and he is particularly anti-JIT because of the dangers he feels could occur if the stock system was to break down. He sent you yesterday the memo reproduced overleaf.
    As production manager, draft a memorandum to him (if possible, on a computer or word processor), explaining the negative and positive aspects of both the automated production process and the JIT system.
3   Prepare notes under the headings
    ● Product
    ● Price
    ● Promotion
    ● Place
    and explain how each of these aspects of the marketing mix may be affected by the new plans of location and production.
4   Do you think a situation of conflict is developing in the management team? If so, why, and how can this be overcome?

MEMORANDUM

FROM: The Manager   Ref.

TO: The Production Manager   DATE . . . .

Although I have not been approached by you formally, I have been informed by our Finance Manager about the changes in the location and production process that you have been discussing with him. These two factors are obviously vital in our expansion process. However, I do have some concerns from a marketing perspective about the automated production process.

In the past the promotion of the Falcon has been based on its exclusive hand-built image. Are the changes in the production process to be minimal or are we now to be "Hand built by Robots"?

The product image is a vital part of the marketing function and, depending on what plans you implement, we may need to change our marketing mix and adopt a totally new approach. Can we please have a meeting on these points as soon as possible?

4.12 Business Strategy and Decision-Making

Strategic programming

Strategic planning has been defined as 'the process of developing and maintaining a strategic fit between the organisation's goals and capabilities and its changing marketing opportunities'. It relies on developing a clear company mission, supporting objectives, a sound business portfolio and coordinated functional strategies.

Canadian business guru Henry Mintzberg's book *The Rise and Fall of Strategic Planning* argues that too much planning in a business is ineffective. He calls for a revival of creativity and imagination and a move away from too much formalisation. Mintzberg believes that great strategies are about great visions and vision is not about planning but about inspiration. He argues that the programming that occurs in a strategic plan is built on computer data and analysis which is distanced from reality.

As businesses, hospitals, prisons and many other organisations go through the process of developing their strategic plans Mintzberg's warnings should be taken seriously. An inflexible plan can have little value whilst the process of drawing together a strategy across a wide spectrum of thoughts and opinions is inevitably flawed.

Source: National newspaper reports and author's research.

Preview

In this chapter we shall investigate the following key areas:

- decision-makers
- stakeholders
- decision-making factors
- decision-making techniques

Achieving the goals of the business

We have already analysed the types of objective a business may have, but in order to achieve these objectives a business needs to have a strategy for moving forward to achieve its goals. Strategic planning is not only a private sector concern but an organisational one which also involves all dimensions of the public sector. Schools, colleges, prisons and hospitals are having to draw up strategic plans to show their long-term goals, usually over a 3–5 year term.

In order for a strategic plan to be developed, decisions need to be made both at a senior policy level and at all levels throughout the organisational structure, both to agree the plan and then monitor how effectively it is being achieved. The successful businesses will be the ones who achieve their goals and make the right decisions along the way.

Effective decision-makers will have certain innate qualities plus the relevant ability and skills. They will need to be able to effectively disseminate information and to be aware of all the implications of each step that is taken. They can call upon recognised decision-making techniques to help them make their way through the maze of potential opportunities. Information technology is a vital tool in the decision-making process and this will be looked at later.

Decision-making will always be coloured by the constraints put on the business by outside forces such as the government and European legislation, its business competitors, the market and the economy. These factors will inevitably complicate the decision-making process and make the need for planning even more vital.

The strategy of the business

We have already looked at the types of objectives a business may have and how they are established, but once objectives have been set a strategy is needed. The business needs to clarify the four key areas listed in Box 12.1.

In order to be able to put the strategic plan into action, a business must analyse its own potential and limitations. A term for this type of assessment is the SWOT analysis outlined in Box 12.2.

BOX 12.1	**Elements in the strategic plan**

- Where it is **now**? (the **reality**)
- Where does it want to **go**? (the **objectives**)
- How will it **get there**? (the **strategy**)
- How will it know if it is **getting there**? (the **targets**)

BOX 12.2	**SWOT analysis**

Strengths

Weaknesses } An **internal** assessment of resources

↓

Opportunities

Threats } An assessment of **external** forces

All decision-making is a dynamic activity where individuals are having to respond to a given situation. SWOT analysis is a way of cataloguing the reality of the position at any time and can be used as an effective decision-making tool.

The decision-makers

Decisions are made at all levels of an organisation by all of the stakeholders. The senior management team may make important strategic decisions but all the workforce make decisions on a daily basis at varying levels. Whatever the structure of a business, decision-making is integral to all its parts.

Some decisions will be structured policy decisions, others will be spontaneous responses to a given situation or event. The type of decision will vary between those which are programmed or routine, and those which are unprogrammed or unexpected. The delegation of decision-making in any organisation will depend on the type of management structure. In organisations with a centralised management structure the majority of higher level decisions will be made by fewer individuals. In a decentralised structure, higher level decision-making may be passed down the management line.

American companies, in particular, often split their operation into small cells or independent units, with each unit having autonomy to make decisions in many areas as defined by higher level management. This type of structure is ideal for the team approach to decision-making. Decision-making by groups is an effective way of gaining consensus. The brainstorming method, where groups of individuals all contribute ideas towards solving a problem, is an effective technique, which is widely used. The factors which will help to make a decision-making group effective are the size of the group, the type of groups and their belief in the process. The type of problem also needs to be appropriate to a group dynamics situation.

The corporate stakeholders

The stakeholders in a business are those who have an interest in its success or failure. They include not only those who work for the company at various levels but also the owners, investors, customers and those to whom the business owes money (creditors). The corporate stakeholders could be defined as those who own or work for the business. Look at Box 12.3.

The decision-making process

Look at Box 12.4.

The types of decisions taken will depend on the role held by the decision-maker in the organisation. The importance of delegation, as a management function, means that a manager must be able to rely on the effective decision-making of subordinates. Much decision-making in organisations is on a formal or structured basis; increasingly, however, lower level roles are being involved in the higher level decision-making process. This is known as the bottom up philosophy.

The individual as decision-maker

When an individual is appointed, decision-making skills will be as much

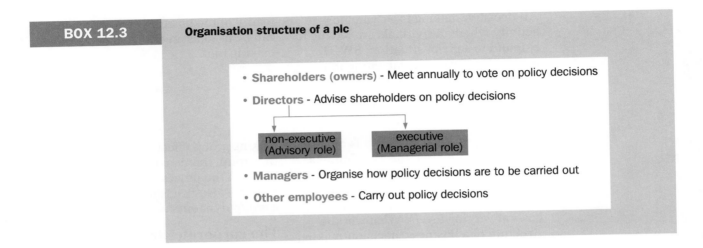

BOX 12.3   **Organisation structure of a plc**

- **Shareholders (owners)** - Meet annually to vote on policy decisions
- **Directors** - Advise shareholders on policy decisions

non-executive (Advisory role)   executive (Managerial role)

- **Managers** - Organise how policy decisions are to be carried out
- **Other employees** - Carry out policy decisions

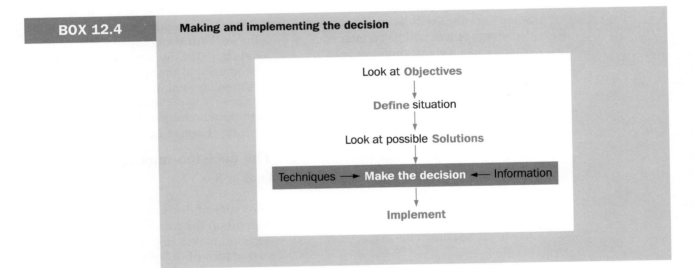

BOX 12.4   **Making and implementing the decision**

Look at **Objectives**

Define situation

Look at possible **Solutions**

Techniques ⟶ **Make the decision** ⟵ Information

Implement

under scrutiny as any other ability. However, because decision-making is a dynamic function it is difficult to test or judge how anyone will perform. Simulations can be done during the interview process to put candidates under some pressure to react to a given situation, but this would usually be done for more senior levels of management. There can also be some indication from past performance or through the monitoring and evaluation process.

The decision-maker requires a number of analytical skills to enable an appropriate response to a specific situation. This includes the intelligence and ability to be able to assimilate the information available and to understand the consequences, and the competence to be able to use available techniques and methodology as a decision-making tool. A confident and self-assured manager will be able to take decisive action, and their own perception of the situation will guide them as to when, where and what decisions will need to be made.

Each decision-maker will have a bank of acquired skills, knowledge and expertise which will help them to make appropriate decisions. They will also have innate or subconscious qualities or weaknesses. Box 12.5 shows some of the factors and constraints impacting on the decision-maker in practice.

Constraints

Whenever a decision is made the individual involved needs to be aware of the constraints. Information flows about external or internal issues will be vital here.

Resources

The basic economic problem is limited resources and this is as true for the firm as for the individual. Choices have to be made with an awareness of the resource implications.

Competition

Whatever decisions are made, one always need to be aware of the competition. In areas like marketing and production, a wrong decision could lead to loss of market share, whilst pricing and financial decisions will often depend on how the competition is perceived to be operating.

The market

A business must be aware of market trends and pressure from government or economic forces. It needs to understand how contractions and expansion in the market for its output occur, and also any changes in the availability or cost of its inputs.

Government and the EU

The government makes regulations which will have a direct impact on the decision-makers of a business. A company will need to consider any legislation relevant to its operation. The EU Directives are now another factor which need to be considered, as are tax implications for any business. Any tax levy may have a direct affect on demand for the product, depending on its elasticity.

The economy

Businesses operate within an economic

BOX 12.5	Making a decision: 1

Subconscious factors	Conscious factors
• Emotions • Perception • Security/insecurity	• Skills • Competence • Intelligence • Ability

The risk factors
Tactical strategy
Constraints (internal/external)

context, so economic forces will provide the climate within which decisions must be made. Interest rates, exchange rates, inflation and other factors will all affect demand and supply and will be analysed in Section 6. We can now set out how such factors as these will impact on the decision-maker. Look at Box 12.6.

Making a decision: 2

Constraints	The decision-maker's thinking
● Resources	If I increase output do I have the funds to take on more labour or would investment in capital be more cost-effective?
● Competitors	If I develop this new product is this market already saturated?
● The market	If I increase the price is the demand elastic?
● Government and the EU	How will European regulations on product specifications affect this new product?
● The economy	If we take on new investment can we cope with the level of interest rates, and are they likely to rise or fall?

The techniques of decision-making

Decision trees

A decision tree can be useful to research the possible outcomes which stem from a particular decision made. The system follows the routes or branches of consequences and identifies further decision-making opportunities en route. A value can be placed on each decision, based on the probability of its potential revenue or cost implication.

In decision trees, unknowns are represented by a circle whilst decisions are illustrated by a rectangle. The flow process moves from left to right. Look at Box 12.7.

By allocating the probability of success to each possible decision and including a value, the expected profit or loss of each decision can be estimated. Look at Box 12.8.

The entry costs are £100 000

Route A
There is a 0.4 probability of achieving revenue of £280 000 in a given period

$$0.4 \times £280\,000 = £112\,000$$

Route B
There is a 0.6 probability of achieving revenue of £160 000 over the same period

$$0.6 \times £160\,000 = £96\,000$$

BOX 12.7

The decision tree: 1

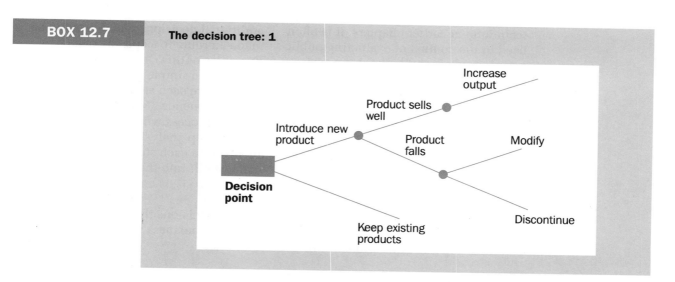

BOX 12.8

The decision tree: 2

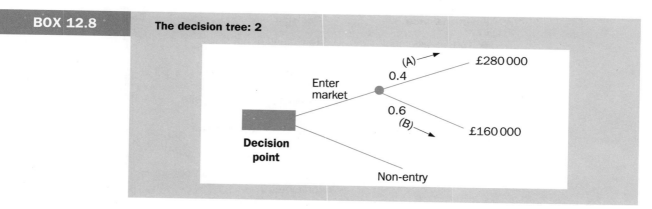

Game theory

There are substantial similarities between an entrepreneur and a games player, particularly in games that are based on strategy rather than purely chance. Decisions made in a business, like those made in a game, are dependent on external factors which are beyond the control of the player, in particular the moves or actions of a competitor. Possible outcomes have to be planned and counter strategies developed in response to events. This comparison is being developed more fully in game theory techniques: computer games can provide interesting scenarios for business decision-making strategies and are being used widely for business simulations.

Opportunity cost

An opportunity cost must be applied to the possible outcome of any decision made – the real cost of the decision, in relation to other possible options. There are a number of techniques which have been developed on the opportunity cost model. One is the 'minimax regret' or the missed opportunity.

Cost–benefit analysis

We have already looked at this

technique in earlier chapters. It is often used in the context of evaluating public sector projects, and looks at the costs and benefits to the firm, and to society of any decision made. This can be applied to both private and public sector costs but can be also used to weigh up the affect of a decision on the firm.

Network analysis

Working through a process in a structured way and analysing each step can be an appropriate way of deciding the outcome of a particular decision. It can throw up any other problems or additional decisions which need to be made en route to a specific objective. Examples of this can be demonstrated through the simple process of 'baking a cake' where each step is planned in a logical sequence. 'Making a journey' is another process which is suitable for step-by-step analysis. The time factor involved in each step of the process can be built into the equation. Critical Path Analysis, is an example of a type of network analysis. Box 12.9 shows typical decisions that the functional areas of a business will have to address.

BOX 12.9	**Typical decisions**		
	Functional area	**Decision**	**Constraints?**
	● Top management: growth or focus	To expand or not?	
	● Business organisation as a whole	The choice to go public	
	● Production location: the social dimension	Expansion of a factory site	
	● Production operations management	Should we switch to flow production?	
	● Marketing: price	Increase price?	
	● Marketing promotion	How should the product be promoted?	
	● Budgeting and costing	Increase fixed costs?	
	● Financial records	How to increase liquidity?	

TASK 12.1

Think of possible constraints for each of the decisions in Box 12.9.

REVIEW

You should now be able to see the importance of decision-making to an organisation and understand the role of planning. You should also be able to apply techniques which support this process, and appreciate constraints.

REVIEW TASK

PRACTICAL APPLICATION

An investor has to decide whether to invest in shares in Company A or B.

There is an initial investment amount of £68,000. The objective is after one year to maximise:-

1. Income from dividend
2. The potential market value.

Company A
- Initial price £2.40 a share
- After six months there is a 0.7 probability of increasing the price by 50%
- After one year there is a 0.6 probability of gaining dividend of 11.5%
- After one year there is a 0.5 probability of increasing the price by 65%.

Company B
- Initial price £1.92
- After six months there is a 0.6 probability of increasing the price by 56%
- After one year there is a 0.8 probability of gaining dividend of 9%
- After one year there is a 0.6 probability of increasing the price by 70%.

Which company should the investor choose?

TASK

CRITICAL ANALYSIS
Totally Innovative Management

Japanese firms have made considerable achievements in Western markets by out-thinking the opposition. The American computer giant IBM were out-thought by the surge in creative strategic planning from the East.

A creative constipation has been the characteristic link between many Western business failures. In the computer industry, where change is part of daily life, the impact of failing to innovate is much more intense. The innovative lags started at IBM in the early 1980s and by the end of the decade it had lost its crown. IBM's decision to concentrate its effort in the computer mainframe market, rather than develop its personal computers and laptops, proved an endemic failure in creative thinking and demonstrated strategic complacency.

Creative thinking should be built into any strategic plan. The Strategic Planning Society calls this concept Totally Innovative Management. The Japanese call it 'Creagement'. They demonstrated the ability to think strategically when they spotted the potential in the small car market from rising fuel prices and the increase in the numbers of female car purchasers. Unlike Detroit, they developed and creatively designed high quality small cars. Management need to be capable of creative strategic thought or innovative talent will be wasted. The creative and the disciplined should not been seen as opposites but rather as complementary factors working in harmony.

Source: National newspaper reports and author's research.

1 Explain how IBM could have introduced increased creative thinking into their strategic planning.

2 Why might the 'creative' and the 'disciplined' be seen as opposite forces by managers?

3 The Strategic Planning Society view total quality management (TQM) as a process by which innovation and ideas can be strategically developed through an improved methodology. Can you explain what is meant by this and how this methodology could work?

QUESTIONS

Essay questions

1 'The Bottom Up approach is about effective decision-making by involving those who will ultimately have to implement the decisions.' Discuss.

2 How will the structure of an organisation affect its decision-making process?

3 'Group decision making will lead to a more dynamic approach.' How far is this true?

4 Study the information below and answer the questions which follow.

> Watcher Ltd is a small firm that manufactures high quality pillow cases, duvet covers and fitted sheets. Solely on the basis of the following figures, the Board of Directors has decided to discontinue producing duvet covers and not to replace them with any other product. This will leave production capacity unused and fixed costs unaltered

	Pillow cases £	Duvet covers £	Fitted sheets £	Total £	£	£	£	£
Income								
Sales Income		100 000		120 000		70 000		290 000
Direct costs								
Direct materials	30 000		40 000		20 000		90 000	
Direct labour	35 000		50 000		25 000		110 000	
Overheads								
Variable overheads		10 000		12 000		7 500		
Fixed overheads	15 000		21 400		10 700			
Total costs							29 500	
		90 000		123 400		63 200		276 000
Profit (Loss)						47 000		
		10 000						
			(3 400)		6 800	13 400		

Show any appropriate calculations

A. Explain to the Board the implications of its decision to discontinue the production of duvet covers
   (i) in the short term
   (ii) in the long term
B. The Directors decide **not** to discontinue duvet cover production. Outline **two** other options that may be available to them.
C. One of the Directors suggests that there should be a more structured decision-making process. What might be the key elements of such a process?

Specimen paper, new AEB syllabus

5 Study the information below and answer all parts of the questions which follow.

Greig Chemicals

Greig Chemicals is about to take delivery of a new machine which will cut down the amount of pollution emitted from a chimney. The production controller is determined to have the new machinery in full production before a visit from the Health & Safety Inspector in 30 days' time. After that, the production department has been set the objective of achieving full Just In Time manufacturing within 6 months.

The production controller's first problem is how to complete the following tasks within 30 days.

		days
A	Delivery of machinery	2
B	Installation	6
C	Initial production	8
D	Production fine tuning	10
E	Full scale (test) production	12+
F	1st phase training	4
G	2nd phase training	9
	Total	53+

A. Draw up a network based on the above, given that:
   - activity **A** is the start of the project;
   - **B** starts when **A** is complete;
   - **C** and **D** follow **B** and **F**;
   - **E** follows **C**, **D** and **G**;
   - **F** follows **A**;
   - **G** follows **B** and **F**.

B. Work out the earliest start times of the activities and add them to the nodes of the network you have already drawn. Can the project be completed in 30 days?

C. To what extent might Critical Path Analysis be useful when carrying out Just In Time production?

D. Both Critical Path Analysis and Just In Time production can benefit from the use of Information Technology (IT). Outline three other applications of IT in business.

(AEB specimen paper, new syllabus)

CASE STUDY

The personal strategic plan

The scenario

A business is an organisation which functions under set aims and objectives and within limited resources. It needs a Strategic Plan to structure its methodology for mapping its future. In your studies you too will need a Strategic Plan to enable the learning process to be more effective. You will need to research, plan, analyse, evaluate and communicate your knowledge and understanding. The decision-making process will be integral to all your studies. You will also need to appraise your work and evaluate the outcomes.

Go through the process of:

Deciding
- What are your aims?   (Career development?)
- What are your objectives?   (Exams needed?)
- What are your targets?   (Grades necessary?)
- Appraisal techniques   (Negotiate with tutor?)
- Evaluation process   (Did you meet the targets?)

CASE STUDY TASK

1 Do a SWOT analysis on yourself.
2 Draw up your own strategic plan for your studies.

Integrated case study for Section 4: Locheye the new

Bob had always had a soft spot for the countryside, and it worried him that there was so little work there. Fewer people were required on farms these days and many of the traditional skills had declined or disappeared completely. Nevertheless, some excellent workers remained, people who were unafraid of long hours and physically tiring effort, and some who displayed an adaptability and a measure of craft skills which seemed to be part of their heritage.

For these reasons, amongst others, Bob decided to locate a branch of his organisation in a rural setting, near the English/Scottish border in the town of Locheye, at the same time taking the opportunity to buy a house nearby. He'd been in business for 30 years, and he felt he and his wife deserved a nicer environment in which to live, away from the industrial Midlands. There were costs in his decision, both for himself and for his company, but it was a price he was prepared to pay.

From 1986 to 1988 things went quite well. The employees were grateful for the work, which they undertook conscientiously and with considerable skill. They produced and assembled 3 parts of a component called the BDO 70, which was itself part of a larger machine tool used in the motor industry. These parts were code named BD12, BD13 and BD14 and were built in batches on a ratio of 2:4:1. Although quality was high, profitability remained, at best, marginal.

Locheye production schedule

		BD13				
BD12		BD13				
BD12	+	BD13	+	BD14	=	BDO 70
		BD13				

Things came to a head in June 1990 when Bob was approached by another component supplier in the Midlands who offered to match the annual output of 5000 BDO 70s per year. The supplier could not assemble them but he could supply BD12s for £4.50 each, and BD14s for £15 each. Assembly at Locheye would cost an additional £10 000 per year in transport costs although, in the long term, Bob could close Locheye completely and move BDO 70 assembly back to the Midlands. At present, however, all the factor capacity there was fully used, and he estimated it would require a £50 000 investment in order to create more. Indeed, the lack of spare capacity had been one of the factors in Bob's original decision to open a new plant in Scotland in the first place.

He decided to speak frankly with the Locheye workforce, especially since in the last 18 months he had become less impressed with their output. As he said to another managing director one day over lunch:

'I don't know, Sally, I lose heart sometimes. I gave these people regular work with a regular pay packet for the first time in their lives, and all they do is complain. They think they remember some kind of "golden age" when they were out in the open air, doing more or less what they liked when they liked. They seem to forget the rain and snow and the times when there was no work at all. Well, the harsh realities of the business world catch up with us all, I suppose. I'm going to be quite honest, explain the proposal and the figures and see what they make of them.'

Two weeks later, after talking to his workforce, Bob had a response. Knowing that redundancy stared two-thirds of them in the face, they had formed into groups, based around their work stations, to see if they could save time or materials. The results were quite startling, with estimated annual savings of £20 000 on BD 12, £10 000 on BD 13 and £16 000 on BD14. What's more, the workers had suggested that even more savings might be made in the future if these meetings were continued on a regular basis. Bob, of course, was delighted, although he was secretly a little doubtful about their ability to deliver these savings. As he drove across the rolling countryside which he was now so delighted to call home, he wondered, not for the first time, if decision-making was ever easy.

INTEGRATED CASE STUDY TASKS

A. Put the case for **and** against Bob's decision to open the Locheye plant.

B. As Bob's chief accountant you have prepared Locheye's 1991 budget which gives the following information for a planned output of 5000 BDO 70s:

	BD12 £	BD13 £	BD14 £
Direct labour	37 000	80 000	44 000
Direct materials	13 000	20 000	22 000
Other direct costs	13 000	50 000	20 000
Total direct costs	63 000	150 000	86 000
Fixed overheads (allocated)	5000	4000	6000

Bob has asked you to prepare a financial statement to show him whether or not he should buy-in BD12, BD13 and BD14 from the new supplier. He is not very numerate and so he will expect all your workings to be clearly explained.

C. He has also asked you to prepare a list of factors, apart from purely financial ones, which he should take into account before arriving at a decision whether or not to buy-in. He will, of course, want your opinion on the various options, as well as the list.

(AEB Nov 90)

ACTIVE LEARNING TASK

1 Decide on a product or service to be produced by a company you have set up. Plan a strategy for the company based on the '4Ps':
Product
Price
Promotion
Place
Produce a product design if relevant, and plan your production/service provision schedule.

2 Explain the process and documents involved in:
A. Drawing up a strategic plan
B. Obtaining a patent
C. Designing a product

D. Implementing a stock control system

E. Implementing a system for computer integrated production/manufacturing (CIM)

F. Making the decision about where to locate a business.

QUESTIONS

1 Analyse and evaluate:

A. The effectiveness of decision-making techniques

B. The importance of a business strategy.

2 Analyse and evaluate:

A. The link between marketing and production

B. The importance of the product portfolio

C. The value of computer integrated manufacturing (CIM)

D. The comparison between flow, batch and job production.

Section 5
The Resources of the Business

5.13 Data Management

'Don't let them get away with IT!'

In the winter of 1993 IBM and the CCU launched a computer crime awareness campaign termed 'Don't Let Them Get away with IT'. Computer-linked crime is now big business and is estimated to be worth billions of pounds. It has many forms, from computer hacking to the stealing of microprocessing chips. Hacking is the unlawful entry into a data base and has become a serious 'white collar' crime. Hackers can damage a company through theft of commercial information, fraud or just plain vandalism. Some computer hackers have managed to gain unlawful entry to financial and business data bases. It is thought that many companies, embarrassed by the security breakdown and the potential damage to their reputation, and worried by the leakage of information accessed, often do not prosecute. It is even believed that pay-offs have been given to stop any future hacking. Computer viruses are another problem. These are rogue programs that enter a computer system and can cause disruption.

The levels of miniaturisation which have been achieved by computer producers has meant the stealing of equipment has become much easier. Microprocessors half the size of a business card, and worth several hundred pounds, are easy prey to many criminals. One of the world's largest microchip companies, Intel, is reported to have had £4 million worth of microprocessors stolen in Europe alone in one year. They now have an identity pin on each of their higher level chips.

In 1984 the Computer Crime Unit was set up at Scotland Yard to attempt to enforce the 1990 Computer Misuse Act. The Act created three new offences:

1. Unauthorised computer access (which includes hacking)
2. Data theft
3. Unauthorised modification of computer data (this includes introducing a virus into the system).

As a result of these crimes, insurance premiums are rising rapidly. The spread of computer networking has led to the internationalisation of computer crime. A new breed of criminal is the information trader who steals data and sells it on. Unfortunately, many businesses do not realise the value of their data until it is gone.

Source: National newspaper reports and author's research.

Preview

In this chapter we shall investigate the following key areas:
- the personal computer
- systems analysis
- word processing

- spreadsheets
- data bases
- desktop publishing
- management support
- financial services

The IT revolution

Technology has always been with us. It is the pace of change which is accelerating. From the Luddites rebelling against industrial mechanisation in the early nineteenth century to the Wapping dispute over new printing techniques in the 1980s, we often fear what we cannot control.

The separate technological areas of computing, telecommunications and electronics have been brought together under the umbrella of Information Technology (IT). Since the development of the personal computer, what was once the privilege of the large company is now open to all. Information can be stored, retrieved, manipulated and communicated by technological means and at high speed without the use of vast resources.

The social implications of this development have been far-reaching, particularly in terms of employment. The financial services sector has been rapidly computerised, from the processing of cheques to the development of home banking. The financial and retail sectors are using computers to link 'point of sale' terminals directly to an individual's bank account. The issue of individual privacy is an important factor here. As junk mail reaches our doorstep the initiator of such direct mailing systems is probably a data base and we have just become an entry, a record. Our credit worthiness is also logged through data base entries, and errors can occur which are potentially damning and hard to identify.

IT can be a dynamic management tool because it allows up-to-date flows of information to be accessed and analysed in a fraction of the time of paper-based transactions and research. The ultimate effectiveness of IT relies on integrated systems. It must never be forgotten that IT is only a business tool, not the business's master, and that its context and use must be selected and continually assessed. The human element is still important, as it is the user that controls the input, and if this information is not accurate the computer acronym of GIGO (garbage in, garbage out) will apply.

The personal computer

Computer technology is fast moving and necessarily embraces all aspects of the business world. Up until about twenty years ago most businesses used mainframe computers. Large central processing units were stored in special rooms with many peripheral data storage units and specially trained staff. Many smaller companies were excluded from the computer world with its high capital investment costs and so their data processing tended to be manual. The development of the personal computer made available, for business use and at an affordable price, small computers with their own memory and specially designed software packages.

These personal computers could be linked together, or networked, to provide a structured system of computerised data processing for any size of business. This development opened up the possibility of computer data processing for all. Many large companies still use mainframes or mini-computers, which are more powerful than personal computers and which allow for increased storage and manipulation possibilities.

Analysing the systems of the business

In order to change a manual paper-based data processing system into a computerised one, a system needs to be designed. It needs to have clear objectives about what is to be achieved, each step needs to be analysed for

potential problems and the resources need to be allocated.

The systems analysis process

Look at Box 13.1.

BOX 13.1

Computerising the system?

Systems analyst

- Designs the system in a series of detailed decision-based flow charts to identify any problem areas and allow the programmer to write out each step for the computer to translate

Programmer

- Writes a program in the computer's language which gives step by step directions to the computer enabling it to carry out the process

---

Business software packages

Since the development of the personal computer, business programs can now be bought 'off the shelf' for certain business functions. There are general

programs for word processing, spreadsheets, data bases and desktop publishing, but also more specific programs for particular business and accounting tasks. This has meant that in most situations the systems analyst and the in-house programmers have become rarer except in the larger companies. Box 13.2 shows two such packages.

Word processing

In most cases the 'electronic office' has meant that the typewriter has given way to the word processor. Processing words on a computer means that before a document is printed it can be edited for errors or alterations and stored on disc. Variables can be added within the text and whole blocks of data can be moved, added or deleted, whilst new text from another document can be inserted. A word search can change specific words globally throughout a document, whilst a spellcheck on many packages can identify any spelling errors that may occur. A document can be transmitted to other terminals in the network for agreement and response before finally being printed. Some sophisticated packages will have integrated facilities for presentation of graphics, desktop publishing in columnar form like a newspaper, and various character sizes and styles of print founts.

Database

A database is a collection of records or information which are held on disk files. A database program allows the information to be created, accessed, edited, searched, sorted and listed. The database facility is important for a business because it forms a vast electronic filing system. The types of information which are likely to be held on a business database are customer records, staff information and lists of suppliers, whilst access to external databases can be important in providing management information support.

Each set of records is held on a file and each record is split into a number of fields, of information. For example, the fields for a staff records database could be Name, Address, Telephone Number, Department, Post, Qualifications and Courses. The program would provide the facility to call up the chosen fields of information or whole records and list them into the order required through the sorting procedure. Look at Box 13.3.

BOX 13.2

Business application programs

1   PAYROLL

- **Input**   Information on staff pay
             Deductions and codes
- **Process**   Wages and deductions calculated
- **Output**   Pay listings and pay slips

2   STOCK CONTROL

- **Input**   Units of stock held
             Prices and suppliers
             Stock usage information
             Re-order levels

- **Process**   Update records
             Check levels
             Calculate values
             Re-order stock

BOX 13.3	**A staff records database**					
	(FILE NAME) STAFF RECORDS					
(FIELDS)	NAME	INITIALS	SEX	START £	DEPT	SALARY
(RECORD)	JONES	CE	M	12.1.95	FINANCE	15 250
	KENEDDY	JS	F	1.7.88	MARKETING	11 661
	KEOGH	FL	M	30.2.90	PRODUCTION	10 778

TASK 13.1 Think of some more staff data fields. What information might be useful for the Personnel Department to hold on record?

A database file of staff records could include hundreds of names (records) with a much wider breakdown of information (more fields).

Once the file is produced more names can be added (created) or deleted. The information held can be altered (edited) and the records accessed (searched). For example, a search could be made of the age breakdown in staffing, numbers of male/female in departments and salary scales. The searching of records can be useful in the decision-making process as it is a quick and simple way of accessing information with the computer program doing the sorting and ultimately producing a print-out of the information. The listing of information on staff can be useful to send out information to them. If a field was added for their address, this field could be called up and printed on envelopes or at the top of headed letter paper.

The use of databases has much wider social implications. Non-business organisations like the police computer at Reading use this type of program in order to help them find suspects of crime by holding records on a database of all previous offenders. By calling up a field within each record, which states the type of crime, they have previous convictions for the name of all individuals of that category which would be sorted and listed by the computer.

Because of the power of databases and their wide use in all walks of life their use is controversial in terms of personal privacy and the problem of incorrect data. The dangers inherent in the misuse of sensitive information led to the establishment of the Data Protection Act 1984. Box 13.4 examines the importance of this legislation.

Spreadsheets

Spreadsheets are programs which deal with calculations on the computer and are useful for any financial records or analysis. They are fundamentally a large grid of cells like a vast array of pigeon holes into which can be placed information in a numerical or textual form. Within the cells you can place formulae in order to achieve the numerical calculation required. A spreadsheet program will enable many

BOX 13.4

Data Protection Act 1984

For the individual, the mass of computer information held on data base can be worrying. The Data Protection Act 1984 was passed to prevent the misuse of computer information held on individuals. The act has eight principles:

1. Information should be obtained and processed lawfully
2. Data should be held for one or more specified and lawful purposes
3. Personal data held should not be used or disclosed for any reason other than the purpose it is held
4. Data held for any purpose should be adequate, relevant and not excessive in relation to its purpose
5. Personal data should be accurate and, where appropriate, up to date
6. Personal data should not be kept for longer than necessary
7. The individual has the right to be informed about data which is held on them and where appropriate have it corrected or destroyed
8. Security should be provided to ensure there are no unauthorised access alterations, disclosures or distribution of personal data and also no loss or destruction of data.

If the individual feels that any of these principles has been violated, they can complain to the Registrar of the Data Protection Act who can then investigate the situation. In reality, if data collected on an individual is incorrect or misused the implications can be far-reaching. Blacklisting of trade union militants who cannot then find a job and loss of credit worthiness are just two implications, but redress for inaccurate information or its misuse is often pointless after the damage has been done.

simultaneous calculations to be done very quickly and effectively. By placing a variable figure in a formulae you can forecast what will happen to the calculations if a change occurs in some part of the process. In Section 2.6 on finance and budgeting we looked at the use of spreadsheets for financial calculations, as they would be used in the real business world.

Desktop publishing

Desktop publishing programs enable the user to produce well illustrated and structured text which can incorporate diagrams and charts. The text can vary in size and style and therefore be used for documents such as leaflets, programmes, invitations and newsletters. This means that by using a desktop publishing program these tasks no longer have to be contracted out to a printing company but can easily be achieved in-house on a PC.

Electronic mail

The use of electronic mail (e-mail) systems enables the sending of messages or documents via a computer terminal linked through a modem to a telephone line. By this type of link-up data can be passed from computer to computer without a piece of paper being sent. These are often called 'mail box' systems. There are also some subscriber-based electronic mail systems like Telecom Gold which not only allow communication between different organisations but also provide access to multi-information database banks.

Management support

Management decision-making procedures in business are being revolutionised by the use of computer technology. In addition to the standard business programs, which have already been mentioned, on-line graphic facilities show 'live' data on screen for information support. These systems consist of tables, information and charts, which are automatically updated. Diagnostic packages consist of software which enables the user to interrogate the information, asking 'what if?' questions of the data.

Computer graphics packages can be used to produce graphs and charts on overhead transparencies for presentations at meetings and conferences. The advantages of computer graphics packages for the manager is that they are a flexible facility and can be used for data storage, presentation, analysis and decision-making. The level of success of any of these systems, however, relies on their integration as a central part of the management process.

Financial services

A major area of IT development has been in the area of financial services. Banking has seen some of the greatest change. The CHAPS (Clearing House Automated Payments Service) system has enabled the sector to process an enormous amount of cheques in an automated process. The development of Bank Service Points and plastic card systems of credit and debit payments has also meant the loss of jobs in the banking sector. The development of home banking will mean further job losses. The Bank of Scotland were the first to initiate home banking through a computer terminal, but this will undoubtedly be an expanding concept. The use of a computerised system of payment transfer in the money markets has meant that the government has found it difficult to keep control of monetary and currency flows, whilst the increase in transactions on the Stock Exchange led to the £60 million demise of the computerised TAURUS system.

EFTPOS

The consumer boom of the 1980s led to closer links being established between the financial and retail sectors. Electronic Funds Transfer at Point of Sale (EFTPOS) has meant that by using debit cards, for example Switch or Connect, an individual can pay for goods by handing over the card at the point of sale, which is fed through a machine and the money is debited directly from the person's account. EFTPOS UK is a company owned by its members who include the major banks and building societies who operate a national scheme.

REVIEW

You should now understand the role of IT in an organisation, its use as a business tool, and its implications both for the business and for society at large.

REVIEW TASK

CRITICAL ANALYSIS
Outsourcing
Companies deconstructing and subcontracting are big business. IT is one of the newer growth areas throughout Europe to be subcontracted, particularly in the public sector.

This process is known as 'outsourcing'. However, the saving on costs of 'contracting out' of IT systems can throw up other difficulties. The loss of control for the buyer, which can result from badly thought-out contracts can be highly damaging and ultimately cost far more through disruption to the company than the in-house cost of an IT system.

The companies that have outsourced successfully are those that had effective IT strategies in the first place. Unsuccessful outsourcers are often outsourcing because of their inability to construct an IT strategy and they are ultimately just passing on the problem in a negative manner. For the vendor to gain from outsourcing, it is estimated that the price needs to be 15–20% lower than an in-house operation to compensate for the risks incurred.

Source: National newspaper reports and author's research.

1. Explain what is meant by company deconstruction and subcontracting, and why they are the current vogue in business philosophy.
2. Why is subcontracting used particularly in the public sector?
3. Define the problems which could be caused by outsourcing.
4. Define the positive aspects of outsourcing.

QUESTIONS

Essay questions

1 Outline the control systems required in a small business and explain the importance and uses of information technology.

2 'Businesses are at the mercy of the computer hackers who have the power to destroy their systems.' Discuss this statement.

3 To what extent might Critical Path Analysis be useful when carrying out Just In Time production?

4 Outline five applications of IT in business.

CASE STUDY

'Quick Shop'

Background

Harry Bedford's grocery and newspaper business is a fairly small corner shop which he operates as a sole trader. There has been considerable re-development in the local area which means that trade should increase. However, Harry is nearing retirement and is not sure that he has the enthusiasm or energy to exploit the new market potential. At the moment he sells newspapers, magazines and a limited range of groceries, sweets and soft drinks.

Harry has two main options:

1. Sell the business as a small retail outlet with 'much potential'.
2. Stay in business, expand the services offered and sell at a later date at a higher price.

The decision process
Sell the business?
Keep the business?

- Receive financial gain from sale
- Lose potential future gain

- Need to expand, raise finance for investment
- Receive increased future financial reward

It was a hard decision to make but his son came to the rescue. Harry's son Steve was a manager in a local construction company. Seeing the potential rewards that could be reaped by the expansion of the business, Steve decided to go into a partnership with his father. Harry could become a sleeping partner.

The first changes Steve felt should occur were:

1. The renaming of the shop to 'Quick Shop', to give it a more up-to-date image
2. Introduce extended opening hours to include Sundays
3. Expand the newspaper and magazine delivery service
4. Increase the range of groceries and introduce free home delivery
5. Computerise the shop's information systems
6. Produce leaflets to inform local residents of the shop's new image and facilities
7. Obtain a bank loan for the computer and other renovations.

CASE STUDY TASK 1

Using desktop publishing facilities, if possible, design a leaflet for local house-to-house distribution stating the new information.

CASE STUDY TASK 2

Steve is unclear about the implications of a partnership and the role of a sleeping partner. Explain these factors to him, in the form of a word processed report if possible; emphasise the importance of the Deed of Articles and what it should include, and give information about other possible business structures that Steve could form.

CASE STUDY TASK 3

What type of data information held by the shop could be computerised? Explain the type of programs that are available and how they could be used, giving examples of the types of information and processes relevant to the business. If possible, use the programs to give examples to demonstrate the facility, i.e. set up a data base of customers who have newspaper and magazine deliveries.

CASE STUDY TASK 4

Word process a letter to the Bank Manager. Steve has already forwarded him a cash flow forecast on a spreadsheet program. Steve now wants to let him have the forecast of potential sales and to demonstrate further the application and use of the computer.

Produce the figures set out below in 3 different forms of graphical presentation on a computer, if possible.

Potential sales from the beginning of the financial year 1 April 1997

		£000
Demand from construction workers:	April	5
	May	8
	June	8
	July	10
New residents move in:	August	20
	September	23
	October	25
	November	25
	December	35
	January	25
	February	35
	March	39

5.14 Human Resource Management

Whose team is it anyway?

The creation of 'teams' permeates all structures of society, but whether the team operates in the field of military strategy, sport or in business the objective is the same – the creation of synergy.

Successful teams are distinguished by three major characteristics: they have clearly defined objectives, firm roles for all members and they rely on trust. The traditional idea of a business operating like a 'symphony orchestra' has been overturned for the newer creative improvisation of a 'jazz band'. Forward thinking corporations are creating the business culture in which teams can flourish and in which individual talents are cultivated. A merging of minds and the gathering of consensus is seen as vital to any successful business philosophy.

Increasingly, network structures are being used to develop teamwork across the department divides. Networks are often set up to confront particular projects or issues where brainstorming and a marriage of ideas is sought. The result is that departments are not seen as isolated sections, but inter-related organisms. Modern management theorists like the behaviourists, shape the organisational structure into manageable divisions in which teams can function with flat hierarchical structures. The 'bottom up' approach is encouraged, based on the belief that the decision-making process should involve those who are likely to have to carry through the decisions – those at the bottom of the structure.

But do we sacrifice the vision of the individual for the compromise of the group? Are we achieving consensus with the loss of individuality? Or is the group strategy a way of making individuals feel they are part of the process when in reality the decisions have already been made? As we saw in Chapter 4.11, Sir Alec Issigonis, the designer of the Morris 1000 and the Mini car, once said 'nothing effective was ever designed by a team'. Certainly the major inventions and design breakthroughs have often been the creation of a single mind. In our obsession with group activity, are we in danger of losing clarity of vision and is consensus just compromise? Has the hidden agenda already been written?

In the age of competition, the team emphasis in business philosophy is being developed into the creative conflict of competing teams within an organisation. Bill Gates of Microsoft has a simple mission statement – 'to be first'. When Data General wanted to develop a new computer range to challenge Digital, they set up two teams with the same objective. One team won, the other lost.

Whatever we mean by 'teams', and however they operate, one thing seems certain: if individuals are to function effectively as a group they need some form of quasi-ethical ideal to provide cohesion and motivation to their operation. This has worked well in the past in the great Quaker business families like Cadbury, Rowntree and Kellogg's with their traditions rooted in religious values, whilst the success of the Japanese could be in part due to their call for a quasi-religious dedication to the firm. One thing is clear – to be a success the results of the team effort has to be greater than the sum of the parts. But the question still needs to be asked: are we really achieving synergy or just another form of symphony?

Source: National newspaper reports and author's research.

Preview

In this chapter we shall investigate the following key areas:

- the organisation
- the management function
- spans of control
- management theory
- communication systems and flows
- the personnel functions
- UK legislation
- the management of conflict
- the implications of the EU

What is human resource management?

Human resource management (HRM) is a modern term which has replaced the traditional and more narrowly based definition of personnel management Human resource management is about all factors which have an effect on the organisation's human resources unlike the 'personnel' function which has in some sectors in the past been viewed as the 'hiring and firing' and staff welfare department. Human resource management is about analysing everything which affects the efficiency of the workforce

Psychology is the basis of much human resource management theory. There is a need to know how individuals think in order to understand their motivations and aspirations. Much of the theory on effective management of human resources has come from American psychologists. The Japanese multinationals have also led the way with their less formal management structure involving the workforce at all

levels in the decision-making process. Whatever style of management the company has, it needs a supporting hierarchical structure and organisation with complementary spans of control and communication links.

The question of 'what makes a successful manager?' is one which has resulted in a mushrooming of business books. The difficulty is that what constitutes a 'good' or 'bad' manager is often a subjective response. If a business operates successfully it is put down to effective management; if it does not, the management is considered weak. The 'science of work' has been developed in an attempt to measure the characteristics of success. Human behaviour has been studied collectively and individually, in the hope of discovering some pattern or principles to explain success or failure. This is a 'soft' science, which attempts to measure the unmeasurable and predict the unpredictable. One thing that seems certain is that large groups of people, including those working in organisations, function more effectively if they share some common belief or ideal. So perhaps the role of human resource management is to provide the right environment and cohesion within which effective output can take place.

Human resource management in practice

The organisation and its structure

An organisation is a series of interrelated functions working together to achieve an output. The organisation may have a mission statement which sets out the business philosophy and clearly defined objectives will be set out in the strategic plan. One of the common criticisms employees make about the organisation is their inability to have an impact on the way it functions. To achieve job satisfaction the employee must understand where they fit into the organisational jigsaw and what part they play in helping to achieve the objectives set. An important part of the human resource management function is to establish individual role functions and place them in a wider context within the whole structure.

Organisations are complex institutions. The structure will have certain common aspects but the form will ultimately depend on the type of organisation and its objectives.

Box 14.1 shows an example of an organisation tree for a limited company.

The structure of an organisation determines how the activities are organised and carried out, the responsibilities involved and the line of authorisation or referral. There is nothing standard about the structure of a business. The larger a company grows, the more complex its organisation becomes. The structure will also depend upon the type of output. For example, a manufacturing company will have a production department whilst this would be irrelevant in the service sector. The organisational chart will be used by a company to show the line management and identify communication links.

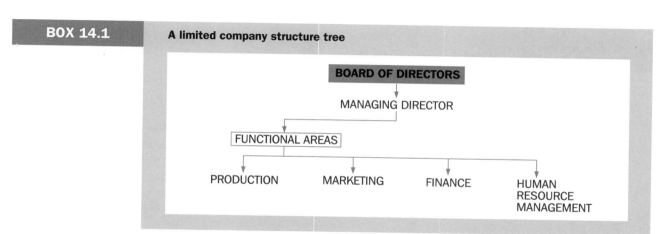

BOX 14.1   **A limited company structure tree**

The management function

Managers are the leaders of sub-sections of any business. As such, they are the central pivots of any organisation. A manager may have a specific departmental expertise but the management functions remain universal. For example, the manager of finance would need to be qualified in financial matters but the type of tasks he carries out would be much the same as the production manager, who would have a very different expertise. Look at Box 14.2.

Spans of control

The span of control describes the number of individuals who report back to a manager. The pyramid or organisational structure will have different shapes depending on the designated span of control. Box 14.3 shows two typical span of control structures found in the modern firm.

Management theory

The way in which management functions are applied will depend on the style of management. Management theorists attempt to assess what type of management is most effective for the company. There are three main

management theories – classical or traditional, the behaviourist and the systems approach.

Classical/traditional

In this style of management, responsibilities are grouped under departments or functional areas. The line management is clear, with each individual answerable to the next person in the line. Managers are often seen as remote individuals, a symbol of status, and the set-up is very formal. The traditional management view has often been based on the belief that the American psychologist Frederick Taylor put forward at the turn of the century. Taylor said that 'men are like machines and can be treated as such'. He believed that man was motivated by 'economic' needs and that financial reward was the only motivating factor. This led to the development of financial incentive payment systems and piecework (pay by product output) agreements. The belief was challenged in the 1920s by A. H. Maslow and Elton Mayo who developed the Behaviourist or Human Relations Theory, based on a belief that workers are motivated by 'social' needs and that they need to respect their place of work and to be appreciated and valued as individuals.

BOX 14.2	**Managers must be able to . . .**	
	Function	**Typical task**
	Forecast and plan	Look at targets, plan how they can be achieved and forecast outcomes
	Budget	Achieve objectives with limited financial resources
	Report	Process information on activities and outcomes
	Direct and delegate	Pass aspects of control to others as appropriate
	Organise	Ensure things happen effectively
	Liaise and coordinate	Link up with other functional areas
	Communicate	Convey information and influence opinions

BOX 14.3

Spans of control

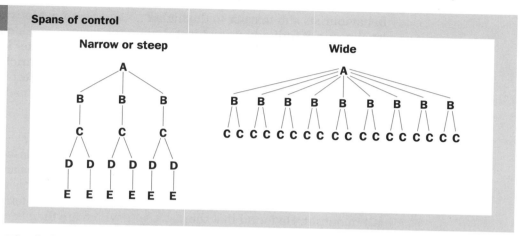

The behaviourist (or human relations) theory

This management theory concentrates on how individuals work together and their motivation. It looks at the aspirations of individuals and the informal pressures that affect their work. The firm is seen as a type of social structure. Behaviourists believe that it is possible to improve human resource output, motivating individuals by increasing their self-worth and making them feel that they are a vital part of the company. Workers are encouraged to become part of the decision-making process as they are the

ones who will be called on to activate any decisions made. They are also given the opportunity to become shareholders in the company. Group identity is an important aspect of this theory.

The behaviourist theory is based on the psychological approach to dealing with the motivations of individuals. The theory initially stemmed from American psychologist A. H. Maslow's belief that people have different levels of needs. Maslow developed what he called the hierarchy of needs demonstrated in Box 14.4.

BOX 14.4

Maslow's hierarchy of needs

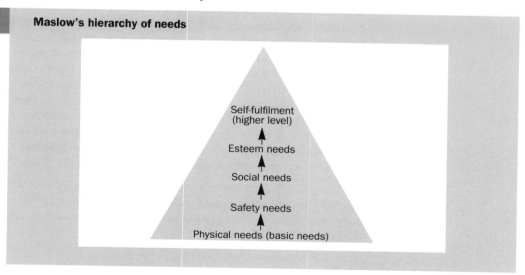

Behaviourists aim to cater to the higher level needs of individuals, not just giving financial rewards but encouraging self-fulfilment in the workplace.

Elton Mayo carried out a work study at the Hawthorn factory in Chicago. Output had fallen, so Mayo carried out an experiment to identify the factors that affect output. He put one section of workers into a group and varied the conditions to see if there was a rise or fall in output. He found that the cohesion which the group identity provided meant that even when conditions deteriorated output rose. Frederick Herzberg defined the concepts of 'maintenance' (or 'hygiene') and 'motivators'. Maintenance factors were seen as the essential ingredients for work to take place – i.e. good lighting and heating. Motivators were seen as the factors which could increase output and create greater job satisfaction. These were the 'job enrichment' factors and included prospects for promotion, increased responsibility and a sense of achievement.

Systems theory

This theory is based on the belief that all organisations are part of a universal natural and social structure. Businesses convert raw materials into products which are then converted back to waste materials. The complete cycle of events, and the implications, need to be considered. This is very much a 'green' approach to managing resources.

Box 14.5 shows how management theory has been adopted around the world.

BOX 14.5

Management theories in action

UK management has traditionally used the classical approach. It incorporates a formal style where the 'boss' is seen as a remote and often autocratic figure who makes the decisions. This style has been blamed for the adversarial approach in British businesses and the degree of conflict with the trade unions. The manager and the workers are seen on opposite sides of the fence with opposing interests rather than working together for the same objectives.

In contrast, the behaviourist approach is used by many Japanese and American companies. An 'open door' policy is applied so that you can go straight to the manager you want to see rather than to the next in the line. The behaviourist style has led to managers being involved at each stage of output, becoming involved in the production process and cutting across formal lines of control. The Japanese culture is based on consensus so workers are involved in the decision-making process. Strategically it states that if you involve the workforce in decision-making you carry them with you, and the implementation of decisions is not problematic but automatic. For a behaviourist approach to work the structure needs to be flexible to suit the management style. UK companies are now moving more towards this style of management, particularly under the influence of the Japanese multinational companies like Nissan and Honda.

The systems approach has had a higher profile with the interest in Green issues, but in practice it is more often a state of awareness than a company culture. However, The Body Shop has based its business philosophy on a 'systems culture; as has the Co-operative Bank (see Chapter 1.4).

Source: National newspaper reports and author's research.

Communication systems

Communication can be defined as the exchange of information, ideas and emotions. The key to human resource management is to understand that lack of communication leads to uncertainty and distrust. To be able to communicate, a common system of symbols, signs and behaviour is necessary. Whether the form of communication is verbal, written, numerical or even demonstrated through body language, the tone and emphasis are important if the right message is to be received. Studies show that managers spend 50 and 75% of their time communicating in meetings and discussions. Communication is not purely a way of passing information but a way of motivating individuals. Effective communication is at the heart of the management function.

Organisational communication

Effective communication is likely to be a difficult goal to achieve, and the larger the organisation the more complex the situation becomes.

Common problem areas are:

Structure

The structure of the organisation may not be conducive to effective communication: lines may be too long, links may be poor.

Language

The language used may be inappropriate for the purpose of conveying information: technical language used by one department or individual may not be understood by other areas of the organisation.

Media

The media used should be suited to the objective. Communications which need to be recorded are not appropriately carried out over the phone but should be written in the form of letters, memoranda, reports, minutes, etc.

Suppressed information

This situation can cause conflict when leaks occur, and increasingly modern organisations are moving towards more open policies.

Other obstacles

Other obstacles to effective communication can be the inadequacy of the communicator, and the prevailing attitudes of those with whom you are attempting to communicate. 'Transactional analysis' may also have an impact. This theory is used by psychologists to demonstrate that individuals react to each other in three types of ego states:

- Parent –
  The dominant approach, e.g. teacher/pupil
- Child –
  An immature or emotional manner
- Adult –
  A logical or rational way.

The theory states that individuals act in different ways depending on the situation and their objective. Yet in whatever mode people operate, it is only in the adult mode that they achieve 'real' communication.

Communication flows

Box 14.6 shows how the formal channels of communication in the organisation work.

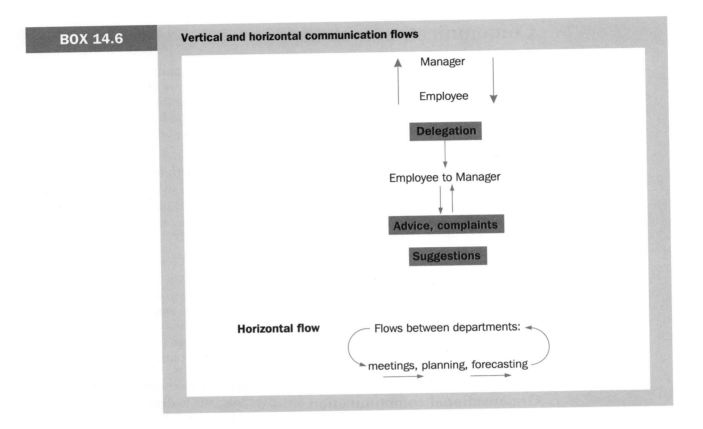

BOX 14.6 — Vertical and horizontal communication flows

These are the formal flows. The informal flows are the ones illustrated by behaviourists and can have a major impact on how the organisation really communicates and performs.

Structure and communication

In wide or horizontal spans of control communication links are relatively direct and distortions are less likely. In narrow or vertical spans the communication has further to travel, and distortions are more possible.

Communication networks

Networks show the pattern of transmission of information and feedback in the organisation.

Box 14.8 demonstrates a common situation.

In this example C is likely to be the most powerful communicator of information as C is the one who disseminates it to the widest number of people.

BOX 14.7   **Close and distant communication links**

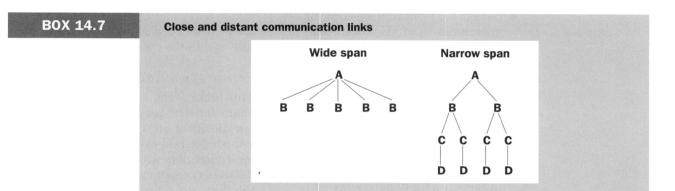

BOX 14.8   **The communication network**

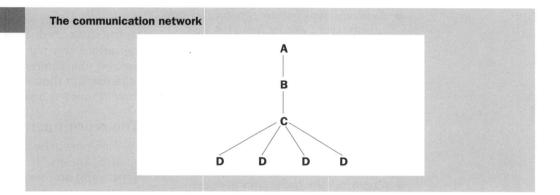

The value of the individual: the human resource at work

Although we call labour a factor of production in an economic model, in a management context people obviously cannot be treated like machines. This fact is central to management theory – how to get the best out of your workforce, the optimum utilisation of human resources. The behaviourists demonstrate that people need to feel valued and have worth in order to be motivated. They should also be fairly rewarded for effort and have a sound relationship within an enterprise.

The personnel function

The role of the personnel section will depend on the size of the company and its objectives. Large companies may separate personnel and training, but in smaller ones this will be a joint function.

Generally the personnel function:

- Provides human resources through recruitment and selection
- Provides advice for organisation managers and staff
- Maintains a reward and remuneration system
- Monitors employee/work relationships
- Creates training and development opportunities

- Sees that the workplace conforms to government and EU workplace legislation
- Maintains employee record systems
- Handles recruitment/termination
- Monitors industrial relations.

To enable the business to plan staffing levels and recruitment, personnel:

- Forecasts future staffing requirements in liaison with departments
- Looks at local and national labour markets to gauge potential supply
- Assesses gaps between potential supply and forecast demand, and makes some form of provision or plan
- Prepares job descriptions and job specifications
- Selects recruitment channels
- Organises pre-interview selection, processing application forms, CVs and references
- Arranges the interview process and job offer
- Organises the induction process
- Arranges training and development
- Issues contracts of employment
- Advises on key legal aspects.

We need to look at some of these aspects in more detail.

Job analysis

This is the process of analysing the job to decide its role and the context within which it operates. It is an important part of the recruitment and selection function as it sets the scene for the job description and job specification, and ultimately the selection of the most appropriate candidate.

Job description

This puts the job into context within the organisation. It lays out a broad description of the job, the skills required and duties involved. The employees' relationship to their line management is also established and their role within the organisation clarified.

Person specification

This looks at the essential and desirable characteristics required for the job. The job specification would include knowledge and experience, special aptitudes, disposition and the more detailed competence requirements for the post, and equal opportunities legislation must be adhered to in drawing up the job specification. The job specification is a guide to shortlisting candidates. The successful candidate may not have all of the desired characteristics but the organisation then needs to target their developmental needs.

The recruitment process

When a post arises in a company, it can be filled internally or externally depending on the candidates available and the requirements of the job.

Internal recruitment

- Advantages
  - A cheaper route
  - Faster
  - The candidate is known
  - It can provide motivation for staff
  - It is possible to re-deploy individuals
  - The company can avoid redundancies.

- Disadvantages
  - It can lead to discrimination
  - There can be a lack of 'new blood' into the organisation

External recruitment

If a business wants to recruit new staff externally, there are various routes to do this:

- Advertise – locally or nationally dependent upon the job and the market
- Employment agencies
- Job Centres
- The Careers Office
- Create links with educational institutions
- Head-hunting (making a direct bid for an individual who works elsewhere).

Steps in the recruitment process

Once the ad has been placed or internal announcement made, there are eight key stages:

- Dealing with applicants
- Request letter of application and CV
- Send out application forms
- Process returned information to parties involved
- Shortlist candidates
- Arrange interview panel
- Interview
- Appoint

The induction process

This is an important part of the selection process. It is a way of familiarising new employees with the workings of the business. Induction courses can be anything from a week to half a day, depending on the complexities of the business and the emphasis put on the process.

Remuneration

This is the monetary- and incentive-based reward for labour. Money is not the only motivator but it is clear that there needs to be an equitable system in place which attracts staff, rewards effort and is cost-effective.

Traditionally the term wages has been used to denote the payment to manual or weekly-paid workers, whilst the term salary has been used to describe the

payment to 'white collar' or monthly-paid staff. At the present time roles are becoming blurred and the distinction is less clear-cut.

The wage or salary is not the only form of rewards that a firm will offer. Many companies now offer performance-related bonuses. In a production post this may be linked to output; in a sales post there is usually a commission payment which is based on percentage of sales. There are also other perks which are related to performance. Some companies offer company cars to employees who reach a certain measurable level of achievement. Other common incentives are:

- Paid holidays
- Sickness benefit
- Nursery facilities
- Opportunities for overtime
- Profit-sharing and share options
- Bonus payments
- Pension schemes.

Payment levels are based on two main methods – time, or output, or a mixture of both:

- Attendance or time – pay for hours at work
- Output – pay for output achieved (piecework schemes)

Evaluation and appraisal

Evaluation

The evaluation process can be used as a mechanism for updating the job description. Increasingly the effort put in by individuals is being evaluated to achieve measurable performance indicators. The evaluation system needs to be a two-way process, with the individual analysing their own performance alongside the observations of their line manager. It is only through a system of evaluation and appraisal that rewards and incentives can be effectively applied.

Appraisal

The objective of the appraisal system is for staff to review their skills and performance in order to maximise their potential and in the process benefit the organisation.

The process is meant to be a two-way negotiation with the organisation setting up the procedure in order to prove that they are interested in the performance of the individual and enable them to establish staff training and development. Employees are encouraged to evaluate their own performance. The process is likely to include:

● Planning and negotiating the appraisal process
● Interview with line manager
● Setting evaluation criteria
● Observation of performance
● De-briefing – the way ahead.

Box 14.9 shows how the formal job analysis, job description and job specification work together to match employer and employee for the mutual satisfaction of both.

BOX 14.9

The job and the employee
● Job analysis – What is **wanted**
● Job description – Outline of **responsibilities**
                              and line management
● Job specification – **competences** needed
                              – Evaluate
                              – Appraise
                              – Train: career development

The training of staff

There should be an assessment of needs at all levels of staffing so that staff training programmes can be developed. Training can be set up either on the job, off the job or a combination of both. The training role of Personnel will be to liaise with external providers, e.g. colleges and other training providers, including government-sponsored organisations like the Training and Enterprise Councils (TECs). A system of on and off the job training has been achieved through programmes like the Youth Training Scheme (YTS), through which the government subsidises firms to train 16–18 year olds. Also the development of NVQs (National Vocational Qualifications) has meant that individuals can gain national accreditation for skills which are tested by nominated assessors in their place of work.

UK legislation

Trade Union Reform and Employment Rights Act

This Act has had quite a dramatic effect on employment contracts, necessitating employers to review the contracts they issue to staff. The Government produced a White Paper stating that all employees, working eight hours or more per week, should be given full written particulars about their job. Look at Box 14.10.

| BOX 14.10 | **Trade Union Reform and Employment Rights Act 1993** |

The following details must be set out in one document:

- Names of employer and employee
- Date employment began
- Date continuous employment began
- Scale or rate of remuneration or method of calculation
- Intervals at which remuneration is paid
- Terms and conditions relating to hours of work
- Holiday entitlement and pay
- Job title or description
- Place of work

The information below must be provided within the first eight weeks of employment:

- Information relating to injury and sick pay
- Details of pension schemes
- Period of notice to be given
- Period of the contract
- Any collective agreements
- Disciplinary and grievance procedures if there are more than 20 employees.

If workers are employed outside the UK for more than one month details on currency payments and any other benefits need to be specified.

Dismissal procedure

The Employment Protection (Consolidation) Act 1978 states that it is the right of every employee not to be dismissed unfairly.

A dismissal is when the contract is terminated by the employer with or without notice. Other contracts, such as fixed term ones, expire automatically at the date specified. Temporary contracts will expire when the employer gives notice. However, if the contract is for two years or more the employee has a statutory (legal) right to redundancy payment and to claim unfair dismissal.

There are generally three types of dismissal:

1. Dismissal – redundancy, end of fixed term contract, etc.
2. Summary dismissal (instant dismissal) – dismissal without notice which usually occurs after an employee has committed an act of gross misconduct.
3. Constructive dismissal – this is where the employee believes the employer is in breach of the contract of employment and the employee resigns (resignation under duress).

If an employee feels that they have been unfairly treated, they may appeal to an Industrial Tribunal.

Redundancy

There are certain procedures that an employer must follow in order to make an employee redundant. The procedures must conform to employment legislation such as that contained in the Trade Union and Labour Relations Act and the Trade Union Reform and Employment Rights Act 1993. They are mainly concerned with consulting the trade unions when such a situation occurs, with a view to reaching an agreement to eliminate or minimise the impact of redundancies. Employees who have completed two years' service and are over the age of 18 and under 65 are entitled to redundancy payments.

Collective bargaining

The purpose of a trade union is to establish collective bargaining. The trade union movement was established in the industrial revolution to protect the workforce against unscrupulous and powerful factory owners. Any employee is entitled to belong to a trade union but since the 1980s it is illegal to have a 'closed shop' (when everyone who works for a company 'must' be in the union). The trade unions have the power to push up their wage rates and achieve other concessions as long as demand for labour outstrips supply. However, in times of unemployment when the supply of labour is higher than the demand, unions are always likely to lose their power. The power of the unions in the UK was very strong in the post-war period up until the late 1970s. In the 1990s unions are looking to re-assess their role in relation to the company and with the increased role of the workforce in the decision-making process, and the development of employee share ownership, workers are not seen purely as being on the other side of the table, but as part of the human resource team. The unions are having to reassess their role within the company structure.

The management of conflict

In the 1920s Mary Parker Follett put forward her theories of constructive conflict in an essay of the same name. She felt that conflict should not be forcibly eliminated but that the energy which is produced should be managed and directed to positive use.

Follett said that there are three methods of resolving a situation arising from conflict:

- **Domination** – this leads to the destruction of an opponent until a new force evolves
- **Compromise** – this is usually only a temporary trade-off
- **Integration** – this is the only 'real' solution, because it can provide a common value system.

Although Follett's essay was written many years ago, the issue of constructive conflict is one which is popular amongst management theorists today. The increased use of team decision-making forums is a way of harnessing this type of energy. Constructive criticism can be of benefit to management rather than being seen as posing a threat.

Europe and the workplace

European employment legislation is far more favourable to the workforce than UK laws, which since 1979 have increasingly sought to limit the rights of the workers and deter trade union activity. So far the government has resisted complying with some of the EU legislation over workers' rights. However, part-time workers have, as a result of EU judgements, gained rights which include joining the company pension scheme and the right to redundancy payments.

EU directives

The Treaty of Rome (signed 25 March 1957) Article 119, sets out that each member state had to ensure that they applied the principle of equal pay for equal value. This ultimately led to the development of Directive 75117 Equal Pay for Men and Women and the EU Equal Pay Act 1970. The implications of this directive are important to businesses because it has called into question the rights of part-time employees. Part-time workers in the UK have to wait longer to get the same rights as full-time employees and some part-time staff never get the same rights. The majority of part-time workers tend to be female, and the British government has been challenged in the courts for breaking this directive by indirectly discriminating against women. The repercussions of this case could be far-reaching in terms of the cost of labour. As the profile of the UK workforce is increasingly part-time it is a ruling which will certainly have a major impact.

The Acquired Rights Directive 77/187 (14 February 1977), was translated by the British government into the 1981 regulations, The Transfer of Undertakings Protection of Employment (TUPE). The EU Directive was established to protect employee rights in any transfer of undertakings or businesses into new ownership. The UK law of TUPE interpreted this directive as 'only applying to commercial ventures'; they said that public sector organisations were not covered by the Directive as they were not commercial ventures. This had major implications for the government policy of privatisation and competitive tendering. Those utility areas which were market-tested in the private sector – for example, Local Authority services like refuse collection – believed that TUPE should apply to them and that they should have protection under the transfer of undertaking regulations. Three Eastbourne refuse collectors took the government to the European Court and the court ruled that the UK government's interpretation of the directive was wrong and that it should cover the transfer of any undertaking, not just commercial ones. This means that if a company is transferred from one ownership to another, the employees must also be transferred and their rights of employment remain. Redundancies cannot be made as a direct result of the transfer but it is possible for the new company to restructure for economic, technical or organisational reasons.

Directive 89/391 (12 June 1989) introduced measures to encourage improvements in the health and safety of workers at work. The UK already had its own health and safety regulations, but this directive is much wider and regulates over issues like the time spent on VDUs by operators, which had not been taken into account by the UK Act.

The Social Chapter

The UK has refused to sign the Social Chapter, which is a charter of what the Community States see as the fundamental social rights of workers. It was drawn up on 10 December 1989 and all governments except the UK signed. Some of the aspects covered in the charter are already covered by UK law but other aspects would mean an extensive re-write of UK employment law. Some of the issues covered by the directive are set out in Box 14.11.

Also, on 29 May 1990, a resolution was made by the European Court on the protection of the dignity of men and women at work, which has particular relevance to issues such as sexual harassment and victimisation.

The Social Chapter was a step too far for the British government; they felt that the European Union governments were (generally) more left-wing than themselves. The legislation they had achieved since 1979, particularly in the laws relating to controlling the activities of the trade union movement, they felt was being undermined. The prospect of moving back towards the more liberal and 'worker friendly' social policies prior to 1979 would be as if 'Thatcherism' had never happened.

BOX 14.11

The Social Chapter

There should be legislation in force to protect or ensure:
- Freedom of movement within the EC
- Employment and remuneration
- Improvement of living and working conditions
- Social protection (including regulations on social security benefit)
- Freedom of association and collective bargaining
- Vocational training
- Equal treatment for men and women
- Health protection and safety in the workplace
- Information, consultation and participation for workers
- Protection of children and adolescents
- Protection of elderly persons
- Protection of disabled persons.

Key employment documents

We will complete the chapter by detailing the content and layout of some of the main documents.

1 Job analysis
A job analysis is completed when any position becomes vacant.

The analysis will result in two key documents:
A. Job description
B. Person specification.

The analysis will determine the work which needs to be done and the skills and personal attributes necessary.

This analysis is then related to the overall effectiveness of the organisation.

2 Job description
Job title
(Position in company)

Responsible to]
(Line manager)

Purpose of the job
(Summary of the role)

Main responsibilities and duties
(Definition of responsibilities and
duties)

Job activities
(A more detailed description of the
actual duties and responsibilities
involved)

3 Person specification

This document defines the skills,
knowledge and experience necessary for
the job. It also describes other personal
attributes which are necessary.

The most commonly used specification
is Rodgers' 'Seven Point Plan'. This
defines human characteristics as
involving:

- Physical make-up
- Attainment
- General intelligence
- Special aptitude
- Interests
- Disposition
- Circumstances.

There are two levels of characteristics:
A. Essential
B. Desirable.

REVIEW

You should now be able to appreciate the importance of the human resource to the
business, and the legal framework governing the workplace.

REVIEW TASK

CRITICAL ANALYSIS
Management by infection?

Anita Roddick of The Body Shop believes in what she calls 'Management by Infection': a
belief that management is not really about controlling, organising and deciding things
but that it is about infecting people with energy, excitement and enthusiasm. This is
what gives the 'buzz' to the best organisations. Roddick seeks to enthuse her workforce
with a belief in her business philosophy. She believes that commitment to a moisturiser
is a ludicrous concept and that it is her Body Shop campaigns on projects like Trade not
Aid, and Social Rights and Environmental Issues, which makes the Body Shop a
company that deserves commitment.

Management by infection can ultimately be cheaper than management by control
because people do not need to be continually monitored if they believe in what they are
doing. Because of the need to choose the right people it is vital that the selection
process for the issuing of franchise agreements is effective. Roddick achieves this in
her inimitable way by designing a quirky questionnaire which asks questions like 'how
would you like to die'? She says she is not looking for management school clones who
have been conditioned to think profit and loss; she wants original thinkers, people with
charisma, passion and energy. Get the right people and the rules take care of
themselves.

So how far is this original thinking? The Japanese would call for a similar commitment
to the company but would not see the belief in the product as questionable. Perhaps
Roddick's originality is in her belief that business is part of the wider eco-system which

should give back some of which it takes out – a founder 'Greenist'. The Body Shop concept has many imitators including major retailers like Boots with their own 'Global' range. Roddick's critics might say that she exploits the issues as part of her own publicity campaign. Whatever the reality the commitment she engenders from her staff is replicated in the market place.

Source: National newspaper reports and author's research.

1. Make an analysis of Roddick's management beliefs, comparing them with the three main philosophies discussed in this chapter – classical, behaviourist and systems theories.
2. 'Roddick not only uses her campaigns to enthuse her staff but to capture her market.' Discuss.
3. How important is it that The Body Shop selects the right franchisees and workforce?
4. Design your own Body Shop questionnaire for potential franchisees (refer back to Chapters 1.4 and 3.10 on franchise agreements and statistical analysis).

TASK 14.1

PRACTICAL APPLICATION

Trade unions and the supply of labour

1 Draw a demand and supply curve for a perfectly competitive labour market – where a firm is in the position to employ as much labour as it wants at a ruling wage rate. Explain what type of supply this is called.
2 Analyse each of the statements below:
   A. Trade unions state that wage increases can be paid out of a firm's increase in profit.
   B. Workers may push up their wage levels at the cost of increasing the price of the goods, and in the process causing inflation.
   C. Wage increases cause unemployment.
   Use diagrams to illustrate your answers where possible.

QUESTIONS

Essay questions

1 'European Directives could ruin our ability to compete internationally by pushing up our labour costs.' Discuss this statement.

2 What difficulties might one experience in managing a rapidly growing firm?

3 Explain how effective teams can be in a management context for the modern firm.

EXAM QUESTIONS

 1 Read the extract below and answer all parts of the questions which follow.

Pioneers and prophets

A. H. Maslow was the author of one of the best-known theories about motivation to emerge this century. Maslow is best known for his notion of a hierarchy of needs that humans seek to satisfy. He argued that the lower needs dominate people's behaviour until they are fulfilled. Once a need is satisfied, people turn to the needs on the next step in the hierarchy.

Maslow's philosophy encouraged organisations to the view that individuals might be capable of taking on greater responsibility if they were given more varied work and lighter supervision.

But Maslow's theory did not escape criticism. An important omission, critics said, was that although basic needs become less important as they are attained, failure to meet them can create intense dissatisfaction. Maslow's work was, to some extent, superseded by Frederick Herzberg who distinguished between hygiene factors and motivating factors.

Although Maslow's theory is now seen as old fashioned, many still find it attractive. Most people feel incapable of achieving self-fulfilment while worrying about basic needs such as security and safety. The idea that a workforce can be motivated by notions such as autonomy, responsibility and the regard for others has also remained powerful.

Source: Adapted from Financial Times (November 1994).

    A. Distinguish between hygiene and motivating factors. How do they relate to the motivation of employees?

    B. Give two reasons why managers might **not** put motivation theory into practice in the workplace.

    C. Using your knowledge of Maslow's hierarchy of needs as a framework, compare the motivation of managers working for a large company with the motivation of those working for themselves.

    D. (i) Many companies today seem to have rejected Maslow's theory in favour of Human Resource Management. How might this approach lead to improved staff performance?

        (ii) For what reasons might Human Resource Management fail to achieve improved staff performance?   AEB November 1987

2 The following passage is adapted from an article which appeared in the *Administrator* (November 1985). Read the passage carefully and answer the questions which follow.

'Traditionally, employers have relied almost totally on a permanent workforce. As Britain adjusts to the recession, a new breed of managers is recognising the benefits which can be achieved with a flexible workforce. Temporary help is called upon as a 'solution' to staffing problems. It is no longer a case of ringing up the local 'agency' and asking for a clerk or secretary but rather of discussing a job description – the skills, experience and even personality attributes required for the proposed temporary position.

This new attitude has contributed significantly to the temporary help industry's doubling in size over the last 2 years. There are pointers that this explosive growth will continue. In America, where flexible working is a way of life, President Reagan was reported to be urging the US Civil Service to make an even greater use of temporary help.

In Britain, a survey conducted recently by the British Institute of Management found that the number of part-time workers has doubled in the past 20 years to 4.5 million, with the result that 1 in 5 British employees is now part-time. This number is expected to increase still further and the Government is being urged to introduce more flexible tax policies and benefits for part-time workers. The BIM also believes that part-time working should be a standard part of company employment policy .

While in London the overwhelming percentage of temps work either in secretarial or personal service occupations such as catering and cleaning, outside the capital agencies report greater variation. There is a small but increasing number of temporary workers with technical and professional expertise, as well as temporary managers who can be employed on short term contracts to oversee a project from inception to completion. As a response to these new trends the number of small specialist agencies is increasing. Perhaps in the future these may allow the currently self-employed freelancer to retain a degree of independence while enjoying some of the same benefits as permanent staff.

One thing is certain, we need to drastically rethink our views on temps and temping if we are to make the most of changing patterns in the world of work.'

A. Explain why a company would use a private employment agency to recruit temporary staff instead of using its own Personnel Department.
B. Management theory emphasises the importance to the individual employee of 'self-achievement' and 'responsibility'. Why then do so many people take casual work with temporary agencies?
C. The article suggests that many companies are now making increased use of temporary staff:
  (i) What benefits does the use of temporary staff offer a company?
  (ii) What are the problems which a firm faces when employing temporary staff?

AEB November 1987

3 Read the information and answer the questions which follow.

A job description

Job Title: Office Services Supervisor.

Department: Administration.

Main purpose of job: To ensure the provision of efficient typing, reprographic and switchboard services to company personnel.

Scope of job: Responsible to: administration manager.
Responsible for: five staff: equipment to value of £300 000.

Main duties:

1. To allocate suitable personnel to switchboard, telex, offset printer and photocopiers, as required.

2. To ensure the provision and maintenance of an accurate and efficient typing and reprographic service.

4. To collate control information on departmental costs, etc.

5. To order stationery, reprographic chemicals and other materials, recording use and maintaining suitable stock levels.

6. To train and assist in selection of new staff.

Source: Adapted from ACAS, Recruitment and Selection, ACAS.

A job description

Seven-Point Plan

Essential	Desirable
Physical make-up	
Good health record. Acceptable bearing and speech.	Pleasant appearance, bearing and speech.
Attainments	
GCSE English language. Ability to type, and to operate office machines. Experience of general office work.	GCSE maths or equivalent. RSA II typing. Experience of using simple statistical information and experience of staff supervision.
General Intelligence	
Above average.	
Special aptitudes	
Reasonable manual dexterity. Facility with figures.	
Interests	Social activities.
Disposition	
Persuasive and influential. Self-reliant.	Good degree of acceptability, dependability and self-reliance. Steady under pressure.
Circumstances	
No special circumstances.	

A. Using examples given in the data, distinguish between a Job Description and a Job Specification.

B. How might a firm recruit for this post?

C. What factors might be important in the conduct of an interview?

D. The firm has appointed someone to fill the post without interview. What information might they have used in making their selection?

E. Outline **four** pieces of legislation that might be taken into account during the recruitment and selection process.

AEB June 1991

4 Referring to appropriate motivational theories, explain the behaviour of the workforce in the Integrated case study for Section 4.

Falcon cars: 2

The Managing Director has today e-mailed the following to all functional heads and union reps in the company.

> MEMORANDUM
> **FROM**:   The Manager   Ref.
> **TO**:   The Production Manager   DATE . . . .

RE: Article, 'Whose team is it anyway?'

I attach a copy of an article I read last week on the topic of teamwork. I think, in terms of our present expansion programme, it raises some interesting issues.

Certainly the scale of our operation will mean that we will need to review our management practices to achieve maximum output and cooperation from our staff. History has shown, as I am sure we are all aware, that the move from job production to flow production in manufacturing can lead to a disenfranchised workforce. I do not want this to happen at Falcon as we have very rightly been proud of our excellent staff relations.

It is interesting that the original Falcon car model was, as you know, designed by a very talented individual, and as we have decided to create a design team for the new model we must ensure that the outcome is not the product of compromise but the achievement of positive group dynamics.

I set out below an action plan which I would like you to achieve within the next three weeks.

Action plan

● **Personnel Manager**
  Please let me have a résumé of the behaviourist approach to managing staff and some ideas as to how we could implement this ethos at Falcon.
● **Union representative**
  Please could you list any areas of concern you have over our expansion programme and draw up an agenda for a meeting so we can discuss your concerns.
● **Production Manager**
  With our plans to implement JIT shortly, can you draw up plans for an effective computer integrated management strategy.
● **Design team**
  Could you please give me your thoughts on the dangers stipulated in the article. I know you are at present working on the new design – do you see a role for competing team designs? How effective are the computerised design packages? A report, please.

Integrated case study for Section 5: Communico Construction

You are a newly appointed Office Administrator for Communico Construction Company.

The following information about the company has been given to you as part of your induction process.

Background business information	Induction information
	Communico Construction was set up 7 years ago by James Alderson and his friend Peter Tinsell. It was established as a partnership. However the partnership structure did not work well and James Alderson bought his partner out.
(This worked much more effectively but the company suffered from lack of capitalisation)	He then set up as a sole trader.
(Initially there were problems for the first few months. His creditors did not like supplying goods. They had originally, whilst he was a sole trader, known that his own personal assets could be seized if he got into financial difficulty, whereas when he became a limited company, he would have limited liability)	James decided to form a limited company one year ago.

Type of operation

The company functions as a civil engineering contractor to:

A.   British Telecom
B.   Cable TV

British Telecom
They contract out, using indirect labour, for much of their cable work. They contract their work out to a contract company but this work is often 'sub-contracted out' again to another company.

This is the case with Communico:

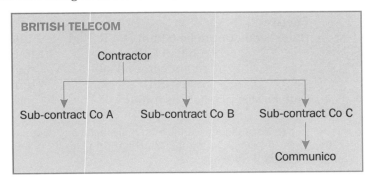

The company that Communico sub-contract for is largely a management company. They are not involved in production but only in issuing contracts and monitoring sub-contractors to do the work.

All 'utilities' (water, gas, electricity, telecommunications) need licences to place cables, ducts, pipes, etc. in the ground. These licences are granted by the government Department of Trade and Industry (DTI).

Cable TV
Cable TV companies are granted licences by the government to provide cable TV in certain areas. These licences are issued as franchise agreements and operate in the same way as any franchise contract.

Company		Area
Nynex	–	Surrey
	–	West Sussex
	–	Manchester
Eurobell	–	Crawley
	–	Exeter

Communico operate as a contractor laying ducts for one of these companies.

An invitation to tender for telecommunications ductwork to be installed from Teletown to Chat City

The tender is to be compiled from the schedule of work:

Specification
Carriageway ducts to be laid at 600mm of depth
Footway ducts to be laid at 450mm of depth
Soft surface ducts to be laid at 450mm of depth

Carriageway
Reinstatement* to be 100mm Hot Rolled Asphalt (HRA) on 320mm ground sub-base (GSB)

Footway
Reinstatement to be 60mm Hot Rolled Asphalt (HRA) on 100mm ground sub-base (GSB)
Soft surface reinstate as found.

Schedule of work
Average cost to excavate trench, cart away spoil and backfill:

- Carriageway – £25 per metre
- Footway – £11 per metre
- Soft surface – £9 per metre

This cost includes the use of plant and equipment to execute the work.

Average cost of materials:
Hot rolled asphalt
£42 per tonne
Ground sub-base
£4.50 per tonne

Guidelines:
1 tonne HRA = 20m carriageway
1 tonne HRA = 30m footway
1 tonne GSB = 6m carriageway
1 tonne GSB = 16m footway

*Reinstatement – once a hole has been excavated to lay ducting, it must be refilled with strengthening materials (ground sub-base) and covered with 'hot rolled asphalt'/tarmac.

Street Authority Sunny County Council Thoroughfare (Road name)	Duct size	Total length	Carriageway	Footway surface	Soft
Tower Road	100mm	95m	15m	36m	44m
George Street	100mm	13m	5m	8m	
Goose Lane	100mm	2015m	1382m		633m
Union Road	100mm	86m		71m	15m
High Street	100mm	15m	11m	4m	

Ducts supplied by the telecommunications company. Contractors to supply all other plant (e.g. lorries, diggers, road works guarding, barriers and road signs) and materials.

INTEGRATED CASE STUDY TASK
Draw up a tender document showing full broken down costs (use a spreadsheet if possible).

ACTIVE LEARNING TASK
1

> **VACANCY**
> Administrator required for small but busy company. The suitable person will be required to set up and run computerised systems of financial control and customer record-keeping. A sound knowledge and understanding of spreadsheet, database and word processing packages essential.

In groups or individually:
A. Draw up the relevant personnel documents which would be needed to support the post.
B. Write your own CV and application letter.
C. In groups, conduct interviews for the above post, taking the roles of interviewer, interviewee, and other member(s) of the interviewing panel.
2 Explain the process of:
A. Setting up a database for a company like that in 1 above.
B. Setting up a communications system for the company.
C. Carrying out recruitment for the vacancy in 1.
D. Carrying out an appraisal for the candidate chosen for the vacancy, at the end of 3 months' employment with the company.
E. Conforming, as an employer in the company, to the requirements of the Trade Union Reform and Employment Rights Act (TURERA) 1993.
3 Analyse and evaluate:
A. The use of spreadsheets as a method of financial control.

B. The effectiveness of the Data Protection Act 1984 in protecting the individual from abuse of personal data.

C. The classical and traditional styles of management in the workplace.

D. The role of human resources management (HRM) as a strategy for the business.

E. The impact of the EU social legislation on the employee in the workplace.

QUESTIONS

Essay questions

1 Read the article below and answer the questions which follow.

Unionised firms consult more widely

Employees in unionised companies are consulted on a wider range of issues than in those without unions, according to an ACAS report.

The survey of 600 private sector firms shows that employee consultation in unionised workplaces adds to collective bargaining rather than supplanting it. Unionised workplaces have also been more likely to witness an increase in the scope of consultation over the last 3 years.

However, managers at many companies, both union and non-union, told researchers that they consulted workers on a growing range of issues to do with running the business.

'It appears that the general process of consultation may have become more important in their thinking and approach to employee relations in recent years', says the report.

Topping the list of companies with the most extensive range of issues for consultation were the British bases of foreign firms, mostly European. This bears out the view that an employer from a country with a well-established statutory framework for consultation will be more likely to have absorbed the culture of consultation.

The survey explores the myth of the non-unionised inward investor riding roughshod over the British workforce.

The report makes it clear that, although British management is doing a great deal more in the way of communicating with employees, it is clearly being outstripped in most respects by foreign firms operating in this country with a more open and participative management approach. AEB June 1993

The report says that a majority of establishments, not all of the small employers, had developed no formal or regular means of actively seeking the views of their employees.

Source: Adapted from Personnel Management Plus (March 1991).

A. Distinguish between 'employee consultation' and 'collective bargaining' (lines 3–4).

B. What might make consultation between managers and employees in *unionised* workplaces more likely than in non-unionised workplaces?

C. Explain four benefits managers might hope to gain by adopting a 'more open and participative management approach' (last line of article).

D. 'Although British management is doing a great deal more in the way of communicating with employees, it is clearly being outstripped in most respects by foreign firms. . .' (lines 21–3).

Discuss the business implications of this statement for British firms. (AEB June 93)

2 Analyse the essential principles of a good training programme.

3 The head of a school/college will be interviewing a short-list of three candidates for the post of A-level business studies teacher. Candidate **A** is professionally well qualified, has worked in industry but has no teaching experience. Candidate **B** is moderately qualified and has two years' successful teaching experience. Candidate **C** has just qualified as a teacher of business studies. Suggest factors which might influence the head's choice and consider:

A. how the head might brief him/herself for the interviews;

B. the questions s/he might ask each candidate;

C. The information s/he might seek before making the decision. (CLES)

Section 6
The Business and the Wider World

6.15 Government and the Economy

Castles in the air

The credit boom of the 1980s has left many casualties. Loose lending, or easy credit, meant that people consumed, without thought of cost. Much of the available credit went into the housing market. In 1979 6 million housebuyers had mortgages, by 1990 9.3 million were paying mortgages with 12% borrowing 3 times their annual income.

The belief that property was an asset that could only increase in value was shattered by 1990. Soaring interest rates and high unemployment had burst the bubble. The term 'negative equity' (the value of the mortgage outstanding being higher than the current market value of the property) was born.

The cost of the housing boom to the economy and businesses should not be underestimated. Expectations of profit meant that private capital flowed into property, which otherwise could have been invested in industry.

The UK is peculiar to EU economies in having so much wealth tied up in property. The more successful economies like Germany are at the bottom of the home ownership league with only 40% of the population owning property. Statistics show that the high flying economies prefer to encourage a rented sector. The poorer performing economies tend to be higher up the league table with the UK figure at 67% and Eire 80%.

The Government encouraged the property boom as part of its political and economic philosophy but the cost has been substantial. Tax relief given to mortgage holders formed lost revenue, whilst their encouragement of the sale of council housing at approximately 70% less than the market value resulted in a £14 billion loss. Councils were forced to sell off their housing stock or incur financial penalties and now have difficulty housing the homeless.

When the true market value of property within a wide economic context was realised, prices tumbled. The rush for ownership could not be reversed. The implications for the flexibility of the labour market were disastrous, with workers stuck in houses they could neither sell nor afford. The result has been massive re-possession rates, reaching a peak of 100 000 in 1991, and falling to 49 410 in 1995.

But where are the homeless to live? We now see another entrepreneurial opportunity arising – that of the landlord. As the Government are forced to pay private landlords to house the homeless, many of whom were players in the property boom, they may lament the cost of their housing policy.

Source: National newspaper reports and author's research.

Preview

In this chapter we shall investigate the following key areas:

- the business environment
- the economic problem
- micro- and macroeconomics
- government revenue and expenditure
- the measurement of income and expenditure flows
- the monetary system and the role of the Bank of England
- Government economic objectives

Pressures on the business

Businesses are part of the wider social and economic environment and are therefore affected by decisions and pressures by national and international governments, which are applied either directly or indirectly. These pressures and decisions can be legal, economic, social or even political.

Governments may have a policy of linking their decision-making to the needs of the business world or they may adopt a 'hands off' approach, leaving businesses to 'sink or swim' in the market place. Now that the UK is part of the EU, it has become an even more complex environment for business operation. The EU has an important role in the decision-making of the UK Government on matters affecting laws, social policy and the economy. The UK Government is only partly conceding to collective European pressures. On economic policy, much of Europe is heading towards a single currency, but the UK is reluctant to commit itself to this objective.

The demand for goods and services is related to the individual's income, which in turn is influenced by the operation of the economy. The level of expenditure has a direct impact on the rate of inflation, or the rate at which prices rise, which in turn will affect the Government's policy on interest rates, or the price of money. The interest rate policy will have an impact on the level of exchange rates. These are major concerns to a business. This Government has not had an exchange rate policy except when, under Chancellor Lawson, the pound 'shadowed' the German Deutsche Mark.

The business environment

Businesses operate within a complex structure of external controls and forces (see Box 15.1). The state of the economy will have a direct impact on the demand for their products, but will also have an affect on costs. National Government and EU legislation and policies will direct the decision-making process:

BOX 15.1 **The pressures on the business – Controls**

Local authority	Government/European Community
Examples include:	Examples include:
Business rates	Laws and regulations
Planning regulations	Social policy
Environmental controls	Regional policy
Health and safety	Economic policy
Food and hygiene	Environmental policy
Control of trading licences	International trade objectives
	Revenue and expenditure budgeting

The basic economic problem

We have already looked at economics in previous sections covering types of production. We know that there would be no economics if there were enough resources to satisfy all our needs. Businesses, individuals and Governments need to know their economic resources in order to decide how to allocate them (see Box 15.2). This decision should be based on the opportunity cost of each choice.

Whether the entrepreneur or the government makes the production decision will depend on the type of economy in operation. In a free market, a firm's decision to produce will normally depend on demand. There are many factors which will influence the level and type of demand, some of which we have already looked at in Marketing and Operations Management. However, the Government will also provide a significant force and will need to monitor the total levels of demand in the whole economy from a macro-economic viewpoint:

Macroeconomics = the study of the whole economy.

A macroeconomic model is one which looks at the whole economy and deals with the interrelationships of all its components.

BOX 15.2 **The allocation of national resources**

```
                RESOURCES
                  ╱ │ ╲
                 ╱  ▼  ╲
            ◄──╱       ╲──►
   LAND      LABOUR      CAPITAL
```

ENTREPRENEUR OR GOVERNMENT
LINK TOGETHER RESOURCES FOR
PRODUCTION CHOICE (WHAT TO PRODUCE)
BASED ON (OPPORTUNITY COST)
= OUTPUT

Microeconomics = the study of the components or firms which make up the whole economy.

A microeconomic model analyses the spending decisions of individuals or groups within society. For a government to attempt to control or manipulate demand or expenditure, it needs to analyse the whole economy.

Government revenue and expenditure

Governments need income to pay for their expenditure. A large portion of this income comes from taxation. There are two main categories of taxation, direct and indirect. Direct taxation is a tax which is levied directly on income. Examples of direct tax are income tax, and corporation tax (a tax on company profits).

Indirect taxation is a tax levied on spending which the seller of the good is liable to pay by law. Examples of this type of tax are VAT, Customs and Excise duties and vehicle licences. The seller will usually pass the tax onto the purchaser by raising the price of the good. However, some taxes on expenditure, for example stamp duty, which is paid when purchasing property, are direct taxes on expenditure.

The PSBR

The Public Sector Borrowing Requirement (PSBR) is the annual difference between public sector income and expenditure, which has to be funded by Government borrowing. In the post-war era governments were constantly funding a Public Sector Deficit (spending more than they were earning). Throughout the 1980s the UK Government earned more than it spent on the public sector, mainly through selling off nationalised industries. Any surplus forms the PSDR (Public Sector Debt Repayment) and allows some of the accumulated National Debt to be repaid. If the Government borrows money to fund the PSBR, this can have what is called a crowding out effect on private sector borrowing – in other words the Government creates a demand for funds by issuing, for example, gilt edged stock which competes with the private sector for funds. Interest rates are then likely to increase.

Measuring income and expenditure

A business will need to know the potential demand for its goods and services. The Government will want to know the level of expenditure in the economy so it can forecast its own expenditure and resources and plan its economic policy. Look at Box 15.3.

In a very simple flow, workers earn income and then spend on consumption which flows back to firms. In reality not all income is spent on consumption and not all income comes directly from firms. Look at Box 15.4.

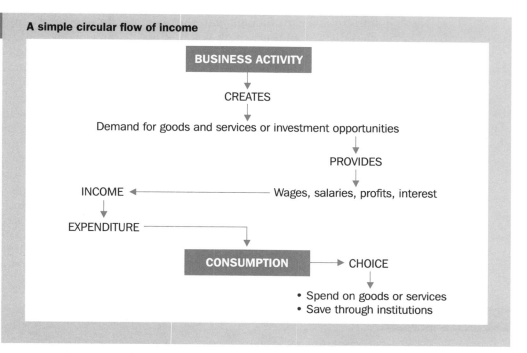

BOX 15.3 **A simple circular flow of income**

BUSINESS ACTIVITY

↓ CREATES

Demand for goods and services or investment opportunities

↓ PROVIDES

INCOME ← Wages, salaries, profits, interest

↓

EXPENDITURE ——

CONSUMPTION → CHOICE

↓

- Spend on goods or services
- Save through institutions

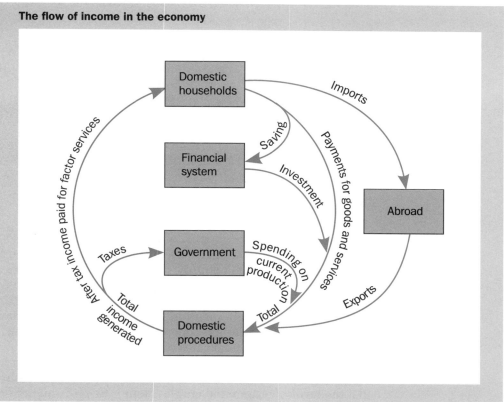

BOX 15.4 **The flow of income in the economy**

Domestic households

Imports

Saving

Payments for goods and services

Financial system

Investment

Abroad

After tax income paid for factor services

Taxes

Government

Spending on current production

Exports

Total income generated

Total

Domestic procedures

Individuals earn income, and they can then dispose of that which is left after their statutory deductions are taken away (this would be seen by Government as an outflow):

Gross income *less* deductions = disposable income

The income that is left after the Government statutory deductions have been extracted then forms potential consumer expenditure, which in turn can form demand. An individual may not spend all of their disposable income on goods or services they may spend the income on imports in which case the funds would flow out of the circular flow. They could save some of that income, in which case it could also flow out of the income circular flow.

On the other hand there are injections into the circular flow of income. Exported goods earn income into the circular flow. Some of the savings which have flowed out may be invested back into business or Government activity, in which case this will be a flow back into the circular flow. Much of Government expenditure comes back into the circular flow as potential consumer expenditure. Box 15.5 summarises all this.

BOX 15.5	**Leakages and injections in the circular flow of income**

THE INDIVIDUAL EARNS INCOME (FACTOR OF PRODUCTION)

SPENDS INCOME (CONSUMER)

THE BUSINESS	–	PAYS EXPENDITURE TO THE INDIVIDUAL AS A FACTOR OF PRODUCTION AND EARNS INCOME FROM THE INDIVIDUAL AS CONSUMERS
AN INJECTION	–	THIS IS MONEY WHICH COMES INTO THE CIRCULAR FLOW
A LEAKAGE	–	THIS IS MONEY WHICH GOES OUT OF THE CIRCULAR FLOW.

Aggregate demand and supply

The most influential economist of the 1930s was John Maynard Keynes. He argued that demand and supply, on a macroeconomics level, could be 'managed' by the Government. He was writing during the high unemployment period of the 1930s, and his theories overturned the traditional rules of economics and initiated the birth of macroeconomics. Keynes demonstrated that the level of output and employment depended upon aggregate demand (total demand) for goods and services in the economy and aggregate supply (total supply) of goods and services in the economy, and that these could reach equilibrium at levels well away from full employment.

A macroeconomic supply curve will slope upwards from the bottom left towards higher prices. The aggregate demand curve will slope downwards from the left because as prices fall demand will increase. The level of national income is where *AS* and *AD* meet: see Box 15.6.

The difference between equilibrium national income and the full employment level illustrated is the extent to which it is possible to increase national income to employ resources.

The gap between national income and full employment is called the deflationary gap (see Box 15.6).

If there is a situation where all resources are fully employed, then an increase in aggregate demand could put pressure on prices. This is an inflationary gap (see Box 15.7). This means that prices will rise without an increase in output.

BOX 15.6

National income and the deflationary gap

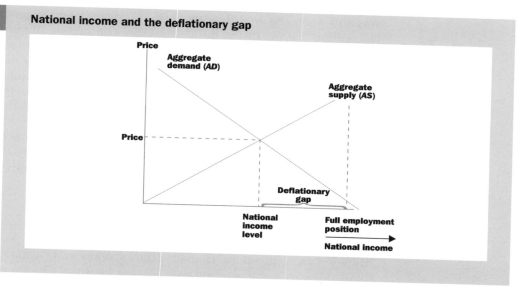

BOX 15.7

National income and the inflationary gap

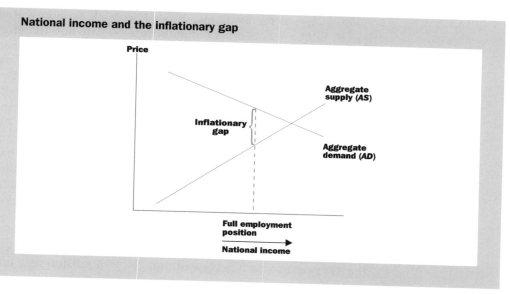

The multiplier

Injections into economic systems will lead to an increase in income but the size of the increase can be much greater than the initial injection. One component of Keynesian theory was the demonstration of this multiplier effect.

If a man's income increased by £100 and his marginal propensity to consume was 80% then £80 would be spent. If we assume that the rest of the community have an 80% propensity to consume then the £80 would generate a further £64 and so on. . . This can carry on until the £100 has become £500 and the multiplier is therefore 5, as the sum of the geometric series.

This could be done by formula:

The multiplier is

$$\frac{1}{MPS} \text{ or } \frac{1}{1 - (MPC)} \text{ or } \frac{1}{leakages}$$

In our example, the formula would be

$$\frac{1}{0.2} \text{ or } \frac{1}{1 - 0.8} = 5$$

Keynes emphasised the investment multiplier and saw the collapse in investment as having a multiple contraction in output whilst the national income multiplier showed the multiple effects on demand and hence the creation of jobs. Any multiplier effect would obviously be diminished by withdrawals from the circular flow.

The circular flow is a measure of value and the measure of value we use in modern economies is money.

The monetary system

'Money is as money does' is a very true cliché. Money is only as good as what it buys. Barter is a way of facilitating trade when money is not available, only goods. But barter, as early communities discovered, only works if there is a coincidence of wants. Many early societies used shells, minerals, and precious metals as a means of exchanging value.

Qualities of money

For a monetary system to work the money used must provide six things (see Box 15.8).

The role of the Bank of England

The Bank of England was established in the 17th century to fund one of the many wars against France. It was set up by Royal Charter and plays a predominant role in the control of the UK economy. It was nationalised in 1946 and therefore became publicly owned. It has many functions, a major one being the Government's director for the control of the economy. Many believe that the Bank's ability to achieve its role as the central bank is jeopardised by its lack of independence from the Government. The German Central Bank, the Bundesbank, functions in an independent role, which may be the role that the Bank of England will take on in the future.

Issue of bank notes

A printing works in Essex prints around 5 million new notes a day and destroys

The qualities of money
- **Durability** – so that value can be stored and used over a long period of time the currency must be durable. Over the past decade we have seen the reduction in use of paper money, which has a much shorter life – the £5 note is now estimated to have only a 12 month lifespan.
- **Portability** – Currency must be easy to carry.
- **Acceptability** – The currency must be accepted not only nationally but internationally.
- **Divisibility** – To provide flexibility the currency must be easily broken down into smaller units.
- **Rarity** – To keep the value stable there must not be too much money printed or minted.
- **Recognisablity** – there must be a set standard of size, shape and weight.

roughly the same amount. The new notes are put into circulation by the High Street banks on behalf of the Bank of England.

Public sector bank

The Bank of England holds accounts for Government departments and controls all the revenue and expenditure which result from public sector activity

Supervision of the banking system

A sound banking system is very important to the stability of the UK economy and how it is perceived in the world. A function of the Bank of England is to supervise the banks operating in the UK and ensure that depositors' money is not at risk. The Bank of England was much criticised in the 1980s for the Johnson Matthey controversy and in the 1990s for the BCCI fiasco. Whilst Johnson Matthey's gold bullion dealing seems to have been fairly well run, its banking arm would have gone bust in the Autumn of 1984 if the Bank of England had not taken it over. Market theory says that inefficient firms should cease to operate, but when a bank is involved the whole banking system could be undermined in a very complex monetary tangle. Questions were asked about why the Bank of

England had not spotted the problems during the normal course of supervision, but the BCCI collapse showed that with so many changes taking place in the City, the Bank of England is coming under increasing pressure: it is always difficult for the gamekeeper to keep up with the poacher.

Holding foreign exchange

The Bank holds the nation's gold reserves and also its foreign currency. If foreign goods are purchased foreign currency is needed for payment. This currency can be obtained for goods or simply for holidays abroad through the High Street Banks who will obtain this currency from the Bank of England. The Exchange Equalisation Account (EEA) is a foreign currency reserve account held at the Bank of England and used to control the level of the pound on the international exchange markets. If the value of the pound is falling, the account can be used to shore up its value by purchasing pounds and creating demand.

Borrowing funds for the government

The Government needs to raise finances for its spending and it does this through the Bank of England. The Bank of

England issues gilt-edged stock and sells it to the public via the Stock Exchange. These stocks earn interest and the buyer can cash them after a certain date. Other forms of Government revenue raising are Premium Bonds (which also allow the holder to take part in a nation-wide draw with the potential to win large sums of money) and National Savings Certificates which are available at local Post Offices.

When the Bank raises funds for the Government it is in direct competition with not only other financial institutions competing for investors' funds but also businesses. This can have the effect of pushing up interest rates.

The bankers' bank

All of the British banks have to hold an account at the Bank of England. This provides a mechanism for the cheque clearing system whereby all cheques can be cleared and accounts can be balanced at the Bank of England.

Control of the money supply

The fact that the banks have to hold accounts at the Bank of England also enables the Government through the Bank to expand or contract the money supply. The central bank can call in extra deposits to be held in the banks' accounts at the Bank of England. Calling in or releasing funds will have a direct impact on the money supply and the economy, Also each bank is directed to hold a proportion of its funds in liquid assets so the amount available for loans can expand or contract depending on what level of liquidity is called for by the Central Bank. Look at Box 15.9.

Control of interest rates

The Bank of England can also attempt to control the levels of interest rates in the economy.

Interest is the payment for money: it is either paid or earned, depending on whether money is borrowed or lent. The general level of interest rates can influence whether individuals or firms spend or save. If interest rates are high it may be attractive for individuals to save their money in order to earn higher interest rates. Therefore consumption may decrease. If interest rates are lower it is less favourable to save because the interest rates are not as conducive to higher earnings from investment. For businesses higher interest rates will mean a higher cost as they seek funds for capital investment. Higher interest rates may also be detrimental to trade as they encourage individuals to save

BOX 15.9	The Bank of England and the money supply

CUT AMOUNT HELD IN BANK
OF ENGLAND — EXPAND AMOUNT HELD IN
BANKS FOR LENDING OUT

INCREASE BALANCE HELD IN BANK
OF ENGLAND — DRAW IN FUNDS FROM THE
BANKS LEAVING LESS
LIQUIDITY AND HENCE
LESS AVAILABLE FOR
LENDING OUT

rather than consume, so demand may diminish. So what makes interest rates higher or lower?

There is not just one rate of interest in the economy but a variety of rates, depending on the source, the time, risk factors and the institutional need for funds. However, interest rates are a vital economic management tool for the Chancellor and are therefore monitored and controlled on the Government's behalf by the Bank of England. The Bank of England will attempt to control interest rates through its role as the 'lender of last resort'.

If the banking system is short of liquidity it is the Bank of England that supplies funds and becomes the 'lender of last resort'. However the central bank reserves the right to dictate the interest rate at which it supplies these funds. This finance is only available through the Discount market. This market comprises the 9 London Discount Houses who form the primary market in short-term securities for the banking sector and the Government. If the Bank of England squeezes the banks, they in turn will go to the discount market and recall short-term loans. The discount houses will go to the Bank of England which will set the 'base' interest rate at which it will lend funds to the discount houses. The discount houses use the funds from commercial banks to buy commercial and Treasury bills.

Bills of exchange, or commercial bills, are used by businesses like a cheque. They form a type of delayed payment whereby the business that is owed the money holds the bill. If they want the funds before the due date they can sell the bill to the discount houses at a discounted rate, the discounted rate being less than the face value. The difference is the income for the discount house, or the price of discounting. The discount houses also agree to 'cover the tender' for the Bank of England issue of Government Treasury bills. The Government can use the Treasury bills as another way of controlling the money supply. By issuing Treasury bills the discount houses buy the bills and their funds, or liquidity, are then cut. They, in turn, will recall funds from the commercial banks and so cut the money supply.

Therefore the Government through the Bank of England can control the money supply by five means, as Box 15.10 shows.

Measuring the money supply

Because money is constantly flowing it is hard to measure its value at any one time. In fact many systems which were set up to try and do this have been abandoned. To measure money is really to measure potential spending power in the economy, which is useful information to the Government and business. For a monetarist government

---

BOX 15.10

Controlling the money supply

- Calling in or decreasing the amount held by banks at the Bank of England.
- Controlling the rate of interest through the discount houses, which in turn makes the attraction to save or spend more acute.
- Increasing the liquidity ratio held by the banks.
- Selling gilts and bonds on the open market.
- Controlling the PSBR.

this is particularly important, but can it be done effectively? Monetarists hold that inflation is caused by the money supply growing too much and pushing up prices, which in turn calls for demands for pay increases to meet the new price level, which in turn pushes up prices further: an inflationary spiral.

Monetarists believe that this situation can be cured by reducing the supply of money in the economy. In order to be able to reduce the level of money in the economy it is necessary to be able to measure the money supply. The 'monetarist' Government of 1979 used two main measures of the money supply, M0 and £M3 (sterling M3). Look at Box 15.11.

BOX 15.11

M0 and £M3

- M0 = Notes and coins in circulation plus money held in bank tills (cash) and the operational balances of the banks held at the Bank of England

  M0 measured money used for **transactional purposes**.

- £M3 = Notes and coins in circulation plus deposits held in the UK banks by UK residents, sight and time deposits (sight = withdraw on demand, time = notice needs to be given)

  £M3 measures money used for transactional purposes plus money held as a form of saving.

Inflation and unemployment

The 1980s demonstrated a direct link between unemployment and inflation. As unemployment has increased in the UK economy inflation rates have fallen. So what is the greater evil – unemployment or inflation? Some economists would say that a certain amount of inflation is manageable as long as it is anticipated whilst others would say that unemployment in an economy is self-inflicted, caused by the labour force pricing itself out of the market.

Causes of inflation

There are two main types of inflation: cost push and demand pull.

Cost push – is where the costs of production are rising and hence pushing up prices.

Demand pull – is the situation where demand for goods or services exceeds supply.

In the 1970s we saw a new type of inflation occurring – stagflation. At this time both inflation and unemployment were increasing together; this was unusual and contravened the theory about trade-offs between inflation and employment. Stagflation was largely caused because of the oil crisis which meant that the price of oil as an input was pushing up price levels. There are five main problems caused by inflation, as Box 15.12 shows.

Problems caused by inflation

- It distorts money values.
- It hits those on fixed income who cannot keep pace with changing prices.
- It can lead to an inflationary spiral, where wage demands are invoked to meet inflation, which in turn causes increased inflation.
- It may be uneconomical for individuals to save or invest because interest rate values cannot keep pace with prices.
- It can be damaging to overseas competitiveness as UK prices will rise.

The situation may mean that interest rates will have to rise to counteract inflation. Higher interest rates could mean businesses being hit by higher costs of investment and a corresponding fall in demand.

Unemployment

Because of the economic objective of destroying inflation, the labour market has been hit by large-scale unemployment. This situation has been exacerbated by large cuts in the public sector and the change in the structure of the economy which has meant the disintegration of the UK industrial base. Unemployment is fundamentally a waste of resources, but there are many reasons for unemployment other than a tight monetary policy. Mobility problems and regional policy have already been looked at in Section 4.11. Technology is an important factor, as already investigated in Sections 4.11 and 5.13 on Data Management and Operations Management. In August 1994 Barclays Bank announced huge increases in their profits, but insisted that they were still going to cut a further 5000 jobs, even though one in five jobs had already been cut. Technology is changing the face of banking but with no new jobs to replace job losses unemployment could be something everyone has to learn to live with, perhaps even the development of a two-class structure, the employed and the unemployed.

Government economic objectives

All Governments will have their own economic objectives. Because businesses have to operate in whatever economic structure or forces which are established or evolve, they need to be aware of them.

Growth

To achieve economic growth, production or output in the economy has to increase. This can occur through an increase in national resources or more efficient use of the factors of production. Growth can ultimately lead to a higher standard of living for individuals in society. But growth can have its costs in terms of the pressure on the environment and the stress on individuals. Governments are now talking in terms of sustainable growth, which means a growth that the environment can maintain without long-term damage.

National income figures can be used to measure growth but also to compare

Measuring national income

- **Expenditure** – This measures the amount spent on goods and services.
- **Income** – This measures the income of individuals from all forms of employment, but also income from business profits, interest and rent.
- **Output** – This measures the output value of organisations.

economic performance with other nations. National income can be measured using the three methods shown in Box 15.13.

Each of these methods provides the same result, via a different route. We also need to be aware of a country's GDP and GNP.

Gross domestic product (GDP) is the value of goods and services produced nationally over a period of time.

Gross national product (GNP) is GDP plus 'net' property income from abroad.

Income can be earned in the form of interest, profits and dividend from abroad. The 'net' figure is the income earned from abroad *less* what has to be paid out overseas.

The periods of economic growth throughout the years have tended to form into a regular pattern, known as the trade cycle. The cycle spans from boom (a period of higher economic growth) to slump and back again.

Full employment

Unemployed resources mean that potential output is sacrificed. Up until 1979 successive governments sought full employment as an economic target, but after 1979 full employment was no longer a target. It could be argued that the full employment policy had led to the build up of power by trade union members whose own jobs were secure. The unemployment which developed in

the 1980s meant that no jobs were secure, so it was less likely that individuals would risk their jobs to be militant. There was also thought to be widespread 'overmanning' in the public sector industries. Once these were privatised, such jobs became vulnerable to market forces.

Income distribution

One of the ways a Government can intervene in the economy is by creating a more equitable distribution of income and wealth throughout the population. They can do this by using the taxation system to redistribute funds or using the benefits system to help those in need.

Balance international trade payments

We will look at the implication of a balance of payments deficit in Section 6.16 on Global Problems.

Control price levels

We have already looked at the types and implications of inflation. Throughout the 1980s and today the control of inflation has been seen as one of the main economic objectives. Ironically inflation was not viewed as the ultimate evil prior to this time in the UK: high unemployment was seen as a much more serious problem.

Control money supply

Monetarists believe that inflation is caused by excessive increases in the money supply. Therefore controlling the money supply is the way to control inflation. They also believe that lower interest rates will increase aggregate demand as individuals are tempted to borrow money to buy goods and services. Look at Box 15.14.

BOX 15.14

Monetarism v. Keynesianism

Monetarism

During several periods since 1979 the UK economic policy could be said to have been based on 'Monetarism'. Monetarism is based on the belief that:

- Unemployment can be caused by workers pricing themselves out of jobs. Market forces for labour may mean that wage rates will fall according to demand levels. If the labour market does not function according to supply and demand then the economy can be uncompetitive. Welfare payments to the unemployed should not be at levels where they can act as a disincentive to work.
- Excessive growth in the money supply can lead to inflation. Therefore growth in the money supply should be controlled by cutting back on Government borrowing (PSBR) and the use of interest rate controls. Higher interest rates should curb any growth in the money supply because 'interest' is the price of money. However, interest rates also affect other aspects of the economy, in particular exchange rates, which we will look at in Section 6.16 on Global Problems.

The Keynesian view

- Unemployment is caused largely by a lack of demand in the economy. Governments have the power to create, or manage, demand by increasing the PSBR.
- Growth can be achieved by creating demand in the economy which will in turn encourage firms to invest because they see there is a market for their products.
- Inflation is caused mainly by 'cost push' factors which can be managed by Governments through policies which control prices and incomes.

REVIEW

You should now understand the place of the business within the context of the economy as a whole. You should also appreciate the constraints this places on an organisation, and hence the need for business to understand how the economy works.

REVIEW TASK

PRACTICAL APPLICATION 1

The government is proposing to introduce further restrictions on consumer credit.

A How might this policy be implemented?
B What effect would you expect such measures to have for:
  – the motor car industry
  – builders' merchants supplying the DIY trade
  – the overall level of economic activity in the country?

REVIEW TASK

PRACTICAL APPLICATION 2

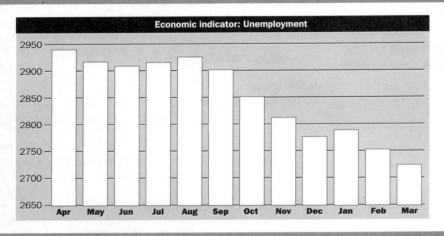

Source: *Observer (21 May 1993).*

- Unemployment in the UK fell by 30 000 between February and March to 2.72 million (9.7% of the labour force).
- At the same time retail sales rose more highly than anticipated. This caused the IMF to warn against further UK interest rate cuts in case of inflation.
- However, most of the employment growth has been in the part-time sector and this has not had an effect on total hours worked in the economy.

1 Work out the percentage changes in unemployment figures from April to March.
2 Explain why the statistics show that unemployment fell, and state the real implications to the economy.

TASK

CRITICAL ANALYSIS

The price of politics

Examine the following article and supporting graphs and then answer the questions that follow.

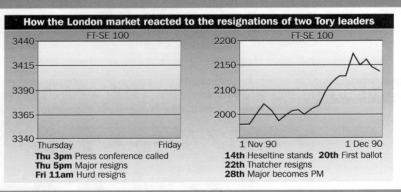

Source: *The Observer, 25/6/95.*

When John Major resigned, temporarily as it turned out, as leader of the Conservative Party, London's financial markets prepared themselves for a rocky ride. The initial impact of the resignation was minimal but it was followed by further news of the departure of Foreign Secretary Douglas Hurd and inflation problems in Germany. Subsequently the FTSE index fell 24.4 points.

The survival of John Major has not rectified the split in the Conservative Party over European issues. A CBI survey has shown a fall in business confidence, and there is evidence that the economy is slowing down. It is likely that when the Chancellor meets the Governor of the Bank of England, the 'inflation busting' Eddie George will be calling for a rise in interest rates to control a rising inflation rate. The Chancellor will need to be mindful of the effect an interest rate rise will have on the business world. With retail sales rising by only 1% for the first few months of 1995 it is unlikely that consumer spending will fuel growth.

Optimists say we are in a 'growth pause' similar to the one that occurred in 1984 whilst others are predicting business and economic gloom for the foreseeable future. However, it is likely that with the next election looming nearer, there are signs that the Government could engineer a pre-election boom.

Source: National newspaper reports and author's research.

A. What is meant by 'growth', and how can it be achieved?
B. Explain how Eddie George could 'bust' inflation, using interest rates as weapons.
C. Why do the CBI and the business community fear a rise in interest rates?

QUESTIONS

British Gas chief receives 75% pay rise

Mr Cedric Brown, Chief Executive of British Gas, has received a 75% pay rise, taking his basic annual salary to £475 000. This pay rise makes Mr Brown's basic pay amongst the highest of any UK public company director. The news has provoked an angry reaction from trade unions and politicians. Mr David Stirzaker, a senior official of Unison, Britain's largest trade union, said that Unison members who worked at British Gas had received rises of less than 3%.

British Gas said that the review by the company's remuneration committee, composed of non-executive directors, concluded that its directors were underpaid in comparison with other British-based international companies.

The company added, 'we are expanding internationally and need to recruit, retain and motivate top calibre international management'.

The executive directors said that from next year the company's annual report and accounts would contain far greater details of each director's salary package, including perks such as company cars.

Source: Adapted from Financial Times (21 November 1994).

A. Give three examples of groups which are stakeholders in a business.
B. Discuss the extent to which shareholders could have the power to reverse the decision of the non-executive directors.
C. 'In a free market people are paid what they are worth.' Discuss this statement. To what extent do you agree with this view in relation to a shop floor employee in a British Gas showroom, as compared with the Chief Executive, Mr Cedric Brown?
D. Consider whether governments should intervene in business decision-making. (AEB new syllabus specimen paper)

CASE STUDY

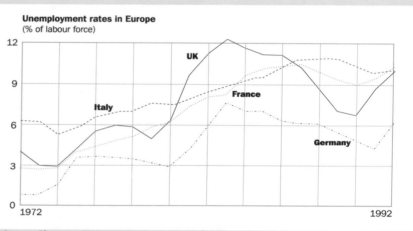

Source: *Observer (21 May 1993).*

Unemployment in Europe has been on an upward trend throughout the 1990s. Yet the Americans and the Japanese have largely avoided this trend.

The 1950s and the 1960s are remembered throughout Europe as a period of high growth and low unemployment. This growth was supported by a productivity gap that existed with the United States after the Second World War and motivated by Keynesian economic policies of demand management.

As European economies matured unemployment began to rise as counter-inflation policies were established. So what are the main triggers of unemployment?

Some would argue that capital investment has replaced labour as a factor of production and that technological production processes have eliminated the need for a large proportion of the workforce.

Monetarists would say that wage rates have risen faster than productivity and that workers have priced themselves out of jobs. The full employment policy of the post-war period led to the consolidation of trade union power, although this has been reversed in the UK since 1979. Workers were, therefore, able to push up the price for their labour which proved inflationary. Institutional problems in European labour markets acted as a barrier to flexible working practices, in particular in areas such as the use of a part-time labour force.

Governments increasing 'non-wage' costs of employment like employers' National Insurance contributions and creating high levels of social security have resulted in what is called 'voluntary unemployment'.

The anti-inflationary policy of the Government since the mid-1970s has had a detrimental effect on employment and growth, whilst poor employment training has not helped the mismatch of skills in a rapidly changing employment market.

Source: National newspaper reports and author's research.

CASE STUDY TASKS

1 Explain what is meant by 'demand management' in an economy.
2 Draw a diagram to illustrate how workers can 'price themselves out of jobs'.
3 Describe how labour policies in Europe in general, and the UK in particular, have changed sharply since 1979.
4 How far do you think technological development is to blame for European unemployment?
5 Explain what is meant by inflation, and explain the theories for its increase during the 1960s and the 1970s.
6 How was inflation cured in the UK, and how were businesses ultimately affected?

6.16 The World Stage

FOCUS

Global warning

The UK has become part of a much wider European context. European laws and regulations are increasingly influencing not just our business and trade, but also domestic issues. As we become integrated into a much larger European state, the rest of the world looks set to form into two further distinct trading blocs, East Asia and America.

The question of whether Europe can compete in a global market place needs to be confronted. Pessimists would say that Europe may be vulnerable, with global companies from the USA and Japan making strong inroads into European markets. A major problem is that European nations tend to think of themselves as distinct from the European market. If Europeans cannot cooperate in harmony, how can they be expected to compete as a global force? This negative attitude has developed through historical mistrust and a diverse cultural identity.

Some European businesses have attempted to fight back with mergers and takeovers, but they have not always been successful. The merger between the airlines Swissair, SAS and KLM collapsed, as did the collaboration between Volvo and Renault. The Europeans fear American moves to use Mexico as a cheap source of labour, with a relatively secure investment base and a growing market. The recent Asia/Pacific Summit may also be seen as a threat to Europe. With American protests of unfair European protectionism it may be that America will be more interested in trading in Asia than Europe.

The battle for the Chinese market will inevitably be a major global event. As world traders vie for the money of the estimated 100 million middle class Chinese, any consideration of human rights issues may sadly be forgotten. The Japanese may also lose interest in Europe as the Pacific boom shifts world trade patterns, with East Asian countries taking off into an industrial revolution and substantial oil deposits being found in Central Asia.

Ironically the growing problems in Eastern Europe and Russia may be a factor that will unite Europe, particularly in the areas of defence and security. The porous eastern frontiers have led to an inrush of illegal immigrants, an increase in crime and an upsurge in the trading of drugs, arms and plutonium. The Russian interpretation of the free market has manifested itself in increased crime and a collapsed social structure. The Russian mafia drug barons are seizing every free market opportunity, whilst developing their own very efficient trading routes, and the market in demand and supply of plutonium has alerted the West to the dangerous implications of the operation of pure market mechanisms.

Source: National newspaper reports and author's research.

Preview
In this chapter we shall investigate the following key areas:
- free trade vs. protectionism
- the European dimension
- the role of multinationals
- international trade
- exchange rates

Trade and interdependence

International trading is becoming an increasingly important business issue. The creation of the EU and the formation of other world trading blocs has created further structures within which business has to operate. Even if a business does not export its goods, EU directives will still have an effect on its organisation (remember Chapter 5.14). Exchange rate policies will also have an impact on the price of goods which are imported. Economic policy may also be driven by considerations of international trade balances.

Opportunities for business have been expanded by the opening up of the Eastern bloc and the extensive market in China. However, political instability will also pose a threat to businesses. In Russia, Western businesses are apparently having to pay large sums of protection money to the Russian mafia gangs in order to operate at all.

Interdependence is a central theme in all global markets: the actions of one nation will have a direct effect on other parts of the world. Countries that are selling, and therefore earning, are obviously trading with countries that are buying, or spending. These payment flows in and out of a nation need to be monitored to ensure that any trading surplus or deficit is controlled.

Free trade vs. protectionism

Free trade
The ability to trade freely on an international scale enables a nation to gain access to vital resources which may be either unavailable or more costly on the home market. It also allows them to expand their output to a wider market area.

The economic rationale for free trade is based on the law of Comparative Cost Advantage. This law basically states that if each nation specialises in what it can produce most cost-effectively, and trades with other nations for the goods that it cannot, world resources will be more efficiently utilised. Free traders would argue that international trade should take place for the same reason as any trade, through the interaction of supply and demand – buyers looking for the best price and suppliers looking for markets. Specialisation, as we have seen, can lead to a more cost-effective output. The economic theories of comparative cost advantage are based on this same theory of specialisation. On an international scale, it will be cheaper for one region of the world to produce a certain type of output than another region of the world using the same amount of resources because of the cost advantages involved. These advantages may be based on climatic factors, availability of natural resources or purely on developed skills or expertise. The Japanese are an interesting case here, because they have very little in terms of natural resources, but they do have highly developed expertise and skills. Free traders would argue that there should be no protectionist barriers to distort the free market mechanisms.

Protectionism

However, given the fact that the concept of a completely 'free' market may not exist, perhaps there is a case for intervention. The simplistic rationale of free trade turns out to be a much more complex process. Countries may operate a free trade policy only to a limited degree. If home industries are being saturated by imported goods, which are being subsidised by a foreign government, it could be argued that this is not free trade or free competition. The effects of free trade may also create unemployment in the home workforce and ultimate economic decline. Therefore governments may argue that they should protect their home industries. There are three types of situation where the protectionist line could be argued.

Dumping

Dumping describes a situation when goods are sold on an international market at a price less than they would be sold on the home market. This may be done by some nations in order to obtain much-needed foreign currency or to establish a market position through a 'loss leader'.

Retaliation

The Americans have threatened retaliatory action against Japan for making it difficult for American goods to penetrate the Japanese market. The Americans would argue that the Japanese are taking advantage of the American free trade policy whilst operating a protectionist policy against foreign goods entering Japan.

Protection of infant industries

Economically it could be argued that free trade does not operate efficiently in a situation where new industries are being developed. Because they are often initially smaller in scale they may be unable to compete on a cost basis with the larger established industries. It could be said that in the short term these industries should be protected from what could be classed as unfair competition.

Types of protectionism

If a government decides to operate a protectionist policy it can do it by:

● Tariffs – Placing a tax on imported goods, thus making them dearer and therefore less competitive.
● Subsidies – A subsidy to home producers will enable them to cut their costs, and therefore offer the goods at a lower and more competitive price.
● Quota – A quota is a limit by

numbers. The government may decide that they will only allow a fixed number of certain goods to be imported annually, and set this as an import quota.

- Exchange controls – In order to buy foreign goods, the national currency is needed. One way of controlling imports is therefore to implement exchange controls which restrict the availability of foreign currency for trade.

- Deposit schemes – Importers can sometimes obtain credit on the goods imported, by being allowed to pay the supplier at a later date. The government can intervene and initiate an import deposit scheme where the importer is required to place a deposit with the customs authority.

The European dimension

EC, EFTA and EEA

The European Community (EC) was established in 1957 but the UK did not join until 1973. The European Free Trade Association (EFTA) formed a peripheral unit which was linked only by trade, not by the wider EC objectives. In 1991 EFTA and its members signed a free trade agreement with the then 12 EC nations which formed its 7 members into the 19 nations in the European Economic Area (EEA). This is seen as a first step towards full membership. Sweden and Austria have applied for full membership and others are expected to follow. EFTA nations are not part of the Common Agricultural Policy (CAP) but the free movement of goods, labour and capital apply to them.

The EC evolved as a result of the desire for international cooperation which resulted from the Bretton Woods Conference in 1947, after the Second World War. The post-First World War period of recession led to the subsequent protectionist policies, with nations moving towards a 'closed' trading policy. Individual nations were fearful for their own economic survival and reacted to the recession by protecting their home industries. World trade contracted. After the Second World War it was felt that a way of alleviating the dangers of another world war was to bind nations together by trade. The Bretton Woods Conference in 1947 set about the task of reconstruction and development in the post-war era. The desire for international cooperation led to the development of Agencies like GATT, the IMF and the World Bank, as outlined in Box 16.1.

Backdoor protectionism

The free trade bloc that the EC initially set out to establish has in many ways not been totally successful. Throughout the Community many member states have managed to protect their home industries from competition through 'hidden' protectionist policies. This type of protection takes many forms, and is often difficult to identify. Four types of hidden protectionism are common.

Subsidies

Governments may be supporting certain industries through the use of subsidy payments, grants or other financial incentives. This makes the products cheaper and therefore more competitive internationally. This effect can also be achieved through public sector support. The French car producer Renault is in

Post-war cooperation: GATT, IMF and World Bank

- **GATT (General Agreement on Tariffs and Trade)**

Set up in 1947 with the objective of reducing protectionist tariffs, GATT operates by holding periodic conferences or rounds of talks. By 1961 there were 38 nations involved, now there are over 100 members. An example of this type of conference was held in Uruguay in 1993 when the Americans challenged the European agricultural policy as being protectionist. A problem with GATT may be that it is looking increasingly out of date as nations are grouping together and planning to enforce protectionist policies against non-member states.

- **IMF (International Monetary Fund)**

Set up in 1946, the IMF's aims were to encourage the expansion of world trade and to help exchange rate stability. It has two main roles:

1. It acts as a banker. Each nation pools a quota of funds to be held as a financial contingency for any future difficulties.
2. It also plays the role of an 'umpire' in the interests of exchange rate stability.

In addition, it has set up a system of SDRs (Special Drawing Rights). Each nation contributes to form a pool of currency reserves which can be drawn upon if needed. The UK had a large loan from the IMF in the late 1970s, and this loan enabled the IMF to have a considerable say in the subsequent UK economic policy.

- **World Bank (International Bank for Reconstruction and Development)**

Set up in 1946, the IBRD provided help to the war-torn European economies in the form of loans and investments. Member nations contribute a quota to the bank which the bank can then invest on world capital markets. Interest has to be paid on loans but there is a separate International Development Association (IDA) which will provide loans at preferential rates to poorer nations.

the public sector, but plans to privatise the company will mean the loss of government funds which could prove detrimental to its future.

Red tape

There are many ways of creating administrative turmoil for those importing goods into a country. The documentation can be so complex and lengthy that the cost of lost time and delays can deter the importer. There may also be different entry points for similar items which would normally be transported on the same load. These difficulties will push up costs and make the importation of goods a much more costly and less attractive proposition.

Government licences

The government may have to issue licences for certain imports, and these licences may be difficult to obtain.

Standards and regulations

Most member states have their own standards and regulations which set the quality and safety requirements for their home market. The standard specifications are drawn up by national bodies like the UK British Standards Institute (BSI). These standards and regulations can act as a barrier to trade if a good does not conform to the national specification.

The single market

The Single European Market initiative and legislation (the Single European Act or SEA) was begun in 1992 with the objective of eliminating the barriers to trade that still existed within the EU. The aim was to move towards achieving the EC's policy of free movement of goods, finance, labour and capital. The Department of Trade and Industry (DTI) set about extensive national advertising, promoting European opportunities to UK businesses, and producing packages of information encouraging businesses to become more efficient and therefore ready to grasp the new opportunities in the wider European market. This data included an 'Action Checklist', a booklet called *The Facts* and a quarterly newsletter called the *Single Market News*. There was also a hotline to put businesses in touch with government officials who would be dealing with specific 'single market' issues. A TV campaign was waged using well known business personalities. Because of the fear that UK businesses might be unable to compete with the rest of Europe, they were encouraged to analyse the efficiency of their operations. The Action Checklist gave advice on marketing, sales, distribution, production, purchasing, finance, training, recruitment and information systems. However, much of what should have been achieved in 1992 is still to be realised. The complexities of the decision-making process and the self interest of member states has meant that the intentions have still to become reality.

The structure and institutions of the EU

There are four main institutions which control the community (see Box 16.2).

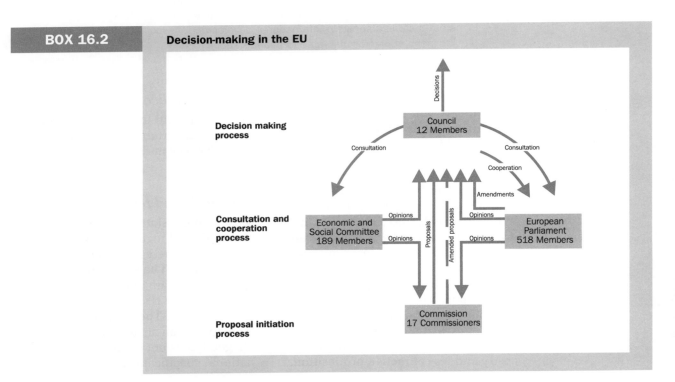

BOX 16.2

Decision-making in the EU

Decision making process

Consultation   Consultation

Cooperation

Decisions

Council
12 Members

Amendments

Consultation and cooperation process

Economic and Social Committee
189 Members

Opinions

Opinions

Proposals

Amended proposals

Opinions

Opinions

European Parliament
518 Members

Proposal initiation process

Commission
17 Commissioners

The Commission

The Commission's members do not represent individual governments but are appointed by agreement with national governments. Their role is to make proposals, draft policies and present them to the Council of Ministers.

Council of Ministers

The ministers represent national governments in each functional area – finance, agriculture, etc. This is the only body whose members directly represent national governments.

Court of Justice

This court rules on matters concerning Community law. The judges are representatives of each nation.

European Parliament

The Members of Parliament are elected directly by the citizens of each region of the community.

The Common Agricultural Policy (CAP)

When the EC was initially set up in 1957 agriculture was the most important European industry. The main aims of the Common Agricultural Policy (CAP) were to increase productivity, improve standards of living, stabilise markets, stop food shortages and enable consumers to buy food at a reasonable price. The over-riding factor was the desire to increase food production. The optimum way to do this was believed to be by using the system of price fixing; this system worked by setting a minimum price for each producer. If a producer could not sell the items for this price, the Community would intervene and buy them at what was set as the intervention price. The goods would then be held in store until the market became favourable. Farmers then began to apply pressure to fix their prices higher than the market price, to ensure a higher income. The higher prices meant that producers supplied more and hence the 'mountains' of food surpluses grew. Box 16.3 shows how this can happen in supply and demand terms.

| BOX 16.3 | Mountains and surpluses |

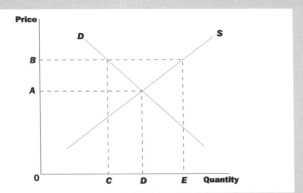

- The only price at which consumers demand the amount farmers supply is *OA*.
- If the Community sets a target or intervention price of *OB*, farmers will supply *OE*, but consumers will only demand *OC*. Hence a surplus will develop.

The spending on CAP forms 60–70% of the EC budget. The main problem for the UK was that its agricultural industry was relatively efficient compared with the rest of Europe. It needed manufacturing, not agricultural, investment in order to support and regenerate its decaying industrial base.

The CAP also caused much consternation in the Uruguay Round of GATT talks. The irony, of course, is that CAP is far from a free market system and the Americans accused Europe of protectionism, contravening the objectives of GATT, arguing that world agricultural markets were being distorted by the protectionist subsidies to European farmers. Claims about a 'fortress Europe' mentality were raised (see Box 16.4).

BOX 16.4 **'Fortress Europe'**

Whilst Europe stumbles towards a free trade policy, it is forming a large trading bloc. The reality is that the world is now forming into three fiercely competitive regional power blocs of North America the Far East and Europe.

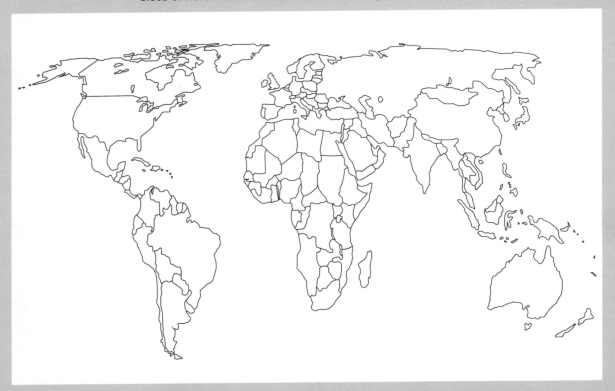

The role of the multinationals

A multinational can be defined as a corporation which has a legally identifiable base in one or more countries, but carries out its production on a worldwide basis. Most of the large multinationals are American and Japanese. They can take advantage of preferential production costs and facilities in various countries. By 'globetrotting' their productive capacity, it is easier for them to switch production if costs rise, trade unions become more militant or governments give regional locational incentives. Multinationals can gain the five main advantages:

- Switch production if the need arises
- Set up where labour costs are cheaper
- Avoid protectionist tariffs if they operate in the market; Japanese multinationals have benefited from establishing their production within the UK, and hence the EU.

- Obtain regional development grants if they establish production in certain specified areas; some multinationals have been criticised for moving into regional development areas, collecting government incentives but switching production when the climate changed.
- Locate where the most preferential tax rates exist.

Most multinationals are welcomed into the host nation because they provide employment and often much-needed investment capital. However, there are dangers inherent in having a powerful multinational corporation (MNC) operating in a host country, particularly if the power of the MNC is more substantial than that of the government. Look at Box 16.5.

| BOX 16.5 | **MNC facts of life** |

MNC facts of life

MNCs have been criticised for operating below western standards of health and safety in third world countries. The Bhopal disaster (see Chapter 1.5) has exposed the operation of these policies and made some MNCs more aware of the implications. Nevertheless hundreds of American companies are rushing to capitalise on the cheap labour force in Mexico where the lax environmental and safety laws mean that considerable cost savings can be achieved.

Multinational production makes it increasingly difficult to identify a product's country of origin, and hence its national identity or liability for protectionist tariffs. Half of the Ford cars sold in the UK are made in the UK, with Escorts being made in West Germany, Sierras in Belgium or Eire, and Fiestas in Spain. Often car parts and components are produced around the world. The Vauxhall Cavalier's engine is made in Australia and Austria, whilst the carburettor is made in France, the fuel injection in Germany, the wiring in Eire and the seats in Germany.

International trade

Imports and exports form flows of payments and receipts in and out of a nation. These transactions represent currency or value being earned or spent – resources flowing in or out (as we saw in Chapter 6.15). Therefore a record of these payments must be kept so that the trading situation can be monitored.

The balance of payments

The balance of payments is the account which registers these movements. The balance of payments is broken down into three sections:

- Current account
- Capital account
- Official financing.

Current account

The Current Account is a record of the flow of goods and services. Goods and services are defined as visibles and invisibles.

- Visibles – Tangible goods, for example cars and videos.
- Invisibles – Service sector products which form paper transactions, for example banking and insurance. Tourism is also an invisible item.

Box 16.6 shows a simple trade account and Box 16.7 an indication of import and export flows around the EU in 1990.

Capital account

All capital transactions are the outcome of forgoing present consumption. Capital transactions form movements of capital and flows of financial assets. When UK citizens invest money abroad this constitutes a capital outflow. If foreign nationals invest money in the UK it forms a capital inflow. The Capital Account includes longer-term and shorter-term transactions.

Longer-term This section represents private investment overseas in productive resources. It can be either real investment, where a UK company buys foreign subsidiaries (this would include the activities of multinationals setting up a production base) or portfolio investment, which is the purchase of shares or securities. The

---

BOX 16.6

A simple trade account
Total goods exported by the UK
Less total goods imported by the UK
= Balance of visibles
Total services exported by the UK
Less total services imported by the UK
= Balance of invisibles

(There is also an account which monitors only **visibles** called the **balance of trade**; it is a useful measure of how manufacturing industry is performing)

Balance of visibles offset by balance of invisibles = **surplus** or **deficit** on current account

- A **surplus** denotes that there has been more **exported** than **imported**. This will mean that reserves can be **built up**.
- A **deficit** denotes that there has been more **imported** than **exported**. This will mean that the national reserves are being **depleted**.

BOX 16.7

Sources of EU imports, 1990

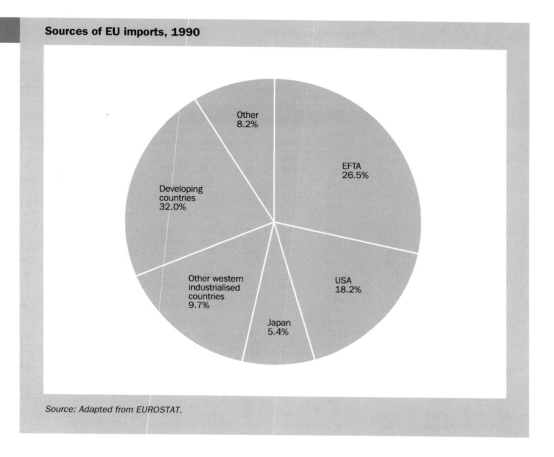

Other
8.2%

EFTA
26.5%

Developing
countries
32.0%

Other western
industrialised
countries
9.7%

USA
18.2%

Japan
5.4%

Source: Adapted from EUROSTAT.

government may also become involved in lending overseas. For both these types of investment, the capital movement will go into the Capital Account, but any earnings from the acquisition of capital, i.e. the profits of a multinational or the dividend on share transactions, would be calculated in the flows of the Current Account as an invisible balance.

Therefore in the short term, investment overseas will result in a capital outflow, but in the longer term there should also be a Current Account inflow.

Shorter-term Shorter-term speculative flows of capital are often called hot money. These shorter-term investment flows are speculative funds which chase interest rates. Currency is bought and sold like shares on the currency markets. The funds move swiftly from one currency to another, hence the term 'hot' money. The effects of these 'volatile' flows can be very destabilising for an economy because the money flowing in and out can overwhelm the balance of payments. Such volatility is a poor indicator of international trade efficiency because the government can manipulate national interest rates to encourage or divert funds, and the effect of this manipulation may be unfavourable to business. A rise in interest rates, for example, may push up exchange rates, which will have a direct impact on the UK's trading position overseas.

BOX 16.8 — Balance of payments

£ million

| | | Seasonally adjusted | | | | | | Not seasonally adjusted | | | | | |
| | | | Invisible (balance) | | | | | | UK external assets and liabilities | | | Allocation of SDRS and gold subscription to IMF | Balancing item |
		Visible trade (balance)	Services	Investment income	Transfers	Total	Current balance	Current balance	Trans-actions in assets[1]	Trans-actions in liabilities[1]	Net transactions		
1984	Q3	−1 534	1 069	1 011	−636	1 446	−88	8	−619	−672	−1 291	−	1 283
	Q4	−1 967	1 158	1 484	−136	2 505	538	1 471	−8 509	4 984	−3 561	−	2 090
1985	Q1	−1 962	1 291	957	−835	1 412	−550	−918	−16 514	14 191	−2 323	−	3 241
	Q2	−214	1 685	535	−851	1 571	1 357	738	−6 485	6 205	−281	−	−457
	Q3	−538	1 765	656	−881	1 540	1 002	1 124	−15 201	10 059	−5 142	−	4 018
	Q4	−631	1 657	148	−744	1 060	429	1 294	−12 416	16 442	4 026	−	−5 320
1986	Q1	−1 585	1 774	986	66	2 826	1 241	455	−15 496	14 508	−989	−	534
	Q2	−2 162	1 407	1 110	−544	1 973	−189	−422	−14 935	13 376	−1 559	−	1 981
	Q3	−2 895	1 408	1 338	−803	1 944	−951	−1 034	−43 619	45 544	1 925	−	−891
	Q4	−2 917	1 634	1 188	−876	1 945	−972	130	−17 783	15 291	−2 492	−	2 362
1987	Q1	−1 848	1 716	1 190	−767	2 138	290	−152	−16 726	19 524	2 798	−	−2 645
	Q2	−2 791	1 616	939	−759	1 797	−994	−1 347	−24 881	28 773	3 892	−	−2 545
	Q3	−3 071	1 598	988	−981	1 606	−1 465	−1 805	−27 556	25 611	−1 945	−	3 750
	Q4	−3 872	1 312	640	−893	1 058	−2 814	−1 679	−13 332	15 297	1 965	−	−286
1988	Q1	−4 329	1 090	847	−1 045	892	−3 437	−3 741	−4 045	11 267	7 222	−	−3 481
	Q2	−4 800	1 021	1 252	−888	1 385	−3 415	−3 709	−20 952	21 736	784	−	2 925
	Q3	−5 648	1 019	1 182	−202	1 999	−3 649	−4 042	−23 323	25 054	1 731	−	2 311
	Q4	−6 703	827	1 143	−1 383	587	−6 116	−5 125	−9 022	10 260	1 238	−	3 887
1989	Q1	−6 371	743	1 127	−706	1 164	−5 207	−5 220	−28 443	38 949	10 506	−	−5 286
	Q2	−6 692	1 008	834	−844	998	−5 694	−6 089	−17 461	21 098	3 637	−	2 452
	Q3	−6 753	850	703	−1 396	157	−6 596	−7 276	−23 566	31 221	7 655	−	−379
	Q4	−4 867	760	724	−1 632	−148	−5 015	−3 927	−21 113	18 951	−2 162	−	6 089
1990	Q1	−6 082	1 127	−142	−1 069	−84	−6 166	−6 411	−16 865	24 789	7 924	−	−1 513
	Q2	−5 407	847	−215	−1 304	−672	−6 079	−6 484	−7 413	8 373	960	−	5 524
	Q3	−4 059	870	855	−1 049	676	−3 383	−4 499	−34 417	38 371	3 954	−	545
	Q4	−3 261	845	483	−1 474	−146	−3 407	−1 641	−21 985	27 340	5 355	−	−3 714
1991	Q1	−3 037	688	−662	−363	−337	−3 374	−3 848	−10 976	11 117	141	−	3 707
	Q2	−2 025	977	−214	234	997	−1 028	−1 548	−4 106	−5 516	−9 622	−	11 170
	Q3	−2 478	1 128	258	−859	527	−1 951	−3 014	−9 129	10 859	1 730	−	1 284
	Q4	−2 744	915	401	−395	921	−1 823	234	3 494	12 876	16 370	−	−16 604
1992	Q1	−2 681	932	482	−1 371	43	−2 638	−3 156	−10 767	3 770	−6 997	−	10 153
	Q2	−2 963	1 114	319	−1 414	19	−2 944	−3 484	−9 384	14 611	5 227	−	−1 743
	Q3	−3 321	1 016	1 777	−1 282	1 511	−1 810	−2 899	−41 306	43 460	2 154	−	745
	Q4	−4 139	1 027	1 715	−1 042	1 700	−2 439	−292	−20 762	23 747	2 985	−	−2 693
1993	Q1	−3 306	1 504	−376	−1 459	−331	−3 637	−3 457	−35 906	32 188	−3 718	−	7 175
	Q2	−3 552	1 110	136	−1 154	92	−3 460	−4 285	−37 038	40 226	3 188	−	1 097
	Q3	−3 176	1 334	1 305	−1 551	1 088	−2 088	−3 082	−23 314	26 206	2 892	−	190
	Q4	−3 175	1 288	963	−1 071	1 180	−1 995	−356	−60 045	66 104	6 059	−	−5 703
1994	Q1	−2 988	1 212	1 874	−1 565	1 521	−1 467	−1 107	12 047	−15 904	−3 857	−	4 964
	Q2	−2 425	822	2 179	−1 683	1 318	−1 107	−2 143	4 485	403	4 888	−	−2 745
	Q3	−1 548	1 392	2 725	−1 750	2 367	819	−60	−26 145	25 144	−1 001	−	1 061

Note:
Prior to 1979 foreign currency lending and borrowing abroad by UK banks (other than certain export credit extended) is recorded on a net basis under liabilities.

Source: CSO, Economic Trends (1995, Table 16.1).

Official financing

As we have already learned, all accounts must balance. If there is a discrepancy in the flows in and the flows out, there must be a balancing item. The Official Financing section of the balance of payments will rectify such a deficit. If the Current Account is in deficit, it can be funded by any surplus there may be in the Capital Account. If both accounts are in deficit, there will need to be funding from the Official Financing section. The government may have reserves of funds which it can use, or it may need to draw on its pool of resources at the IMF. It can also manipulate its economic policy to have some impact on either of these sections of the account. Box 16.8 shows a balance of payments summary for the UK.

The problems of a deficit and surplus

A deficit on the balance of payments indicates that a nation is importing, or spending, more money on imports than it is exporting, or earning, on international markets. This situation will lead to a loss of reserves and a need for borrowing. The extent of the problem will depend on the size of the deficit and the items involved. A deficit on the long-term capital account may result in a later inflow to the current account in invisible earnings:

Current account
Invisibles – Income from profit flows back

Capital account
Long-term – A UK multinational company builds a new plant overseas so investment flows out

A surplus is viewed as an indicator of economic success. However, any nation which has an excess of foreign earnings over expenditure is achieving this at the expense of other nations, who will have a subsequent deficit. This may lead to threats of protectionist measures against the nation which has a surplus.

The trade surplus will result in an injection of income into the domestic economy. The successful trading of domestic goods in the international market place will create domestic employment opportunities, whilst the surplus income flowing into the economy will create other investment opportunities.

If the economy is already operating at a full employment level, this additional income could be inflationary, pushing up domestic prices and eventually increasing the price of exports. The rise in the price of exports may be intensified by the subsequent rise in the value of the exchange rate, caused by the demand for the currency. Look at Box 16.9.

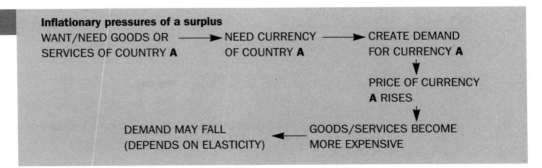

BOX 16.9

Inflationary pressures of a surplus

WANT/NEED GOODS OR SERVICES OF COUNTRY **A** ⟶ NEED CURRENCY OF COUNTRY **A** ⟶ CREATE DEMAND FOR CURRENCY **A**

PRICE OF CURRENCY **A** RISES

DEMAND MAY FALL (DEPENDS ON ELASTICITY) ⟵ GOODS/SERVICES BECOME MORE EXPENSIVE

Exchange rates

Exchange rates explained

Look at Box 16.10 before reading on.

What is an exchange rate?
An exchange rate is the rate at which one currency is **exchanged for another**, or the **market value** of a currency:

- £1 is worth 2000 lira
- If the value of the lira falls
- £1 is now worth 2500 lira and 2000 lira is now worth 80p
- If the value of the lira rises, the pound may be worth 1500 lira.

It might help to think of this as if they were both on a weighing scale – you need to put more on to one side, or take some off (the side that has lost value), in order to restore the equilibrium.

Foreign currency is needed to buy foreign goods, so in simple terms it is the demand and supply for the goods or services of that nation which determines the value of the currency, e.g.

- If a UK company wanted to import Japanese video cassette recorders into the UK to sell on the UK market, the company would need yen to buy the VCRs
- It therefore spends pounds to buy yen
- In terms of supply and demand this means the demand for yen has increased whilst the supply of pounds has also increased
- Therefore the value of the yen should increase and the value of the pound fall (see below).

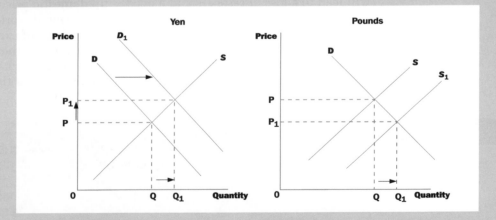

Increase in demand for yen means a rising price $P \rightarrow P1$.

Increase in supply of pounds means a falling price $P \rightarrow P1$.

If the value of the pound is high, this will mean that UK goods are dearer abroad and, to a business which is trying to sell its goods or services internationally, this can be detrimental because the price of the goods rises. If the value of the pound falls, UK goods or services become more competitive.

- If the rate of exchange is £1 = $2, goods selling for £100 in the UK will cost $200 in the USA (ignoring other cost factors)
- If the rate of exchange falls to £1 = $1.80, the same goods now cost $180 on the US market. Therefore these goods become more competitive.

Any business that buys or sells goods internationally will be directly affected by the exchange rate. This is the rate at which, for example, sterling can be traded for another currency. There are three main reasons why an individual or organisation would want to obtain foreign currency:

- If a UK company buys goods abroad it will need to obtain the currency of the country it is buying the goods from, in order to pay for them. Therefore a business buying internationally will need to look at both the price of the goods and the price of the currency.
- A UK citizen travelling abroad needs to obtain the currency of the country being visited.
- An investor may either want to buy a particular currency in order to earn interest rates in that country, or may want to hold a currency for speculative reasons in the hope that the value will rise and it can be sold at a profit.

Exchange rates are normally measured in terms of the value of one currency against another. However, the relative exchange rate of a group, or basket, of currencies can also be measured. This method may be useful to gauge the relative exchange rates of a group of trading partners.

Balance of payments and exchange rates

The exchange rate of a currency is its market price. If a currency is allowed to float freely on the market, according to the laws of supply and demand, it could be argued that balance of payments problems should be rectified by exchange rate adjustments. If we assume that currency is only demanded for trade and ignore other factors, we can see that if the exchange rate falls goods should become cheaper and demand for currency should increase.

In the real world, however, there are also other factors to consider which affect exchange rates and so complicate the issue.

Government intervention via the Bank of England

The Government can actually step in and buy or sell its own currency, thereby creating its own supply and demand and manipulating the exchange rate value.

Confidence in the currency

Individuals who hold UK currency for speculative purposes (as explained below) may feel that the currency is going to lose value and may not be worth holding. Conversely if confidence is rising, this will have a reverse impact.

Interest rates

Speculators hold a nation's currency in order to earn that nation's interest rate. If the nation's interest rates are high, speculators will usually buy that currency in order to capitalise on the high rates. This speculative demand, as we saw, is called Hot money.

Political issues

The value of a currency is also affected by the strength of the nation's government and by their ability to convince the currency market that they are politically stable.

Relative inflation rates

These also affect the price of goods internationally. If a country has a high inflation rate, this will mean that the goods they are trading overseas will rise in price. They will therefore be less competitive. Inflation can also rise if the price of raw materials needed for imports becomes more expensive because of a falling pound, even though this situation can improve the export market.

EMS and ERM

The role of government intervention needs further examination. A government can attempt to control the price of its own currency by intervening in the foreign exchange market when it deems this necessary. However, in some situations the government may decide on a relatively fixed value for its currency and then establish economic objectives to support this value. The Exchange Rate Mechanism (ERM) is an example of a controlled exchange rate system.

European Monetary System (EMS)

The EMS was established in 1979 in an attempt to create monetary stability between members of the EU. To establish exchange rate stability, member states attempt to fix their currency rates within a narrow band of flexibility. The ERM is part of this process.

Exchange Rate Mechanism (ERM)

The ERM is a system which attempts to maintain stability of exchange rates between member states. The currency of each member state is measured against a European Currency Unit or ECU. The ECU is a unit of account where a 'basket' of member countries are measured against each other according to their trading status within the Union. The ECU system also creates exchange rate parities. Member states fix their currency rate at an agreed value within a narrow band of flexibility either side. When the UK joined the ERM it went in at a rate of 2.95 DM to the pound with a 6% flexibility band either side of that value, as the graph, in Box 16.11. shows.

Ultimately the UK economy could not sustain this rate and on Black Wednesday (16 September 1992) the UK left the ERM.

A single European currency

A single European currency is part of the Maastricht grand plan. It is unlikely that this will happen before the turn of the century, due to the complexities of the scheme. The economic implications of varying levels of inflation rates and interest levels are coupled with problems over the actual creation of the currency. Debates are already abounding over whose national monuments and symbols will dominate the currency, and who is to control the process. It is likely that any single currency will need to be phased in

BOX 16.11

Exchange rates in the ERM

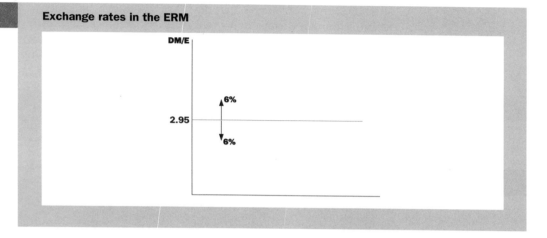

alongside national currencies: there is much work still to be done.

Importance of exchange rates to business

In order for goods or services to be purchased internationally, the buyer needs to look at

- the price of the goods/services, and
- the exchange rate.

A freely floating exchange rate will mean there is considerable unpredictability involved in international trading. A relatively fixed exchange rate gives stability to traders. Businesses can also use this currency level restriction as a factor to restrain wage demands.

In the past, collective bargaining by trade unions had the effect of pushing up production costs and hence the price of goods. In order to restore the competitive price of UK goods in a situation of rising prices, the government could allow the exchange rate to fall:

- If the £ = 4 DM
  £30 (UK good) or 120 DM

- If the price of the goods rose to £40
  £40 = 160 DM
- If the £ was devalued to 33.3p = 1 DM
  Then, rounding up £1 = 3DM
  £40 = 120DM
  Equilibrium would be restored.

Risks involved in currency exchange

If a UK company sells goods to a German company, the Germans will want to pay in DM whilst the UK company will want to receive pounds. Therefore someone needs to exchange Marks for pounds.

Two issues arise:

1. Who is to make the currency exchange and therefore bear the transactional cost?
2. Who is to bear the risk of a shift in the exchange rate?

Currency can be exchanged at either a spot rate (the price now) or at a forward rate (which it could become).

Currency speculation has become big business in the futures market, which allows forward buying in all types of commodities including traded options on shares and currency. Currency speculation can destabilise a currency. This happened when the Government could not control the level of the pound and it 'fell out' of the ERM on 'Black Wednesday'. A currency level which is unpredictable can cause problems for businesses trading internationally.

REVIEW

You should now understand the place of international trading and its importance to an economy, particularly the constraints and opportunities it presents.

TASK

PRACTICAL APPLICATION
1. From the figures in the text, work out the upper and lower limits of the pound against the DM when it was in the ERM.
2. Explain the interaction of supply and demand for currency, using diagrams, for the following situations:
   A. a tariff (tax) being levied against goods imported,
   B. a fixed exchange policy.

TASK

CRITICAL ANALYSIS
Study the graph and table below, and answer the questions that follow.

UK manufacturers: total sales of Sports equipment, 1961–77

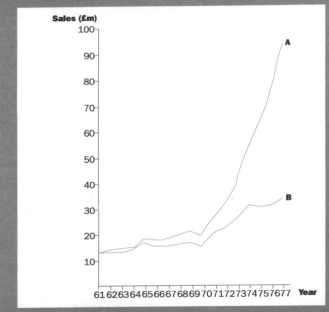

A = Sales at current prices.
B = Sales deflated by sports equipment price index.

Exports and imports of sports equipment

	Exports (£ thousand)	As proportion of total UK manufacturers' sales	Imports (£ thousand)	As proportion of total UK manufacturers' sales
1970	9888	50.99	3105	15.99
1971	13562	48.47	4285	15.31
1972	15209	46.01	5775	17.47
1973	20393	48.76	8981	21.47
1974	25935	47.05	13850	25.12
1975	32184	50.42	18168	28.46
1976	36187	47.30	20500	26.80

Source: *Business Monitor*, PQ 494.3

A. Briefly explain why the two lines on the graph diverged between 1971 and 1977.
B. On graph paper, construct a bar chart to compare Exports and Imports for the years 1971, 1973 and 1975.
C. (i) Calculate the relative increase in both Exports and Imports between the two years 1970 and 1976.
    (ii) Identify **four** economic and social factors which might have led to these changes. (AEB 86)

Essay questions

1 What measures might a Government take to protect an industry from foreign competitors? What possible effects could this have on individual businesses with international customers:
   A. in the short term, and
   B. in the long term?

2 State the advantages and disadvantages for world trade with the expansion of international markets.

3 What are the benefits and costs of the operations of multinationals:
   A. To the host nation?
   B. To the multinational itself?

4 How could fluctuations in the value of the dollar affect a company? What could be done to change this?

CASE STUDY

The long hot Tokyo summer of 1994 resulted in the lifting of regulations inhibiting the importation of bottled water. If meteorologists' predictions are correct the Tone reservoir, which is the main supplier, will soon dry up. The outcome has been the importation of water from Hong Kong, China, South Korea and even Vietnam. The water will be used not just for human consumption but in the cooling process of industries which would otherwise have had to be closed down.

The impact of this situation could have a positive, longer-term effect on European suppliers. Japan will need to reduce its regulations which restrict the presence of a number of trace elements like manganese and iron, and relax its tight specification on taste, colour and smell in bottled water which has blocked the importing of bottled water brands such as Badoit.

Western suppliers have already found a chink in Japan's protectionist armour. The Japanese Ministry of Health and Welfare had prohibited the manufacture in Japan of bottles of less than half a litre because of the low recycling rate. This gap in the market has allowed bottled brands like Volvic to grab a high profile in the Tokyo nightclub scene.

This need for water for industrial use has led to questions being raised about Japan's lack of water recycling and desalination plants. Hopes were raised that this could prove to be another opportunity for the West to gain a foothold in the Japanese market, but the head of the Ministry of International Trade and Industry insists that Japan has the technology to do the job itself – so much for free trade.

Source: National newspaper reports and author's research.

CASE STUDY TASKS

1 What is meant by 'Japan's protectionist armour'? Explain how Japan is enforcing a protectionist stance.
2 Outline the arguments for and against opening up the Japanese markets to free trade.
3 What impact could:
   A. a free trade policy,
   B. a protectionist policy
   have on the value of the yen?

Integrated case study for Section 6: The UK and the ERM

Part 1

In 1990 your company's finance and HR divisions received the following Head Office memo.

MEMORANDUM

TO: Financial Manager
HR Personnel Manager

FROM: Managing Director

UK Entry into ERM

As you are no doubt aware, the government recently announced the UK's entry into the ERM after much deliberation and hesitation. As we are a major multinational corporation this is obviously going to be an important factor affecting our operations.

Exchange rate policy is a vital aspect to any international trading company. We have seen, historically, the impact the government's high exchange rate and high interest rate policy had in the early 1980s. The result was that 18% of UK manufacturing capacity was lost.

Therefore the UK's entry into the ERM will at least provide much-needed stability, but I do feel that the rate at entry is too optimistic and may be difficult to sustain. In order to maintain our competitive edge we need to be very stringent in our costing and be particularly aware of any interest rate fluctuations that may be on the horizon.

From the point of view of our workforce, the relatively fixed structure of the ERM will mean that there will be no room for 'competitive devaluations' by the Chancellor in order to maintain competitive pricing, if wage levels were to rise inappropriately and push up our costs. Our workforce therefore need to be working towards the same financial objectives and be aware of the need for pay restraint.

INTEGRATED CASE STUDY TASKS

1. Why was the ERM an important factor for this business?
2. What does the Managing Director mean when he states that high interest rates and high exchange rates had destroyed 18% of UK manufacturing industry?
3. Explain the term 'competitive devaluation' to restore price equilibrium.

Part 2

On the tube from work, on 16 September 1992, you open your evening newspaper and read the following.

'Black Wednesday'

The pound today crashed out of the European Exchange Rate Mechanism. The government has spent billions of pounds trying to save it from sinking. They even increased interest rates twice in order to attract speculative currency, but to no avail. The speculators had decided that the pound was over and out. The Chancellor, Mr Lamont, must have suffered extreme embarrassment as he had been insisting that the pound was 'not for leaving'! The only ones smiling are apparently the currency speculators.

INTEGRATED CASE STUDY TASKS

1. Why did the Chancellor pull the pound out of the ERM?
2. Explain the importance of the use of interest rates and purchasing of pounds by the Government in this situation.
3. What could be the possible effects on British industry of 'Black Wednesday'?
4. How does currency speculation affect business?

ACTIVE LEARNING TASK

You anticipate a new Head Office memo from the Managing Director in response to the above article, reviewing the implications as he sees them. What aspects do you think the memo will cover? Draft your note, acting as MD of the company.

QUESTION

Read the two extracts and answer the questions which follow.

Counter trade

'A recent study by the Economist Intelligence Unit uncovered estimates suggesting that counter trade accounts for 40% of world trade.'

Source: Adapted from The Economist 5 October 1985).

Pakistan selects companies for counter trade project

John Elliott in Islamabad

Three international trading companies have been chosen by Pakistan to launch the country into its first official programme of counter trading, which the Government hopes will boost its flagging exports by $500m (£350m) in the coming year.

The companies chosen from a list of about 50 applicants, are Sukab of Sweden and Marco of Switzerland which have each agreed to do $200m of export business and Mitsubishi of Japan which is to do $100m. A further batch of agreements for another $500m might follow within a year, taking the total of counter trading business to $1bn.

Islamabad is apprehensive about the possible disadvantages of counter trading, and this has held up a final decision on the plan which is awaiting the go-ahead from President Zia ul Haq and Prime Minister Muhammad Khan Junejo.

Counter trade is being tried because the Government can think of no other way to improve its exports which last year totalled only $2.4bn, far short of a target of $3.1bn. This result is unlikely to be improved much this year, according to present trends.

The country's trade imbalance is more than $3bn a year against imports of $6bn. The overall position has been worsened during the past three years by a sharp decline in remittances from Pakistanis working abroad.

Pakistan has been experiencing problems exporting its major surpluses of cotton amounting to about its annual crop of 5.5m to 6m bales, as well as products from its new steel mill in Karachi and leather hides and manufactured products. It also has a $190m surplus of carpets, exports of which have suffered a 19% decline this year.

In all these areas it has been hit by falling international prices, international protectionism and lack of Pakistani exporting expertise.

So it has decided to try to persuade countries in the Middle East, where it buys oil, and other countries such as Sri Lanka, Malaysia and Japan, where it buys tea, edible oils and engineering products, to match these imports with counter trade purchases.

Individual Pakistan companies have traded by barter for several years. The trade has involved 8 East European companies, Sukab of Sweden and Kemira of Finland. It amounts to about $300m a year.

Source: Financial Times 7 November 1985.

You are employed as a Sales Director of a multinational trading company. Write a report to the Managing Director of your company using a suitable format to cover the following areas:
(a) What is meant by 'counter trade' as used in the text?
(b) Why might the growth of counter trade be important to your company?
(c) What points should the company take into consideration before it embarks upon counter trading deals? AEB November 1987

Section 7
The Enterprise Initiative: A Mini-Company Project

The Enterprise Initiative

Introduction

The purpose of Section 7 is to encourage you to apply the theory covered in this volume by setting up a mini-enterprise business initiative. The ideal scenario would be for you to set up and run, in small groups, over a short period of time, a small business venture. This can be done in the form of a simulation, whereby the company documents are completed and held by the tutor as the Registrar. All the other processes involved with setting up a business – the idea, the research, raising capital and financial projections – can be done on an 'actual' basis. It may be preferable for the groups to plan and research for the start-up of an enterprise without actually trading the goods or service. It is the process and the planning which are important, so if trading does not take place you will still have achieved important knowledge and understanding by the preparation undertaken.

The idea – 'the seed of enterprise'

Before deciding on entering into trade there must be an idea. This can be based on the particular skills or expertise of the individual, the specific knowledge they may have of a product or market, or just an innovation or idea.

Whatever the idea there needs to be a belief in its success. This can be achieved by a thorough process of research, market testing, financial planning and feasibility study.

The test – research

An idea may be a complete non-starter if the market is already flooded with similar ideas or if no one is demanding the output. Market research is a vital element in the business start-up. Identifying the target market will be an important factor in deciding the type of promotion of the product or service.

The form – business units

When starting up a business you may want to purchase one that already exists, in which case there will need to be a careful analysis of the trading figures, comparing costs with benefits. It is also possible to buy a franchise. Value for money must be paramount. A famous and successful franchise will be costly whilst the smaller franchise may not provide the support and service which would you would normally expect to receive from a franchise agreement (remember Section 1.4). Smaller companies are selling franchise agreements on the basis of a contract lump sum and in return they supply stock and customers. Many of these companies quote large earnings figures when selling the agreement, but in reality the money they make from selling the franchise agreements is a good income for them, but for the franchisee the more they sell the less work there is. Therefore a franchise can sometimes be a way of paying for yourself to be employed by a company, and it may well be better to start up a company directly. However, for many individuals embarking on an experience like enterprise is a daunting process and they may feel more secure to be part of something larger which is already in operation. A cooperative is another option.

Sole traders are the smallest unit of ownership. Setting one up is straightforward, just a matter of clearing it with the tax office and abiding by local regulations and laws. You may need to obtain licences for certain types of trade. Partnerships enable a pooling of skills, expertise, knowledge and resources without the process of incorporation. Limited companies provide protection for personal assets and the potential of capital expansion.

Getting a name

When a business decides on a name, it has to be registered. A name will not be registered if it already exists on the registration list, if it is too similar to one already registered, if it is considered to be offensive or if its use would constitute a criminal offence. It is also important to distinguish between a

company name and a trademark, which is a name or symbol by which the goods of a company are identified. The trademark is registered by the Registrar of Trademarks and you would need to ensure that the company name does not clash with another company's trademark.

Registering a private limited company

To register a private limited company is a straightforward process and given the protection that you receive from limited liability status it would seem to be a sensible option. Setting up a limited company can be done through a solicitor which could cost a few thousand pounds, but it is also a fairly simple task to do this yourself for a charge of £50 for registration! All

companies are formed and approved by the Companies Registration Offices. The registration offices have three functions:

1. To register and dissolve companies
2. To check and file documentation required by the various Companies Acts
3. To keep the information held available for public inspection.

The process of incorporation

This has six stages:

1. Send off to the Companies Registration Office to apply for the forms which need to be completed (PUC1, 10 and 12).

2. Select and establish the acceptability of the name of the company.
3. Draw up the:
   - Certificate of Registration (see Box 17.1)
   - Memorandum of Association, and

- Articles of Association (see Boxes 17.2 and 17.3).
4. Send a statement of capital, a list of directors and the registered office address.

5. Sign a declaration of compliance with the Companies Acts.
6. Send the fee of £50 to register.

BOX 17.1

**CERTIFICATE
OF
REGISTRATION (INCORPORATION)**

I hereby CERTIFY that

....

a MINI-COMPANY

is registered with the

MINI-COMPANY Organiser for

....

A registration fee has been paid

Dated this .... day of ....

One Thousand Nine Hundred and Ninety ....

SIGNED ....

BOX 17.2

**MEMORANDUM
OF
ASSOCIATION**

WE (Name of Company) ....

OF (Address) ....

BEING FORMED FOR THE OBJECTIVE OF (Type of business activity)

AND HAVING A MAXIMUM AUTHORISED CAPITAL OF (Maximum amount to be raised by share capital)

HEREBY APPLY TO THE MINI-COMPANY ORGANISER OF

SCHOOL/COLLEGE FOR REGISTRATION AS A MINI-COMPANY

The Directors of the Company are:

SIGNED   Managing Director

Witnessed this day the .... day of .... 199............

ARTICLES OF ASSOCIATION

- Types of shares held and rules for holding and transferring shares

....

....

....

- Details of company meetings

....

- Format and procedure for accounting records

....

....

- The power of directors and their responsibilities

....

....

Finance and pricing

The structure of the business will decide the availability of certain funds but other financial backing may also be necessary. All avenues of finance need to be explored. Before deciding on the funding needed you should create a projected cash flow analysis to investigate potential inflows and outflows of revenue. A pricing policy will also need to be worked out through a break-even analysis, determining fixed costs, variable costs and potential revenue in relation to price.

The business plan

This is the document which draws the whole process of enterprise together. It can be presented to any financier or other stakeholder and reflects professionalism and planning. Planning can never be based totally on fact; forecasting is a vital element in any business, but financial backers will be skilled at assessing whether the forecast is realistic or valid. As much flexibility as possible should be built into any business plan as external forces may push businesses into decisions which may disrupt a rigid plan. An outline business plan should be drawn up as follows:

Fundamental details

- Name
- Address
- Telephone/Fax/e-mail
- Type of business
- Date of commencement

Activities of the business
Personnel and management team

- Expertise
- Responsibilities
- Income
- Future HRM needs through growth
- Contingency plans for HRM in case of injury/illness

Location

- Premises – size, leasehold/freehold
- Rates
- Rent
- Insurance
- Expansion plans

Finance

- Financial projections
- Cash flow forecast
- Financial commitments

- If trading – financial records such as Balance sheet, Profit and loss account
- Debts outstanding

The market

- Type of market
- Expanding/contracting
- Identify competitors
- SWOT analysis
- Marketing strategy planned

Suppliers

- Main suppliers
- Credit terms
- Stock procedures and pricing

Risks

- Key risk factors
- Contingencies to cover risks

The mini-company project

Theory into practice

Your objective is to formulate your own mini-enterprise in groups, and if possible actually trade for a 6 week period. If trading is not feasible, you can do all the preparatory work up to the point of actually running the business.

In a simulated exercise your teacher/lecturer can act as the Registrar of Companies (limited company formation) or as a Solicitor (partnership) and control your documentation. Boxes 17.1–17.6 are sample documentation for you to refer to for information.

At the end of the project you should have prepared:

A. All documentation involved in the business start-up process
B. A business plan

C. Market research information
D. Agenda and minutes of all meetings held
E. Financial projections.

All of the above can be achieved without actually running a mini-enterprise. If you do trade, you will have more information to add – all financial records, for example.

The important factor is to do things professionally, check back through the volume for reference and to be efficient, planned and organised.

The process

Getting together

Form into a group and decide on an agenda for your first meeting. An agenda is an agreed list of items to be discussed (see Box 17.4). A 'brainstorming' session (individuals contributing ideas) is a good way of getting started. The actual meeting should be very formal with a business approach. You will need a chairman who controls the meeting and calls it to order and a secretary who takes the minutes. The minutes are a report of the meeting and any decisions made. Sample minutes are shown in Box 17.5. At business meetings, it is vital that agreements and statements are 'minuted' and decisions carried forward.

The outcome of the first meeting should at least include decisions on:

- The idea
- The business entity
- Market research
- Role of individuals in group

Role of individuals

Each person in the group should be allocated, by agreement, an individual function so that each person knows their role and their job specification.

Some roles needed include:
- Managing Director – The Managing Director is the Chief Executive of any company. Chairs the meetings of Directors.
- HR Manager – Organises HRM, contracts of employment and other records. They will be responsible for taking on any extra labour.
- Marketing Manager – Decides on the market research needed. Analyses the research and organises the necessary promotion of the product.
- Finance Manager – Does all the projected costing and pricing figures.

During trading, records must be kept and decisions made. Meetings should be held regularly and be fully documented. At the end of the period of trading, records should be presented and analysed. There should be a 'debriefing' session where experiences can be shared and evaluated.

If you are a plc, you will need to prepare share certificates (see Box 17.6).

BOX 17.4

Agenda

1. Apologies [those unable to attend the meeting should send an apology]
2. Minutes [The minutes – which are an account of the previous meeting – are discussed]
3. Matters arising [points from the minutes are discussed]
   Aspects to be discussed
4.
5.
6.
7.
8. Any other business [A 'catch-all' item which will cover points which have not been included in the agenda items]
9. Arrange date of next meeting

BOX 17.5	**Minutes**

These are the minutes of the ....

meeting held at ....

on ....

at ....

Those present ....

....

....

....

....

....

....

....

1. Minutes of previous meeting recorded and confirmed ....

....

2. Matters arising ....

....

....

3. Items discussed ....

....

....

BOX 17.6	**Share certificate**

The   Company

at

School/College certify that

has invested in .... shares at .... each

The profits will be divided up and distributed as dividends at the end of the session according to the rules laid down

Integrated case studies for the volume

Case Study 1
Business opportunities in Europe

Read the article below, and carry out the tasks that follow.

The potential expansion of the European Community is moving swiftly towards being one of the world's largest trading unions. A possible ultimate market of 700 million will be incorporated in 42 sections. The Union could possibly stretch from the Atlantic to the Urals, as the map overleaf shows.

UK business must be aware of the potential for trading and be ready to meet the challenge of an ever-increasing competitive market.

The potential market
The 7 EFTA states fearful of being left out of the expansion process are all likely to join:

- **Sweden** – has applied
- **Austria** – has applied
- **Finland** – has applied
- **Norway** – expected to apply
- **Switzerland** – expected to apply
- **Lichtenstein** – as they only have a 78 000 population they may be awarded Associate status
- **Iceland** – they are reticent because of their fears over intervention in their fishery industry.

In order for the Soviet Republics to join they need to:

(A) consolidate their democracy;
(B) develop their economies.

Both of these conditions will be difficult to achieve, but not impossible.

There are already associate agreements with Poland, Hungary, the Czech Republic and Slovakia. Negotiations are also to take place with Rumania, Bulgaria, Albania and the Balkan States. There is also interest from the former Soviet Republics in Europe – Ukraine, Belarus, Georgia, Moldavia, Armenia and Azerbaijan.

Malta and Cyprus may also apply, but the Turkish occupants of Northern Cyprus and Malta's suspected links with Libya may block any hopes they have of entry.

All of this adds up to vast scope for the UK business sector to capitalise and a huge demand for goods, services and capital.

Businesses must be ready for this challenge if they are to succeed.

Source: National newspaper reports and author's research.

Key:

Al	Albania
B	Belgium
Cz Rep	Czech Republic
FYRoM	Former Yugoslav Republic of Macedonia
L	Luxembourg
M	Moldova
NL	Netherlands
Sw	Switzerland
UK	United Kingdom

Shaded area denotes the EC15

Task 1

Research

Find out as much as you can about the potential EU members including, their location, resources, types of currency and culture.

Strategy design

Design a strategy for a chosen business to deal with the new challenge of an expanding EU market. Look at the following points and state under each heading the aspects which need to be considered and the questions which need to be posed.

Marketing

1. Where are the potential customers?
2. How do we get the right marketing information?
3. What are the threats of increased competition?
4. How do we best promote the business?

Sales

1. Are there problems of selling in the new market?
2. What provision of after-sales service is needed?

Distribution

1. What changes will be needed in distribution requirements?
2. What problems would you envisage in so large an area?

Production

1. Will the production processes need to be changed?
2. Should we have a policy of make or buy?
3. What is the scope for entering into collaborative arrangements with other suppliers?
4. What are the implications for businesses of the new standards?

Purchasing

1. Will there be wider opportunities for new sources of supply?
2. Will our purchasing requirements change?

Finance

1. What could be the effects of a wider market on our profit and loss account?
2. What could the effects be on our balance sheet?
3. What are the effects of the wider market on the cash flow?

Recruitment and training

1. Do we need a 'personal planning' policy?
2. What new skills could be needed?
3. What type of training plan would be most suitable?
4. What are the new opportunities for recruitment in Europe?

Information systems

1. Information systems will be vital to achieve sound information on what is happening in the market. Decide on the types of systems that may be needed, then develop an IT strategy and policy.

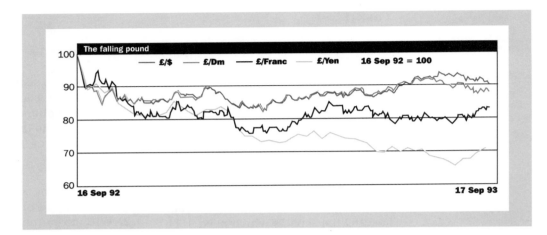

Task 2

Conduct a detailed analysis of the impact on a business operating in the international market of:

A. a rise in UK interest rates;
B. the Government allowing the pound to float freely;
C. a rise in German interest rates;
D. rising inflation in the UK;
E. the workforce securing a large pay increase.

Case Study 2

A reflection on exchange rates

When the pound fell out of the Exchange Rate Mechanism on 16 September 1992, it was thought to be a positive improvement for businesses. Although the ERM, with its relatively fixed exchange rate, had meant currency stability for businesses operating overseas, it was generally felt that the pound went into the mechanism at an inflated rate. This meant that British goods were not as competitive as the entry to the mechanism would imply.

It was felt that the initial impact on businesses of Britain's exit would, in the short term, mean exports would become cheaper and, in the medium term, the volume of exports should increase.

The supposed benefits of a freely floating exchange rate have not materialised because Europe is in recession. Generally businesses operating outside of the Community have fared better than those inside.

Sales to non-EC nations went up by 9% in the first half of 1993 compared to a 6% fall in sales to Europe. In general the type of businesses that lost out were engineering and machine manufacturers which are heavily linked to Europe, as the following economic indicators show.

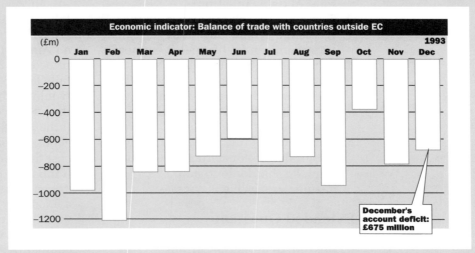

Source: Observer (30 January 1994).

Britain's trade gap with nations outside the EC narrowed from £773 million in November to £675 million. Exports improved by 4.8% to around £5 billion, helped by the growth in demand in the USA. Imports rose by 7.4% to £5.7 billion.

Since the 1992 customs barriers came down, details of trade with Europe have been unavailable. The figures below show the trading figures with the rest of the world including Europe. There was a trade deficit, seasonally adjusted, of £4.5 bn in the first quarter of 1993.

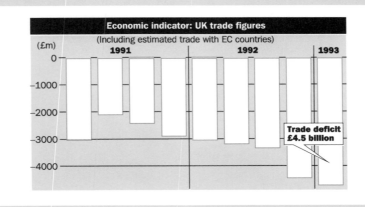

Source: Observer (13 June 1993).

Source: National newspaper reports and author's research.

Referring to the information given:
1. Explain the effect a falling or rising exchange rate has on businesses.
2. What are the implications for interest rates of rising inflation?
3. These figures refer to an economy in recession. What is meant by 'recession', and why does it happen?
4. What should be the policy of a business in a recession period? What advice would you give a firm operating in the international markets?
5. Write a report (using IT, if possible) to the Chancellor stating what you think he should do to help businesses survive.

Extended Question

A. The UK is part of a joint European venture to build the 'Airbus'.

If the price of each Airbus to be sold to the Americans was set at $25million at an exchange rate of $1.10 per pound, what would be the loss to the project if the dollar value fell to $1.80 per pound?

B. If a UK importer wanted to purchase an American typewriter which was priced at $200 and the dollar value falls from $1.10 to $1.80, what would be the effect on the price to the UK buyer?

C. If the £ was worth 4 DM and the UK goods are priced at £30, they would cost the Germans 120 DM.
If inflation pushed the price up by 1/3 and the government were not in a fixed rate system, how much would the pound need to be devalued by in order to remain competitive?

Case Study 3

Population and consumer spending

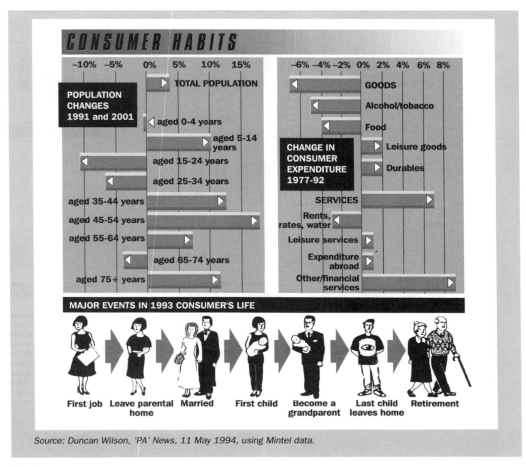

CONSUMER HABITS

POPULATION CHANGES 1991 and 2001

TOTAL POPULATION
aged 0-4 years
aged 5-14 years
aged 15-24 years
aged 25-34 years
aged 35-44 years
aged 45-54 years
aged 55-64 years
aged 65-74 years
aged 75+ years

CHANGE IN CONSUMER EXPENDITURE 1977-92

GOODS
Alcohol/tobacco
Food
Leisure goods
Durables
SERVICES
Rents, rates, water
Leisure services
Expenditure abroad
Other/financial services

MAJOR EVENTS IN 1993 CONSUMER'S LIFE

First job — Leave parental home — Married — First child — Become a grandparent — Last child leaves home — Retirement

Source: Duncan Wilson, 'PA' News, 11 May 1994, using Mintel data.

Task

Write a report (using IT, if possible) on these consumer trends, including graphs, pie on bar charts as you feel necessary, explaining the implications to businesses of the statistics on:

A. population changes;
B. consumer expectations.

Case Study 4

Population and Consumer Spending

Set out below are some statistics that have been gathered for the government's Family Spending Survey 1993. In this information family expenditure is represented by region, age and income. Study this data in detail, and then carry out the tasks that follow.

What percentage of their income do people spend on housing, motoring and food – by age group

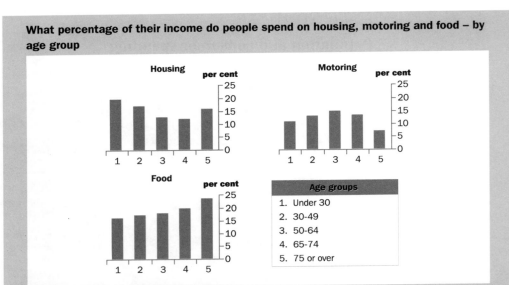

Source: CSO, Economic Trends (1993, chart 2.1).

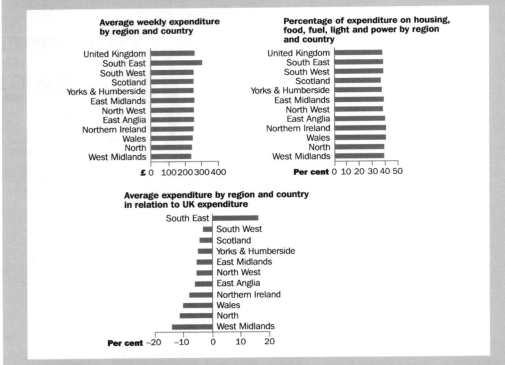

Source: CSO, Economic Trends (1993), charts 5.1, 5.2 and 5.3.

Task

Analyse the data, and evaluate the implications for a range of businesses. Present your findings and present the comparisons in another statistical form to be included as part of a report from yourself to the Family Spending Unit. The report should be word processed and the graphics completed on a computer if possible.

Case Study 5

The housing market

Study the graph of house price changes below, carry out the tasks that follow.

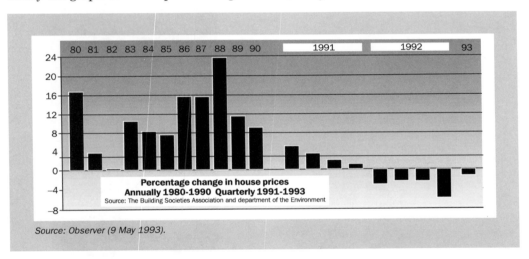

Source: Observer (9 May 1993).

Task 1

Explain the development of the housing market since 1980, illustrating with statistical graphs, pie or bar charts as necessary.

Task 2

Do your own research into the interest rates and housing development over this period.
1. Present a report which links house prices to interest rates and unemployment rates.

2. Draw a graphical representation of your figures, and analyse the links. Evaluate the impact of these figures on businesses.

Case Study 6

Pay differentials

Study the data below on building labourers' employment costs, then answer the questions.

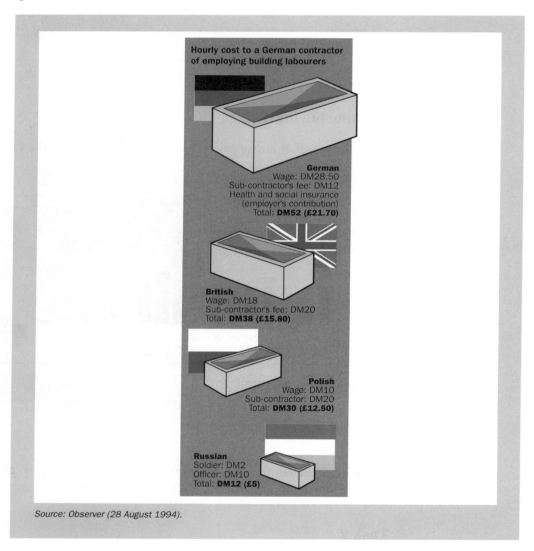

Hourly cost to a German contractor of employing building labourers

German
Wage: DM28.50
Sub-contractor's fee: DM12
Health and social insurance (employer's contribution)
Total: **DM52 (£21.70)**

British
Wage: DM18
Sub-contractor's fee: DM20
Total: **DM38 (£15.80)**

Polish
Wage: DM10
Sub-contractor: DM20
Total: **DM30 (£12.50)**

Russian
Soldier: DM2
Officer: DM10
Total: **DM12 (£5)**

Source: Observer (28 August 1994).

Task

1. Explain why these differ.
2. What are the implications for the contractor?
3. Analyse the role of a recessionary housing market on these pay differentials.

Case Study 7

'Shop till you drop'

Read the extract below and then carry out the tasks that follow.

The British, once called a nation of shopkeepers by Napoleon Bonaparte, have now become a nation of superstore shoppers. As small shops rapidly disappear, superstores are mushrooming across the retail landscape.

Instore bakeries, greengrocers and butchers have taken trade from the small retail specialist in the high street whilst the business rate has generally hit many small traders. Dewhurst the butchers had nearly 20 000 outlets in 1985 but 10 years on they have less than 12 000. There were 2800 fishmongers in 1984 but this figure has now fallen by 25%. Doorstep delivery of milk is falling by roughly 12% per year. The department store, once the symbol of sophisticated shopping is also in decline.

	1984	1994
Milkmen	36 000 (83%)	22 000 (50%)
High street grocers	47 224* (22.2%)	32 663* (11.6%)
Independent butchers	19 000 (41.5%)	12 000 (22%)
Fishmongers	2 800 (54%)	2 100 (33.6%)
High street bakers	5 000 (28%)	3 000 (8%)

Notes
*1982

Source: National newspaper reports and author's research.

So what are the benefits to consumers of the larger store apart from cheaper prices? The attraction of having all food produce and other items under one roof plus somewhere to park is hard to resist for the modern couple. Prize draws like the £1 million prize being offered by Sainsbury are capitalising on the 'lottery dream'. There is also talk of 'singles nights' where romance may be allowed to blossom over the frozen ready meals for single dwellers. The superstore is being promoted by the marketing men as the place where everyone wants to go, from gurgling babies to grandmas: the mecca of family entertainment.

The big stores are also offering 'instore cards'. These are already well established and popular in the USA. These store cards offer a discount service to regular customers and in exchange for customer registration details, money can be saved on items purchased. These cards have become the subject of controversy in the USA. For the marketing function, the ideal scenario is to know just 'what' an individual buys. With a store card, items can be registered to a customer. However, the sheer scale of a weekly shop and the numbers of average items purchased can mean vast amounts of information held on a data base to be accessed when marketing information is needed. However, with technology moving apace this problem is now not insurmountable and huge databases of information on goods purchased are not far away. Look out for the junk mail.

Technological advances will also mean an increase in Teleshopping and direct computer linking to the consumer. Mail order markets are also ripe for technological advance. It is now possible to view the items on video link and the development of 'interactive shopping' is not far away.

Out-of-town complexes have developed around superstores and are an added attraction. The centre of social gravity has shifted from town centres. In the 1980s the government encouraged out-of-town development in order to reduce the congestion of town centre traffic and allow shoppers somewhere to park. The lingering death of many towns has caused the government and local authorities to re-think their strategy: the social landscape is being re-assessed.

For the small retailers, personal service is not enough to ensure survival. Even big high street chain stores are finding it tough. Electrical goods are an example. The market leaders, Dixons, rely on sales of warranties and insurance for their survival. The uniformity of prices had led to charges of price fixing and a referral to the MMC but 60 high street retailers have not survived. The retailers complain that the problem is that suppliers are not discounting their prices. The survival of small retailers will rely on their ability to find a niche market or offer a specialist service. The alternative is to bring prices down, and joining a Trade Association is beneficial. While the small shops struggle to survive the big ones are being criticised for unsociable practices. They are accused of dictating terms to small producers and encouraging road transport for their deliveries.

Franchise contracts are now being issued for Post Office Counter services. The franchise agreements are being offered to other retail outlets, which could result in the demise of the Victorian Post Office facades from our towns. Another landmark of the town centre will be lost.

Source: National newspaper reports and author's research.

Task 1

Analyse the statistics in the extract and explain the reason for the decline in town centre shopping. Evaluate the social and marketing implications of this information.

Task 2

Complete the chart below from your own research.

Type of retailer	Advantages to entrepreneur	Advantages to consumer	List examples
Specialist chain			
Superstores			
Market stalls			
Mail order			
Milk delivery			
Department store			

Appendices

1 Format of a business report

Details of sender/receiver

TO:

FROM:

SUBJECT/TITLE:

DATE:

REF.

Contents

1. Introduction
2. Main part
3. Conclusions/evaluation
4. Recommendations

2   Designing a questionnaire

Background research

1. What do you need to know?

2. Who do you need to ask?
   - Type of person
   - Age group
   - Male/female
   - Occupation

3. Where will you ask your questions?

Writing the questions

1. Keep your questions short and clear

2. Do not ask more than 12 questions

3. Write your questions so that they have either:
   - A 'yes' or 'no' answer (e.g. 'Do you do your main shopping here?' Yes/No?)
   - A choice of answers (e.g. 'How did you travel here? – walk, cycle, bus, car?')

4. Give a choice of age groups, e.g. 20–30

5. Consider the order in which you put your questions

6. Consider the way in which you ask your questions (e.g. 'Would you like a record shop?' might lead to the answer 'Yes', but wouldn't necessarily mean they would use it)

7. Avoid 'open-ended' and leading questions.

Asking the questions

1. How will you ask the questions?
2. How will you record the answers?
3. Practise before you go out
4. Allow people to miss questions if they are not relevant to them or if they object to answering.

3 Statistical representation

Increasingly computers are being used to present statistical information. It is easy to transform figures into a graphical illustration, which means that with the popular use of the PC statistical representations are increasingly being inserted into company information, reports and correspondence.

Tables

Figures are often put into a tabular form, as it can be an effective way of displaying quantities in grouped categories. Tables can be inserted into written information to give a quantitative support picture. For ease of presentation it is usual to round off figures to be represented.

A bumpy ride through the single car market

Manufacturers' recommended prices in six countries, with and without tax

	UK	France	Belgium	Italy	Germany	Spain
Fiat Cinquecento						
Price paid by national (including tax)	£5110	£5676	£5518	£4839	£5778	£5288
Price paid by foreigner (no tax paid)	£4349	£4786	£4580	£4067	£5025	£4025
Nissan Micra						
Price paid by national	£7775	£7979	£8566	£6982	£8542	£7919
Price paid by foreigner	£6617	£6727	£7108	£5867	£7427	£6186
Ford Fiesta 1.1L 5 door						
Price paid by national	£8131	£8735	£7972	£6546	£8806	£8265
Price paid by foreigner	£6920	£7365	£6616	£5501	£7657	£6457
Volkswagen Golf						
Price paid by national	£9316	£9189	£10366	£8689	£9857	£9847
Price paid by foreigner	£7928	£7748	£8603	£7081	£8571	£7693
Rover 214						
Price paid by national	£11795	N/A	£12877	£9111	£12625	£10818
Price paid by foreigner	£10038	N/A	£10686	£7656	£10978	£8451
BMW 316i 4 door						
Price paid by national	£15479	£17129	£17792	£14734	£17179	£17851
Price paid by foreigner	£13174	£14441	£14765	£12381	£14938	£13944
Vauxhall Omega						
Price paid by national	£18430	£20771	£21694	£16730	£21127	£21743
Price paid by foreigner	£15685	£17513	£17638	£13889	£18371	£16987

Source: Observer (30 July 1995).

Pictograms

Pictograms are pictures which represent figures. They are the simplest visual representation of numerical data. A more involved pictogram is one which includes figures.

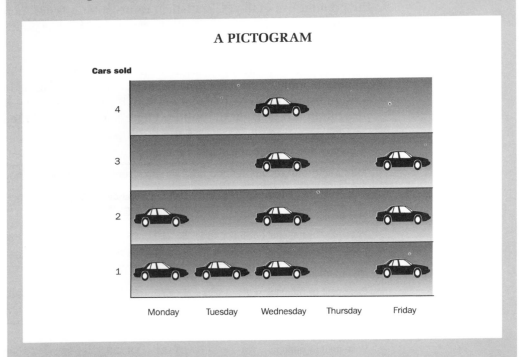

A PICTOGRAM

Bar charts

Bar charts demonstrate numerical information in horizontal or vertical bars. Some bar charts use colour or shading to accentuate types of values, and some use three dimensional effects. They are useful for showing positive and negative values.

Multiple bar charts show comparisons of figures through the use of adjacent bars.

Graphs

A graph is a diagram which shows the relationship between **two variable** axes **at right angles**. Graphs are usually drawn on specially squared paper which allows for ease of scaling both horizontally and vertically. The zero point (0) is termed the **origin** of the graph. The *x* axis comprises the independent variable and the *y* axis is the dependant variable. To be effective, a graph must be labelled clearly with headings and source data. A scale should be chosen which allows data to be plotted over the full range.

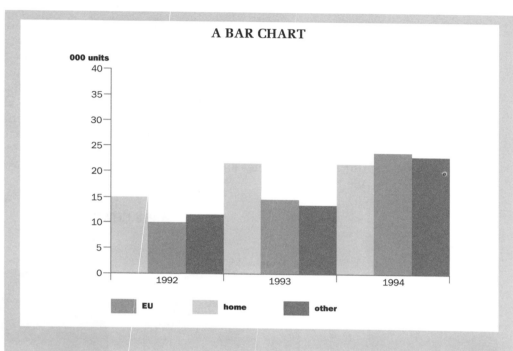

A BAR CHART

000 units

EU   home   other

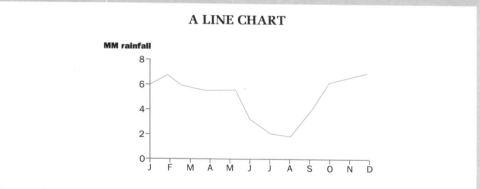

A LINE CHART

MM rainfall

Pie charts

Another way of breaking down figures into component parts is the use of a pie chart. Each component is depicted as a **slice of the pie**, which is a complete circle of data. The whole pie is represented by an angle of 360° so each component part needs to be translated into degrees. The pie is a very effective visual presentation and colours can be used to categorise information.

Index figures

Much of the problem of presenting statistics is involved with arranging data so that it can be **interpreted**. The use of index figures allows a comparison of information over a period of time and different standards of measures contained in one figure. Index figures can measure a variety of quantities against what has been deemed a base, or originating figure. Most people have heard of the Retail Price Index (RPI) and the FTSE 'Footsie' share index. These two compare numerical trends against a base line figure. The FT index, sometimes known as the '30 share index', started in 1935 at 100 base. The shares are chosen as a representative of British industry and commerce, and government stock is not included. It is a popular index to use as a market indicator because it changes throughout each day. It is calculated hourly during trading times and there is a closing index at 5pm. Another example is the FTSE 100.

A PIE CHART

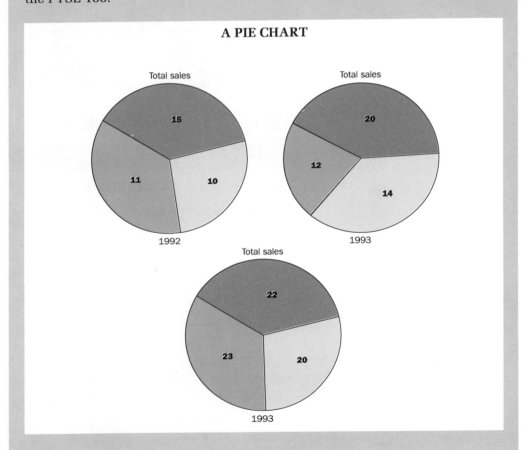

Index